Catalogue
It will seem a dream

Juan Cruz

Introduction

The work of Juan Cruz is often associated with translation and all it implies, with the literal, metaphoric, cultural and linguistic exploration of texts and even of objects through words and mediated experiences; with the structure of cultural identity. Translation in Cruz's work acts as a metaphor for visual representation, which he exploits through a wide range of media including video, installation, performance, drawing, sound, objects, photography and, more recently, streaming.

However, throughout his career he has also used writing and words in many other ways. This project, *Catalogue: It will seem a dream*, conceived for the Museo de Arte Contemporáneo de Castilla y León (MUSAC), focuses on his use of writing as a means of generating original texts that give rise to, refer to, stem from, or accompany many of his pieces. Taking centre stage, through a book and an exhibition that is ostensibly a single spatial installation, are a number of these original texts alongside related original and specially conceived documentary material.

Even in his most ephemeral and dematerialised works, Cruz examines the links between narrative and physical space, questioning how spatial experience can be subtly manipulated, by even the slightest of means. In *Catalogue: It will seem a dream*, works and other images connected to the chosen texts are presented (and, in turn, re-presented) in the exhibition space through a series of small projections and artefacts, giving rise to an installation-type work made up of references to previous pieces. This project is intended to reflect upon Cruz's development and his lines of enquiry and research. As such, it reveals that key resources, for artist and viewer, are the documents and traces that remain of works and proposals (sometimes their actual origins) that have no fixed material form, having been retrieved from now obsolete formats such as audio cassettes, MiniDiscs, MiniDVs, Hi8 s, Quark, ClarisWorks, etc. By revisiting the work like this, we are brought closer to the rawness of the archive and gain a sense of its potential, with a view to generating new experiences and interrelated expressions of his oeuvre rather than creating a unidirectional narrative thread.

In this way, the project manages somehow to upset the usual exhibition logic according to which works are selected and then displayed, essays are written and a catalogue is eventually published. Here, the reverse operation has taken place: the artist has selected original essays and other texts and compiled them in a book of the textual material that refers to a set of works. This book is in fact the essence of the exhibition and steers the selection of works represented in the gallery.

Hence, the publication approximates an artist's book; the exhibition a single installation made up of material associated with earlier works and the show a new project that comprises the interplay between the book and installation. The point here then is not to reinstall the works faithfully to reproduce their original presence, but to return to the original texts in order to find new interpretations and possibilities for the work, for it is precisely writing that has always guided the work and is the leitmotif of the exhibition. The installation, which has something experimental about it, also, and perhaps more importantly, treats the gallery as a space in which the work may be seen generatively in its most sparse and simple documentary form.

This book, therefore, doesn't illustrate the exhibition but forms a part of a broader project that includes the gallery display and that to which it alludes. The installation comprises a series of modest and discrete projections, prints and objects that always refer, directly and indirectly, to essays and other writings published here.

In creating complex and delicate networks of relations between the texts written by Cruz and a series of works that refer to these texts, the project allows us to observe and analyse the evolution of the mechanisms adopted by the artist to convey his experience through his writings and work, if the two are not one and the same. The compilation of essays in this book and related artworks create platforms for incorporating the presence and activity of other/s, the receiver/s who will discover, weave and even improvise with the fragile relations that appear as if suspended. His works are bare, and their starkness questions the properties of physical and conceptual spaces, historical and material contexts,

documentary and/or fictional narratives, and the processes
that relate the works to the visitors, the exhibition space
to the stories around it and, in short, the means or ways
by which all this is communicated.

Catalogue: It will seem a dream also explores various
representations of time – not the linear time that moves from
past to future, crossing the present, but the contained and
drawn-out time of artistic practice and its interaction with
historical events expressed through journeys and travels,
dreams, memories, fictions and imaginings. The title of the
project evokes the artist's interest in visiting these forms
of presentation through references to some of his works
and, by extension, to references from art history, literature,
architecture, music and science, interweaving past and present,
over and again. Although the project resembles a retrospective,
it does not present a chronological vision of Cruz's work but
rather suggests paths between multiple layers and interests
that have remained consistent throughout his trajectory.
This way of operating evokes archival practices, for it involves
collecting and arranging materials to reconstruct facts and
fictions. Ultimately, this 'retrospective' is a convergence
where suggestions and images are elaborated through revisions,
juxtapositions, displacements, accumulations and even
superimpositions of layers of real and imagined meaning.

Manuel Olveira
MUSAC Director

Descriptions of Works in the Collection of South London Gallery

A. 1

1058/757

Five women stand on stone steps that lead to an entrance. They are dressed in luxurious robes and look forlorn. One of them carries an oil-lamp; another oil-lamp lies fallen on the ground at the bottom of the steps.

1075/645

A grey rabbit with its litter of seven bunnies. They all lie on straw and eat green leaves.

1989/3

A church with a tree in front of it. A couple emerges from the church entrance and a man wearing a cap stands just outside the gates holding a hoop and stick.

1190/642

A small boat with ten oarsmen attempts to dock in rough seas. The people on shore are agitated about the possible outcome. There is a large sailing-ship in the distance.

1501/63

A modern, brick building with a large Neo-classical portico. Various people walk or stand on the street in front of it.

1186/531

A small harbour in which small sailing-boats are moored. A couple sit in the shadow of the plain buildings that surround it. The sky is blue and it is hot.

228/567

Five small sailing-boats float passively in the sea at dusk. There are white cliffs behind them.

260/559

On the banks of a river, merchandise is unloaded by men in loincloths from small vessels that have been brought ashore. Many large sailing-ships float in the river.

A. 2

1251/957

A girl carrying a basket walks through a marsh with her very blond younger brother. A ragged old woman who looks like a witch has scared them, and the girl drags her astonished brother away. The orange sky is filled with crows.

1230/576

A bald, elderly man with a
moustache sits wearing a
red military tunic with gold
buttons. His hands are resting
on a walking stick.

PC131/P131

A station in which people are
bustling around. Puffs of pink
and yellow smoke bellow from
the locomotives.

1106/916

An androgynous youth with
short dark hair and chubby
hands sits holding a bunch
of wheat.

B. 1

188/326

A city street curves round
and away to the right. Horse-
drawn carts circulate on it.

1931/730

A grand, palatial Neo-
classical building with a huge
courtyard. Smoke is rising
from three chimneys. While
the gardeners tend the yard
a horse-drawn cart trundles
across the front of the gates.

1254/953

A walled street. Behind the
walls there are gardens.

The sun picks up the bright
yellow facade of a house
further along the street.

1218/586

A pink-faced man with a
large grey beard. Only the
top button of his black jacket
is done up.

1082/605

A very pleasant forest with
a dark pond, the banks of
which are covered with
white flowers.

222/1099

A very large, ornate lamp-
post in a derelict street. Signs
behind it warn that buildings
are to be demolished.

148/66

A tree-lined suburban street.
Cyclists and pedestrians
share the road with a sole
automobile.

B. 2

1072/660

Large and small sailing-ships
are on a grey sea with strong
winds. The shoreline is made
up of white cliffs.

986/912

A prim woman sits sewing.

She has red cheeks and a very
blue dress.

1235/924

A seductive, Spanish-looking
woman; she has heavy black
eyebrows and her large red
lips match the colour of her
velvety dress. She holds an
unfurled fan in one hand and
a set of castanets in the other.

1544/1198

A proud, sombre-looking man
with grey hair and long side-
whiskers sits in a heavy grey
cloak. His startlingly blue eyes
stare into space.

C. 1

1101/1048

A woman in a long dark dress
stands holding her bonnet
demurely in front of her. She
looks frightened – as if being
judged. Her shoes are worn.

1197/649

A woman in a flimsy red robe is
chained to a large stake that is
planted on the beach. She has
beautiful long blonde hair and
one of her breasts is uncovered.
Her hands are clasped and her
feet, which are surrounded by
shells, are already covered in
water from the incoming tide.

103/745

An almost grand Victorian
building. Ladies and
gentlemen in hats stand on
the street in front of it.

C. 2

1001/1172

On the top of a small hill is
a square white building with
palm trees around it. At the
bottom of the hill, a man in a
fez sits talking to three women
outside a row of shacks.

970/1507

A middle-aged woman
with black hair that is
covered by an elaborate hat.
Her red-painted lips are
slightly parted.

1135/1049

A woman and child can be
seen playing the piano inside
a house. Outside, a child
stares into the house, a
woman sits on the porch and a
man, flanked by his small dog,
stares at an orange field.

1045/342

A farmyard surrounded by
green leafy trees. A dog sleeps
in one of the barns.

165/1517
A tall concrete lamp-post.
Red, pink and orange tulips
grow in the flowerbeds of the
railed-off square behind it.
The square is surrounded
by town houses.

1010/723
In the haze of the sun, large
mountains are barely visible.
A large group of people walks
away from the mountains.

1208/593
Two boys and two girls gather
sticks in a dark, leafless wood.
Caps are worn by the boys
and bonnets by the girls.

D. 1

1061/971
A man and three women sit
on a pavement with baskets of
roses, buckets of carnations
and boxes of violets. It is sunny
and they are in good humour.

1216/578
A golden reflection of the
moon on a stream in a wood.
Beyond the wood there is a
windmill.

274/1054
The last remnants of snow
on the green outside a large
brick-built Victorian public
building. People in coats walk
on the snow.

1321/1530
A dark-haired man with long
sideburns is dressed in a black
cloak and a large white collar.
His hair is combed forward
over his bald head and his
grey eyes look up and away in
fake disdain.

1284/1313
A young woman with a full
green dress sits on a couch
in a pleasant, sunlit drawing
room; a baby lies beside her
in a white robe. Her head
rests in her hand and she has
a bored, depressed expression
on her face.

1272/51
Large, organic, multi-
coloured platforms rise above
water; there are shafts of
light and flying creatures
with seaweed-shaped limbs.

261/566
A rocky outcrop on a beach.
Gulls hover above the
placid sea on which small
boats are sailing.

1156/690
On the steps of a temple,
large men are slaying women

and children. Smaller men in luxurious red clothes stand surveying the carnage.

1263/648

A boy with blond hair and a white apron sits and sleeps, slumped on a chest. Shiny boots are on the floor around him.

D. 2

126/1040

A man sits, drawing two other men. One stands and the other sits. They all wear suits.

242/1174

A thatched house in the country. Four cows are standing in front of the house.

1117/1106

The hills and countryside are a mess of green and purple in the snow.

185/1079

The banks of a river are full of cranes. Behind them, a large domed structure is under scaffolding.

1195/595

A woman carrying a large basket on her back crosses a bridge over a brook to approach a wooden house at the foot of some hills. She drives a small herd of goats.

1023/49

The decorated doorway of a small church that has a small tower with two windows. Large sunflowers wilt just outside the door.

1202/319

A broad, dusty street bordered by a white fence behind which there are buildings and trees. A flag with a white cross on a red ground is hoisted on a pole, and underneath it men in large hats stand leaning on the fence. A woman drives some sheep up the street.

E. 1

1277/1270

A large orange house, the grounds of which are surrounded by a wall that is broken by a small gate. All this is set in a wood.

207/1286

Behind a grey wall are the backs of a number of large industrial buildings. They are all equipped with large doors and their own cranes.

164/1523
In the dark, two adults tend
to an illuminated child who
wears a strange hat.

209/1018
A golfer walks along a path,
pulling his clubs on a trolley.
Behind him is the large
white clubhouse.

1185/530
On a gently sloping hill a
blue plough rests unattended
on a long ploughed field.

205/1250
The back of a Georgian
terrace. The exterior of the
garden wall is bordered by a
pavement and is punctured
by a small wooden door.

1199/233
A number of people perform
indistinct actions in an
orderly fashion on a meadow
that is bordered by trees and
a small brook.

1525/317
A terrace of brown houses is
located so as to survey a large
brown garden that becomes
the countryside at its furthest
extent. The sky is white
and mottled.

797/P008
Three Neo-Gothic
church towers. Two are
predominantly blue and
the other is of a dark,
sandy colour.

1053/655
Under a stormy sky trees are
blown in the wind. Under
these, a number of ducks
huddle on the ground whilst
five other ducks search for
food in a small pond.

196/1064
A quiet city street on a
sunny day. A young family
walks along the pavement.

1519/481
A grassy expanse with
occasional trees.

1198/232
Beyond a bridge that crosses
a stream is a thatched house.
A man crosses over the
bridge while a child plays
precariously on the banks
of the stream.

E. 2

771/P136
A tall ship with a red sail sails
out of an ornate harbour. It is
dusk and the sky is golden.

182/990
A troupe of ballet dancers
performs on an ornately
decorated stage. They have
no faces.

F. 1

268/379
Three people wade in the
water just off a small beach.
Behind them is a boathouse,
and behind that a small town
with a harbour, in which a
number of sailing-boats
are moored.

217/1288
A building with large
balconies and a furled-up
Union Jack on a diagonal pole
overlooks a narrow street.
Next to it is a scaffolded
building with a man working
on its roof.

275/425
A tall, thin man who wears
a morning suit. His chest is
puffed out monstrously and
his ugly face finishes in a
ludicrously large nose.

1060/1067
The base of an indistinct
purple and black structure
rises up above pale ground.
The dark, right-hand side of
the structure is punctuated
by a creamy spotlight.

983/1056
Shadowy figures fish with rods
on a river bank. Behind them
are two equally shadowy trees.

1029/1535
A brightly coloured city
is seen from a vertiginous
height. The roof of one of the
buildings is a pink and green
mosaic; one of the facades is
entirely purple.

1048/1051
The broad high street of a
small town. Most of it is tree
lined but some buildings also
flank it. Horse-drawn carts
use the sides of the street to
travel along while two cyclists
speed down the middle.

/

A very pale farmhouse with
a small pond in front of it.
A woman carrying a basket
walks with her child towards
a hay-laden cart.

197/1094
A grand tent-maker's shop on
a high street. Its green-painted
front incorporates large
windows and pictures of tents.
A Union Jack is hoisted up a
long pole on the roof.

257/561

A small village in a valley that is surrounded by dramatic green and purple mountains. One stone house stands apart from the village, amongst trees on the slope of a hill.

157/182

A number of gently rolling green and yellow fields. There is a steeple in the distance.

1505/946

A respectably large, cream-coloured town house. A man dressed in a smart suit and hat walks erectly beside it with his hands clasped behind his back.

1421/563

A stone bridge crosses a river that leads into a medieval town which has a large tower and castle. Three people stand on the bridge. At a different time of day the scene is similar, but the light washes everything out.

F. 2

1193/1331

A small alley traverses the infrastructure of a green iron marketplace.

1319/1506

A high old bridge crosses a small stream. A child plays with his dog at the water's edge.

G.

1240/1255

A man with dark hair and long sideburns sits on a leather chair in a dark room. He is dressed in a dark coat and stares senselessly to his side.

1153/603

In a large columned room a crowned man sits on a stone throne holding a spear. He has long, dark, flowing hair and a beard; his expression is stern. He is surrounded by two doting courtiers and a fey soldier. They all regard an androgynous youth who plays a harp.

236/1062

A temple-like building on the corner of an almost deserted street. There is a set of traffic lights in front of it.

131/1176

A couple who are walking in the countryside look at a large building with an immense central tower. A fox passes by, oblivious to it.

128/1215
A pale old lady who looks mildly contemplative. She wears a white bonnet, and her tightly pursed lips almost suggest a smile.

115/1083
A wide river in a large city. Many barges are either moored on its banks or navigating along it.

1114/7
An angular steeple rises up from green trees into a white and blue sky.

235/1263
Beneath a blue-grey sky, a city street is lined with orange-brick buildings and an elegant white church with black railings.

1042/532
A young blonde child with a toy horse in her hand is held by an old man with a bald head and a large beard. She is whispering something into his ear; he listens attentively.

151/1362
A grumpy old woman with a red cloak and a basket sits in the shade on the banks of a pond where three ducks are swimming.

212/1044
A grassy cemetery with large mausoleums. Barren trees grow scattered in the grounds.

176/1385
From narrow streets there rise tall buildings that are connected by small bridges.

267/368
On the upper banks of a narrow river, two lovers cuddle. The river, which is being navigated by a man on a punt, leads into a small harbour town.

1470/58
A tranquil, suburban tree-lined street. A car is parked on the pavement and a lorry makes its way down the street.

H.

1437/967
A woman with a blue dress and hat sits with a coquettish expression on her face.

1270/501
A young boy with long black hair drinks from a cup that

he holds with both hands. His
dark eyes look over the rim of
the cup.

1041/575
A young boy and his younger
sister stare with concentration
and excitement into a toy-shop
window.

1066/609
Two young ladies, one blonde
and the other red-haired,
collect thistles from the field
in which they are walking.
The one with red hair has a
sad, longing look in her eyes.

1297/714
A mountain pass is traversed
by a shepherd with his flock
and his dog. Storm clouds
muster up above.

1282/647
Long grasses, trees, clouds
and birds are blown about
and agitated by the wind.

1194/754
White bathing-huts are on
a beach that backs onto
undulating fields. The sea is
calm. There are very white
cliffs further along the coast.

1062/520
A woman with fiery golden
hair looks towards a light-
green sea. A white dove pecks
at her ornate cloak.

977/1533
A heraldic coat of arms
picturing a deer, a helmet
above a shield on which
two turrets are described,
a lion and three flowers.
The inscription 'All's Well'
is written beneath it.

1056/265
A house located on the
border between a wood and
a meadow. Washing is being
hung by a woman on a line
outside the house.

1027/1059
The gatehouse of an estate;
the gate is open. A man on
horseback is talking to the
keeper. They both regard a
dog that sniffs something at
the foot of a hedge.

1271/538
A proud, intelligent and noble-
looking boy with black hair
and rosy cheeks. He wears a
high-necked dark top, and is
in a musty environment.

1206/524
A boy with red braces and a
sad-looking girl sit on a rock
at the edge of a pond on
which reeds and lilies grow.

I. 1

1463/1027

A dead-end street that finishes in a small industrial building. A rickety wooden fence runs along one side of the street.

259/728

The end of a terrace in front of which is a pleasant garden with a path running through it. A woman carrying a parasol walks along the path with her child, looking at the plants. Two other children play on the lawn.

168/1376

A roundabout behind which is a building that is located on the corner of a street. Someone pushes their child, in a pram, past a large church further down the street.

1024/358

A scrap-heap of locomotives under an agitated yellow sky.

121/247

A slatted wooden building with a balcony on which two men and a woman stand. In front of the building is a trough from which a horse drinks. Three chickens peck at the ground beneath the trough.

235/1060

A large yellow, blue and orange modern block of flats. There is a small grey modern house in front of it.

993/353

Various people work on their allotments. Four men have stopped working to look at a breezy, orange-haired young woman with bare knees who is digging and enjoying the attention.

269/77

A large dark house on a quiet shopping street. There are bare trees in front of it.

1177/1230

At one end of a street is a fairy-tale-like green steeple. Two rustic white cottages with red roofs are at the other end.

232/1011

A large beige house at the entrance to a cobbled yard. The house is surrounded by a fence; an inscription on its facade declares the business of the yard to be the manufacture of vats and wooden tanks.

1439/183

A village street that is shared by motorcars and horse-drawn

carts. The street is bordered
by leafy trees and a few shops.

223/1175
The quite intact ruins of an
old building. The hedge in
front of it is overgrown.

1456/68
A detached white suburban
house with a black roof and
green paintwork on the doors
and windows. The front
garden consists of well-kept
lawns and a large round
flower bed surrounded by
a circular drive.

154/239
A town street with a steeple
at its end. A man pushing a
wheeled cart crosses the street
in front of an automobile.

237/511
Under a dirty sky, a broad
murky river meanders under
a bridge and flows towards a
cathedral. There is greenery
on one side of the river and
buildings on the other.

155/249
Men use ramps to load things
from carts on to a boat that is
moored on the quay. A sailor
with yellow trousers stands
on the boat.

1275/996
A town square with a single
lamp-post in the middle of it.
A man with a top hat and tails
stands near the lamp-post and
a fox runs across the square.

/
A half-demolished brick
house is behind the remnants
of what was a corrugated-
iron fence. A tramp walks
away from the house – leaving
various empty bottles behind
him.

I. 2

1100/1195
An angry, fat old man with
a bald head and a large
white beard sits on a leather-
upholstered chair. He has a
red handkerchief on his lap
which he holds down with his
right hand; he wears a small
diamond ring on the little
finger of his left hand.

1025/1207
A well-coiffured elderly
gentleman with a blue jacket
and bow tie.

1259/1069
A blue sky is barely
distinguishable from a blue
sea on which a boat sails.

The yellow coast is swept by
the elements.

803/P063
Several houses with tall green
pitched roofs under a patchy
purple sky. A huge teapot
and milk jug are before them –
almost obliterating them.

J. 1

1249/640
In a garden just outside the
city walls, a man dressed in
rags stands under a vine with
his arms raised in surprise.
Another man and a woman,
both dressed in rich robes,
dismiss him angrily. A tall
pink flower stands between
them. From an open door in
the city walls people regard
the encounter.

1283/916
A woman in a long red dress
holds a door ajar and looks
forlornly at the opening.
Fluttering above some blue
lilies that are next to the door
is a yellow butterfly.

1295/753
A ruined castle on the banks
of an estuary. A man is
crossing shallow water on
a white horse and a boat

is approaching the castle's
slipway.

1067/917
From the top of a hill where
bushes and trees grow, green
meadows descend down
the hillside and become an
extensive plane that leads to
a purple horizon.

1278/1271
A bunch of assorted, dull-
coloured flowers in a blue
and white vase.

1322/1206
In a dark rustic house, four
people sit to supper around
a table. On the table, several
tiny figures and a tiny white
horse each emanate a bright
light that illuminates the four
people's faces.

867/811
A rickety old cart is in the
middle of a farmyard. Behind
it is the farmhouse with a
red-tiled roof and next to this,
an inclined oak tree.

J. 2

1103/951
A terrace of five houses backs
on to a yellow wheat-field that
is bordered by more houses

and a farm. The sky is creamy
and the sun barely shines.

1454/574
A small boat is passing
through a lock in a canal
that leads through woods to
a walled city. Men with horses
prepare to plough an adjacent
field.

1130/622
A mousy-haired man with
light blue eyes and a moustache sits on a red upholstered
chair. He wears a brown three-
piece suit and has his hands
clasped on his crossed lap.

1126/1542
A bald old man with silver-
framed spectacles sits wearing
purple ceremonial robes
and medals. He has a mole
on his forehead and holds a
mortarboard on his lap.

K. 1

1244/1519
A woman with heavy features
and white, set hair sits staring
to her side. She wears a
strangely folded white shawl.

100/542
Under a blue sky, a tall
Arabesque tower rises up from

a cathedral that shares the
street with a few residential
buildings.

1064/535
In a meadow, coloured watery
flowers grow from the grass.
Behind them is a wood, and
beyond that, small hills.
The sky is grey and stormy.

153/238
A busy road crosses over
a placid canal via an iron
bridge. On the other side
of a cream-coloured wall,
adjacent to the road, is
a gasworks.

1048/434/2
A page of a brightly coloured
illuminated manuscript.

1382/968
On the edge of a wood, a
man dressed in travelling
clothes sits in front of a pot
that is suspended above a
fire with an arrangement
of three sticks and a rope.
He is concentrating on
something that he is doing
with his hands.

226/438.1
The long narrow gap between
two ornate religious buildings.

225/429

A tall medieval city on a
hill. A castle stands at its
highest point.

324/428

Massive mountains and high
cliffs rise up from a partially
wooded meadow.

226/438.2

A narrow street which is
bordered on one side by
a cathedral.

143/267

In a bushy garden, a man
dressed in travelling clothes
sits concentrating on the
stick that he is whittling.

/893

Masses of working people
bearing banners march
triumphantly with horses,
oxen and carts.

/880

Four tall arched windows
reveal a mother superior's
supervision of four of her nuns
who pick flowers in a garden.
They bear them as gifts to a
crowned and haloed woman
with a haloed child.

1276/1041

A busy high street with shops
and people of all kinds.

A dustman with a green cart
sweeps the side of the road;
a woman with a yellow jacket
walks with her child on the
pavement, carrying a bunch
of flowers.

PC27/P27

A happy, white unpopulated
pier stretches out over a
murky green sea. There are
two small boats on the beach
and three oriental turrets
on the land.

K. 2

199/1183

A quiet town junction. On it
is a green lamp-post that bears
direction signs for various
locations.

1214/580

A kindly, stern-looking
and clean-shaven elderly
gentleman. He wears a heavy
black jacket and a frilly
white necktie.

/1511

A man with a luxurious
furry collar sits at a table.
His hands are joined over
numerous sheets of paper,
next to which are an inkpot
and a feather quill.

1518/480

Grassy fields are divided by hedges that at certain points become small woods. Five cows lie on one of the fields.

1151/1180

Black railings, through which are threaded indistinct jagged wires and plants, shield a house from view.

161/568

A heavily laden cart pulled by two shire horses makes its way down a sombre, almost deserted city street. A dog stands on the pavement, as if about to cross the street in front of the horses.

1110/596

At the entrance to a small village some people stand around a pond. Three ducks file into the pond and a woman walks away from the village with her grandson, who pushes a wheelbarrow.

L. 1

1115/48

A broad pink path leads down from a bridge to a point on a canal bank, which is just prior to the point at which the canal passes under the bridge.

1034/932

Three women stand in an idyllic garden with a sundial. The woman on the left walks away from the other two, carrying a bouquet of flowers that is shedding petals. The one in the middle stands innocently in a white robe with an ornate cup in her hand; she is divided from the third woman by a small trench, which has been dug with a spade that now leans on the sundial. This third woman has a yellow cloth over her head, a crown in one raised hand and a sword in the other. A young boy stands beside her.

1150/1386

A young red-haired woman stands playing the violin in front of a full-length mirror that casts her reflection. Her violin case is open on a chair beside her, and her sheet music rests on a flimsy metal stand.

1265/588

A fat, flabby old man with a moustache looks older than his years. He sits proudly, wearing a fur-collared red robe and a heavy gold lord mayor's medallion. A coat of arms hangs beside him,

bearing the inscription
'All's Well'.

258/907

Sheep lie or graze on a
meadow on the banks of a
river. A man crosses over a
small wooden bridge that
traverses a stream, which
flows into the river.

246/565

A deserted monastery on a
tall mountain. From it there
is an immense view of the
plains below, the horizon
disappearing into purple mist.

L. 2

1397/135

A boy crosses a quiet street.
A man rides a penny-farthing
down a street with a small
dog playfully running beside
him. A woman walks along a
driveway towards a group of
buildings. A large building
with an extensive lawn, which
has railings in front of it; on
the other side of the railings is
a park where people stroll.

249/553

A calm river leads into a
town. Boats are moored on
the river's banks and a man
crosses the river on a raft.

/1087

A very straight white bridge
crosses a mirror-like river in
an important city. Sailing-
boats and steamers navigate
the river.

1496/523

A tightly packed seaside
town is located at one end
of a bay. It is a grey day but
the sea is calm. There is a
white lighthouse at the other
extreme of the bay.

1141/87

A terrace comprising four
houses and one industrial
building. A man calls out
from the porch of one of the
houses to his two children
who are in the street, in front
of the industrial building.

989/1202

A modest church with a long
canopied entrance.

/1545

A good-looking young man
with wavy shoulder-length
hair and stubble on his chin.

162/1515

Three men are unloading
sacks from a lorry-trailer into
a yellow industrial building.
The lorry-driver stands by
the trailer.

1055/615

A proud, elderly man with a
white beard stands in a very
dark room. He wears a puffed-
up black robe and holds one of
its lapels. In his other hand he
holds a sheet of paper.

1178/587

A balding middle-aged man
wears a half-smile and a black
jacket and tie. His hair is
vaguely blond.

1179/581

A thin old man with a bald
head and a neatly trimmed
beard. He wears a blue tie
with a pearl-ended tie pin.

M. 1

1172/521

A beautiful young woman lies
enticingly on a divan next to
a window with red curtains.
Her light-blue dressing
gown is parted so that her
nightdress is revealed. A cup
on a saucer and a dessert plate
are on a small table before her.

1312/1222

A lustred bowl and plate rest
on a shelf, which is hung on a
wall that is decorated with a
motif of lilies.

995/942

A house with pretensions to
grandeur. A dome crowns one
end of it.

161/726

A man dressed in fancy riding
attire lounges with parted legs
on a blanket, which he has laid
on a rock. He has dark hair
and sideburns, and he holds a
cigarette between his fingers.

/1547

An eager-faced middle-aged
man with flowing grey hair.
He wears a smart black outfit
with a white shirt and necktie.
One of his hands is behind his
back and the other points to
a line in a fat book.

1221/1001

Two schoolboys in shorts
play with a football in a
small, unkempt grassed-
over city square. The square
is surrounded by terraced
houses.

1516/477

A house in the midst of gently
rolling countryside.

1286/661

In the shimmering half-light
of dawn two men sit huddled
under a leafless tree. The
horses which they have just

dismounted stand beside them and graze.

M. 2

256/555
Five teams of horses are driven with whips to drag a large sailing-boat onto the beach. Women with baskets on their heads look on.

208/479
At the end of the day, men walk away from the vegetable fields on which they have been working.

737/P691
A country church surrounded by a deserted cemetery. The tombstones lean at odd angles.

1280/1273
The yard of a city dock. The masts of sailing-ships can be seen over the yard's fences, which enclose a number of upturned trolleys.

1219/988
The curved end of a meandering cul-de-sac. One of the three children who are there inspects his knee after falling from his cart; another leans suspiciously on a wall; the third holds a hoop and stick in his hand whilst he regards two women who are conversing.

1539/352
Behind leafless trees is the facade of an old building, the core of which has been demolished.

229/684
A richly dressed couple lean on each other, looking proudly at their daughter who sits at a desk doing her homework. Red curtains partially obscure the window behind them.

206/1285
A row of bland grey office buildings on a cobbled street. A rather ornate tower with a clock on it rises up from the pavement adjacent to the buildings.

127/711
A smart young man with trimmed hair and moustache stands in a musty room wearing a black suit and a white shirt.

N. 1

179/1541
A group of farm buildings next to fields. Tall trees are

scattered around the farm
and the fields are divided with
straight wooden fences.

1233/274

Under a grey sky, men in
white smocks stand in a
wooded field.

1113/992

Black angular rocks rise from
red ground under a blue and
yellow sky. An intense fire
burns amongst the rocks.

1252/1039

On the edge of a walled
enclosure, a coffin is being
loaded onto a horse-drawn
hearse. Two women mourners
stand distraught alongside two
serious men in black top hats
and two children. An old
man with a scythe looks on,
and two other men peer over
the wall.

1264/934

Two identical young red-
haired women prepare a
young blonde woman for her
marriage. They are placing a
veil over her head while she
stares forward proudly and
demurely in her white dress.
Golden braids on the dress
draw attention to her breasts.

141/1521

A chubby man with dark
hair and bushy sideburns
sits studiously at a table that
is crammed with books and
papers. He wears small metal-
framed reading-glasses.

N. 2

1044/1181

The statue of a naked woman
stands on a table next to a
bunch of brightly coloured
flowers. She faces some dirty
brown drapes.

1119/356

An androgynous man with
long hair walks down a street
wearing a blue uniform and
cap. He carries a bag hanging
on a strap from his shoulder.

1227/356

A bridge with four arches
crosses a river. There is a
large domed church behind it
and three small rowing-boats
moored in front of it.

1154/643

Three generations of women
sit outside a large house on
which many crawling plants
grow. Alongside them, a small
toy horse is poised to drink
water from a red saucer.

O. 1

1517/478

A narrow lane slopes down a hill, bordered by a painted concrete wall. Fields flank it on the other side, and beyond them is a group of houses. In the distant horizon is a cathedral that is barely visible in the mist.

1514/475

Tall trees on a grassy field. Geese fly overhead.

1512/473

A steeple is framed by tall trees. In front of the trees is a lawn.

/

The incomplete skeleton of a bridge that is being built to cross a river. There is a cathedral on the far side of the bridge.

1147/587

A serious man with a moustache sits at a table on which lie some papers and two large leather-bound tomes. One of his eyebrows is raised, suggesting mild disdain.

1032/607

A plump woman plays with a baby who is laid down on blankets that cover a piece of furniture. She wears a low-cut green velvet dress and has very long hair, with which the child plays.

1040/623

An eccentric old man with a ludicrously long and square-shaped beard, which would be white if it weren't for the yellow nicotine stains on it. A thick gold watch-chain hangs from his waistcoat pocket. His hands are long and elegant.

O. 2

133/175

A small church with a long canopied entrance. The ground in front of the church is cobbled.

167/1375

A street of grey timber houses. People walk very slowly on the pavement.

1030/539

Tall trees form a curtain through which may be glimpsed a burning orange sky.

145/322

Through an oval window, the expanse of a large estate

can be seen. A horse-drawn carriage drives down towards the manor, which is set amongst trees.

214/1248

A blue building on the corner of a street. A balcony which runs all the way across the first floor is flanked by two white lions.

P.

1210/928

A young goatherd with a long stick stands looking at two of his goats that are munching leaves from a large bush with pink flowers. He has his large packed lunch in a basket on the ground beside him.

1133/1395

Whilst a naked young woman stands frightened on a high mountain-top balcony that is full of roses, a naked young man with beautifully coloured wings made of peacock feathers jumps off the edge of the balcony. He is surrounded by white doves.

1268/1531

Various sections of a wooden fence that surrounds a school have had pictures painted onto them by children: a man with a dragon; an American Indian and his teepee; two goats crossing the road; foxes, hares and a bird; a bus, cars and pedestrians.

1133/1395

A sickly child sits almost naked on his mother's lap whilst his sister removes his sock. The mother leans over the table, which was being used as an ironing board, and addresses her elder son. Another woman is just entering the room, which is full of clothes hanging on lines to dry.

Q.

1123/52

At the foot of some hills, a small hamlet is bordered by a river that continues through some fields. There is a chicken coop on one side of the river and two boys with a small rowing-boat on the other.

1255/83

A large Georgian house with an extension. Net curtains hang in the windows and handsome topiary hedges adorn the front garden.

1124/354

A long straight snow-covered street passes through a dull town. An area in the middle of the street is fenced off; the fence bears a large placard with the word 'Danger' on it.

1258/1071

A man who is between old and middle age fades away on a green easy chair. His hair is combed lankly to one side.

1239/941

Two books, a pipe and a bunch of flowers in a jug share a table-top in a wood-clad room.

1536/366

Behind some small hills, on which charred trees stand almost erect, are a group of huddled and strangely shaped mountains. There is a constructed cave entrance on the face of each of the mountains.

1248/638

In a clearing of a forest the following events are taking place: a man in red and gold robes holds his hands up towards the sky above a large fire; a man with a leopard-skin cape fights with a man in a blue robe over another man who lies frightened on the ground between them; a man in a red and gold robe is surprised at the flirtatiousness of a woman in a white dress; a woman with a long black head-dress stands with her head resting on her clasped hands in a sad, resigned manner; a woman wearing a white dress kneels on a wooden pyre, shielding her eyes and facing away from a man in a red and gold robe who is standing over her and wielding a knife while he implores the heavens.

R. 1

/

An illuminated tram travels along a rainy street that is being crossed by a man in a hat and a raincoat.

/

Behind a fenced-off playground with swings is a large brown-brick building

255/1012

A small station in a semi-rural location. A man on a bicycle buys something from an adjoining kiosk and a woman walks her dog in the forecourt.

265/1316

Four men unload timber from a barge onto a large sailing-ship. A ladder is perched between the barge and the ship, and another timber-laden barge awaits its turn.

1449/982

A man uses a large scythe to cut hay that is to be loaded onto an already replete horse-drawn cart. Other piles and loads of hay are around him, each attended by another man.

1457/69

A woman walks on a pavement next to a wooden fence. Behind the fence is a white house, whose columned porch bears the inscription 'White Lodge'.

1102/1514

The violently coloured modern interior of a house.

1234/915

A richly dressed woman sits on a red divan with her intelligent hands clasped together on its backrest. She wears a white-feathered hat, which looks splendid on her dark hair; on her lap, curled up sleeping, is a small white and brown dog, which she not unaffectionately ignores.

1183/527

A trilby hat, braces and a dirty yellow tie give a shifty appearance to a youngish man who holds a bunch of bright yellow tulips behind his back.

241/158

A small, awkward terrace of houses on the corner of a street. The most minute puff of smoke emerges from one of the chimneys.

1447/978

In a valley, woodcutters saw large trees, which are brought to them on a horse and cart.

R. 2

1537/910

A fairly busy shopping street in a small town. The butcher's shop, with carcasses hanging in the windows, is next to the barber's shop, with its spiralling red and white pole projecting proudly from the front.

1444/974

A picturesque and heavily constructed garden adjoins an affluent home. On an island in the middle of the garden's large pond is a statue of a cherub.

247/562

Various people stand on the banks of a river that passes through a large city. There are houseboats on the river, and beyond them a large grey bridge.

120/85

Two closed shops adjoin each other. The one on the left has the shutter pulled down over the front window.

166/1080

A brightly coloured mermaid with flowers on her breasts strikes a pose in the depths of the sea. A small mask covers her eyes and the long hair on her crowned head straggles in all directions.

253/1093

A group of spindly and almost barren trees in a wood.

distance are some buildings under a sky which is turning stormy.

195/1046

A pub on the corner of a residential street. A woman pushes a pram along the pavement and is about to cross the street.

189/327

An avenue bordered by trees and one small building. A very erect and proper woman walks on the pavement; she wears a red jacket.

1083/658

A young woman with blonde hair tied in a bun is crouched and collects in her apron red and yellow apples that have fallen from trees. Large oak trees loom beyond the sloping orchard.

S. 1

112/1251

The corner of a quiet one-way street. Two men talk on the pavement.

1108/983

A long pale beach, which backs on to sand dunes and is lapped by a green sea. In the

S. 2

1074/644

The long nave of a large cathedral. Shafts of diagonal light illuminate the interior where a woman sits and speaks to a child and various other people wander around contemplating the architecture.

1148/1238
An elderly man with neat
white hair and beard sits in
heavy black garments. He
wears discreet metal-framed
oval spectacles and has
his fists lightly clenched on
his lap.

129/1216
A young man with self-
consciously dishevelled dark
hair looks away into the
middle distance. He wears
an elaborate silky collar
with a brooch, and has a
very prominent nose.

1399/256
A white wooden building
in which various shops are
housed adjoins a much
larger brick building. People
bustle around in front of it,
performing various tasks:
tending horses, pushing
barrows of flowers, pulling
carts of hods.

1314/1253
A chubby man with a
powdered wig has his hand
inserted into the front of his
red and gold waistcoat in
Napoleonic style. A black cape
rests on his shoulders.

1242/579
A balding middle-aged man
with large ears has a smile on
his face that is both shy and
conceited. He wears a dark
grey suit, a white shirt with
curved collars and a black tie.

1279/1272
A curving street at night is
partially illuminated from a
source that is concealed by
an exterior spiral staircase. A
man with dark clothes walks
furtively along the pavement.

1065/536
A tranquil pale-blue sea meets
white cliffs and a beach. Two
small boats with white sails
sail placidly near the beach.

183/1214
A smiling dead man, clad
only in a loincloth, is lowered
from a cross by men in robes
who have climbed ladders
to perform this task. At the
bottom of the cross four
women are praying.

1037/1508
Speckled white and red
flowers in a park.

T. 1

1520/41
A canal on which two barges
are moored. A church steeple

on one side is reflected in the water; on the other side the bank forms a broad walkway.

1445/976
On a plush meadow is a wooden barn with an orange-tiled roof.

198/1105
A broad city street passes by a church with a white steeple.

1302/1102
From the bottom of a garden, amongst shrubs and undergrowth, a square house with a small turret looks rather eerie at dusk.

1121/620
A young soldier with golden centre-parted curly hair, pale eyes and boyish features sits in an easy chair wearing his uniform under a heavy green military coat. He holds his cap between his legs.

971/1505
A bald clergyman with grey sideburns wears full regalia and holds the book open on a red velvet cushion.

T. 2

/
A poster announcing a pony race bears information and humorous illustrations.

1293/583
A man with short dark hair and a white beard looks expressionlessly ahead with his piercing grey eyes. He wears a black suit and tie, and a very crisp white shirt with winged collars.

1244/323
The interior patio of a house has hay on the floor and a trough and bridles hanging on the walls and doors, these being large enough for horses to pass through.

1301/1090
A young woman with a pearl necklace and a low-cut dress shows off the way in which a bird eats a berry from her hand. Her other hand supports her weight on a table.

1047/1050
A stagecoach is pulled by four horses through a small but affluent settlement. Trees line the entire length of the road.

811/P193

Beneath a coat of arms and above a long inscription a man and a woman kneel and pray over a tomb. The man is flanked by eight boys and the woman by three girls, all of whom are also praying.

1253/952

Barely visible in a blurry haze, a person sits with head in hands, huddled on a table. On the table, and also in the haze, are bottles and round fruits. A single white bowl, which is also on the table, escapes the haze with an extraordinarily crisp appearance.

117/1284

A large red building, which looks rather dramatic when seen from a low angle.

U. 1

1225/641

Large piles of red and yellow apples are scattered alongside barrels on the ground of an orchard that is surrounded by stone walls. Two boys wearing hats stand by an open wooden gate. Beyond and in the distance is the sea.

1096/936

A woman and a girl walk through a wood towards a large ruined castle. The sky is blue and filled with fluffy clouds.

1188/549

A teenage girl wearing a summer dress sits propped up on cushions. Her hair is jet black and tied in a bunch of braids. She has pronounced black eyebrows, heavy features and pretty red earrings.

1098/573

Two men cross a river in a small boat. The rural side, which they leave, is populated by grazing sheep and reeds; the side they approach has factory chimneys billowing smoke into the air.

1490/257

A crisp white church with an extended covered porch at its entrance. A horse-drawn cart passes in front of it, as do a couple holding a parasol.

1050/949

Faceless stocky women walk along a curving orange path with full baskets on their heads. Next to the path, other women are tending fields and washing clothes.

U. 2

1373/1199

A man with a fat, jovial face that is covered by a beard but not a moustache. His hair sticks out towards the sides.

1155/10

A garage on a street. Two old women stand at its entrance gossiping and a young couple walk across the road with their arms around each other's shoulders.

1217/1088

A young man with frizzy grey hair, dark eyes and a large nose wears a white cravat and stares into the distance.

1323/1200

A man with a white beard and no moustache wears a white winged-collar shirt and a black bow tie.

1140/1278

A broad driveway curves around a mature tree and leads to a long white house. A man in black stands in the shade of the tree and a woman in bright red stands in front of the house gates.

119/200

Two policemen stand facing a church steeple that is across a canal.

1324/1524

A stumpy black tree shakes next to a white circle in the sky.

239/513

A huge cathedral towers over a city's market square where women in white bonnets shop.

1530/1164

A tall, white and slightly ruined cathedral spire. Beggars walk in front of it, beside a dilapidated house.

1142/1267

Two large cargo-ships are moored in a deserted modern harbour. The sky is quite grey.

930/478

In the distance is a cathedral; nearer is a church, and closer still a group of houses. All is vague and misty.

1303/1103

Behind an iron gate and trees is a house; its roof bears a balcony with a small turret.

V. 1

1285/610

In a very dark red room a woman stands on a stage, at a table – as if addressing a crowd. Below her, on the floor, a man holding a broom leans despondently on the stage.

1059/754

A winged angel gives something and also speaks to a woman in a white dress who looks worried as she stands on the narrow edge between a river and a field of reeds.

1180/613

A middle-aged woman sits wearing a slightly dowdy but nevertheless pretty dress. Her hair is plaited and bunched over her ears; she has a knowing, demure expression.

1015/881B

Oranges and orange-blossom grow from green-leaved branches.

1015/881A

Peacocks form a tower by standing on each other's entwined tail-feathers.

1508/1441

The sky is orange over a river at dawn. Nothing crosses the large bridges, but a steamer does steam underneath them.

1052/1269

On a blue balcony, a woman with red hair and a green skirt sits on a deckchair and writes a letter. There are palm trees beyond the balcony.

V. 2

1081/914

An elderly man with trimmed white hair and beard stands in a black suit and a red tie. He holds his spectacles in his hand.

1243/654

A plump, balding young man in casual clothes holds a book to his chest with a finger marking a page.

1143/1101

Behind two trees is a large square house with a roof pitched from all four sides. On top of the roof is a balcony, in the middle of which is a small turret.

193/1094

A large iron bridge with two ornate towers as its supports. Cars and buses pass over the bridge.

1116/944

A fairly large church on
the green of a quiet town.
The steeple ends in a
sharp point.

1080/1407

A stream flows through
a sparsely wooded forest.
The trees that there are
are quite bare.

234/1032

A row of shops on a street.
The last shop in the row is
covered in scaffolding.

1112/987

A large house on the corner
of a street that slopes up
towards a park.

251/557

On a hilltop, a woman and
two donkeys stand beside a
ruined castle. There is a large
church in the valley below,
and birds hovering overhead.

194/1045

A car travels through
residential streets on a road
that winds round towards a
cathedral. A man crosses an
adjacent street.

W. 1

1220/989

In a playground in an
industrial town, two boys sit
chatting at the bottom of a
slide. Another boy sits alone
on the ground, leaning on a
post and wearing a yellow-
and-black checked shirt.
He looks at the other two
boys and has a ball at his feet.

1069/577

A young girl with amazingly
red, windswept hair stands
holding forth a vase with
white wispy flowers.

1443/973

Beneath a tree, on the
outskirts of a small village,
a fat old woman sits in front
of a sheet of paper, which is
supported on a small easel.
She draws the village.

1087/543

A tree bends over a stream,
shading the water. Yellow
waterlilies float on the surface
of a broad, placid river.

1035/253

Across the street from a pub,
a wooden building adjoins
a much larger one made of
bricks. In front of it, two men
take a break from their work

and converse while another
carries a bundle of wood past
a mother and her son, towards
two shire horses.

1241/53
A black house with many
small red-tiled roofs. The
yellow moon, which hovers
directly above the house,
illuminates a row of four
different types of trees in
front of it.

1196/963
In a farmyard, a man rides
his horse into a pond, around
which there are some white
geese, so that it may drink.
The far side of the pond is
overgrown.

1226/653
Beneath a gaggle of migrating
birds, a man leans out of his
boat into the waters of a calm,
grey river. Cows graze on an
adjacent field.

W. 2

125/716
A man with a grey face is
dressed in heavy woollen
clothes that also cover his
head. He stands before a large
sailing-ship that has collided
with an iceberg.

/860
A grey sky over a large patch
of white ground in a meadow.

1006/1409
A grey house stands behind
a black tree and a long,
grey bridge.

1307/1211
A bald old man with a stern
and golden face. He wears
a heavy blue suit and an
elaborate scarf.

1287/1536
Behind a corrugated-iron
fence, a fading city may be
seen. Houses become tower
blocks as one travels further
from the fence.

X. 1

175/1276
A large grey-blue house which
is accessed by a drive that goes
through a garden.

204/1276
A large grey building with
a white portico.

215/1275
A complex of buildings
set amongst trees. One
of the buildings has a
black-tiled steeple.

1088/81

A long straight street with bare trees and terraces of Georgian houses on either side. The street is empty.

210/1031

A path, along which a family walk with their dog, borders the front garden of a large house.

1276/1042

A jug containing purple flowers and green foliage rests on a table in front of orange curtains that are being blown by the wind that comes in from the open window behind them.

1215/548

On a dark night, a low yellow moon is reflected in a pond that is set within a dense wood.

1063/534

Cows graze in a meadow. Beyond them are some trees and, in the distance, more fields.

1152/1003

A thin old man with big ears and a bushy white moustache. He wears a brown suit and a mauve cravat.

1105/646

A calm river on which lilies float leads through a bridge into an orange city which has a tall steeple. Small rowing-boats are moored along the river, and a girl walks with her baby brother along its banks.

1049/948

A fruit-bowl, flowers, an ashtray, a jug of water and a book rest on a table at which two blue seats are placed. The room in which they are all located is coloured with sickening hues.

X. 2

1433/355

In a long makeshift tent, men sleep under grey blankets on neatly ordered rows of camp beds. Other men in uniform watch over them.

988/1513

The snowed-over, walled back gardens of a group of houses, the pitched roofs of which are also covered by a thick layer of snow.

1004/1378

A narrow alleyway between two buildings. Short bridges span the distance between the

two buildings and cast long
shadows on their sides.

Y. 1

221/1077
The facade of an ornate
building. Two old men walk
in opposite directions on
the street in front of it.

218/1077
A little girl plays with her pink
tricycle on the pavement in
front of a pale-green detached
house. The house's front
garden boasts a beautiful tree.

1458/908
Beyond a wasteland, in land
that is demarcated by a wire
fence, a large brown temple-
like building stands behind
a prefabricated hut.

136/242
On the shores of a river where
boats use a gangway to dock,
a classical temple with a
steeple is fenced off with
ornate rails. There is a
windmill behind the temple
and the riverbank is populated
with very awkward people.

1499/61
A very symmetrical and
proper pale-yellow house.

A man walks along its front,
following the wooden fence.

273/78
A mildly overgrown garden
provides an appropriate
setting for a once noble house
that is now crumbling and
in ruins.

1502/65
On the corner of a street,
a church with a red door is
separated from the pavement
by a wire fence with concrete
pillars. A man and a woman
walk from different directions
towards the corner of the
street. The corner of the
church is adorned by a figure
of Christ on the cross.

1315/1254
A benign-looking man sits
at a desk with a paper in his
hand. The fingers of his fat
right hand – which rests on
his knee – are incredibly short
and pointed.

Y. 2

1046/59
A large dog lies on the top of
a wide wall with its tongue
hanging out and its legs
dangling over the edge. Small
birds fly in the sky behind it.

1124/1196

A fairly old man with grey
hair and beard wears red
ermine robes and an elaborate
gold chain, with a crest on
the large medallion which
hangs from it. He sits on
a large wooden leather-
upholstered chair.

975/1504

An old man with white hair
and beard, and a particularly
prominent moustache, stands
on a balcony wearing red
ermine robes and an elaborate
gold chain which hangs from
his shoulders over his chest.
He holds a paper scroll in his
white-gloved hands.

Y. 3

1257/1008

An extended interior window-
ledge supports a black teapot.
The curtains that cover half
of the window are made of
a black-and-white checked
fabric.

1107/1038

A group of children, dancers
and acrobats lift a seated
clown – who is dressed in red
– as high as they can in front
of a stone wall. Children look
on from over the wall.

1129/621

An unpleasant, thin old man
with greasy white centre-
parted hair sits on a grand
wicker chair. His arm rests
on a pile of papers on the desk
in front of him.

Z. 1

1084/1070

Two barges, one larger than
the other, are motionless on
a frozen river. The riverbanks,
the trees and a house are all
snowed over.

1266/940

A tall, thin white pointed
tower rises up like a rocket
from a village at the foot
of some high mountains.

262/369

A young woman carrying a
basket walks down a path,
past some buildings, towards
a river. Her excited black
dog runs ahead of her.

138/245

In front of the metal railings
that demarcate the grounds
of a large building, some
roadworks are taking place.
The labourer is taking a break
and drinking a cup of tea.
Various people look on.

Z. 2

113/1231

A solitary dark figure stands in a narrow street that passes through archways which connect the buildings on either side. A pile of broken-up crates is strewn on the pavement.

976/1532

A winding path borders a river and continues past a windmill and a house. A man travels down the path with a laden horse and a couple court on the riverbank.

1526/1410

Two men, one standing and the other kneeling, fix a barrel on a boat that floats on a river in the industrial quarter of a city.

264/374

A horse-drawn cart travels down a fading street. The passengers protect themselves from the sun with a parasol.

152/6

Two red trams approach pedestrians who are crossing a cobbled street. Another group of people wait at the tram stop.

123/236

Two schoolgirls in purple uniforms and boaters walk down a street of grand terraced houses.

202/1055

A wooden barn with a red-tiled roof. In front of it, a shire horse is calmly walking away from an overturned cart.

160/241

Barren trees and a wall separate a church from a fading cemetery.

1435/1388

A pick-up truck is parked in front of the garage doors of a building that adjoins a wind-mill. A small conveyor belt is on the neat lawn that surrounds the building. The sky is blue and filled with clouds.

Z. 3

252/558

On top of a hill that offers fantastic views over an extensive plain, two men attend carts that are pulled by donkeys.

190/909

A solid house is surrounded by a high wall, the gates of

which are open, revealing the driveway.

1527/1411

Two men bind and hook up a large package so that it may be hoisted up on a rope. Beyond the watery expanse that is behind them, a vague city skyline can be seen.

134/244

A broad cobbled street, half of which is shaded by the buildings on one side. A horse-drawn cart has just stopped outside one of the buildings on the sunny side of the street.

339/1391

A deserted street with grey pavements and buildings of various types.

159/273

A low church shields a wood of oak trees from view. In front of the church, on parched ground, is an abandoned graveyard.

1176/993

In front of a yellow sky that contains many moons and suns, a woman floats in a seated position with a bowl of fruit on her lap in front of a leafy tree on which

three birds are perched. A woman on a swing is to her left and another stands with a disapproving countenance to her right. Eight depressed women sit or lie on the ground in front of the three.

Z. 4

1273/494

A large, luscious tree shades a square in a small town at noon. Few people walk in the streets.

280/259

Beneath a streaming blue and yellow sky is a farmhouse that is located on a lawn which it shares with a large pond. There is a large cathedral in the distance.

211/1034

A lawned park with trees of various types shielding a long building from view.

278/512

A path travels through a forest of robust trees. Deer on the path stop at the trees to eat the moss that grows on them.

243/526

A small sailing-boat, attended by two sailors, bobs in a

peaceful lake. The sky is an explosion of orange behind the clouds.

1504/945

A man cycles past a bakery and a pub on a city street.

201/1256

A residential street ends in a roundabout on which a woman in a white dress is standing. A green lorry is parked outside one of the surrounding houses.

1429/954

A large and excessively ornate brick building on the corner of two streets. Beyond it there stands a tall factory chimney.

231/1010

The rounded corner of a building forms the facade of a cinema. A Belisha beacon stands in front of it.

187/1031

A modestly grand brick house with a well-tended lawn stands beside an ornate and almost palatial low white building.

220/1076

A man wearing a cap walks down a street past a large building which has a prominent balcony on the top floor.

181/1249

The staircase, landings and halls of a house are entirely blue.

244/1004

A dilapidated house. Its castle-like appearance suggests that it once had pretensions to refined splendour.

248/564

The ruins of a castle stand on either side of a straight and narrow road that goes through the countryside. The sky is grey.

178/1314

Many cranes adorn the banks of a working city river. Boats are moored on a barge that forms a small island on the river; a bridge connects the barge to the mainland.

1513/474

Neat rows of trees demarcate fields in pleasant green countryside. The flatness of the land is slightly interrupted by a few small hills.

1095/955

An overgrown garden with dark trees shields a grey house

from view. The sky is white
and yellow.

Shelf A.

1046/962
The dark head and shoulders
of a man who has a heroic
expression on his face. His
hair is wavy and his goatee
beard long.

Shelf B.

1377/440
A circular grey leafy frame
bears the profile of a man with
lank hair, bushy sideburns and
a prominent nose.

/430
A man in a long dark coat
stands with one foot raised
on a rock at the edge of a fast-
flowing white river. He holds
his hat in his hand.

/442
A young man in a long dark
coat sits next to a tall bureau.
He holds a pen in one hand
and supports his weight on his
knee with the other.

7/443
A small lock of yellowing hair
tied with a blue thread has

the name of the person from
whom it came written next
to it.

1376/439
A satyr concentrates gently
on the foot of a coy young boy
who leans with his hand on
the satyr's curly head. The
boy sits on a white sheet and
is attended by four lambs.

1378/449
A young man with glistening
eyes rests his head on his hand
with a contented expression.

Shelf C.

1462/1017
A woman stands at a bus stop
that is separated from a row
of prefabricated houses by a
rickety wooden fence.

1453/1403
A fat man wearing a white wig
and a three-cornered hat looks
over his shoulder angrily.

124/166
A cross-eyed woman with
controlled wavy hair and
an elaborate dress sits with
her hands neatly folded over
her lap.

137/340

A poster announces the
various events that are to take
place at a fair; the text on the
poster is blue.

/1456

A crane loads white bundles
onto barges that are moored
on the riverside. Two men
oversee the operation.

Shelf D.

1281/554

A shepherd uses a staff to
attempt to drive his flock
along a lane that leads to a
village, which is surrounded
by tall trees. Red poppies
adorn the sides of the lane.

Shelf E.

1181/624

Teams of men wearing
overalls work very hard
in a vast, bleak shipyard.
They are building three
huge iron ships, two of which
are still merely skeletal.

Sancti Petri

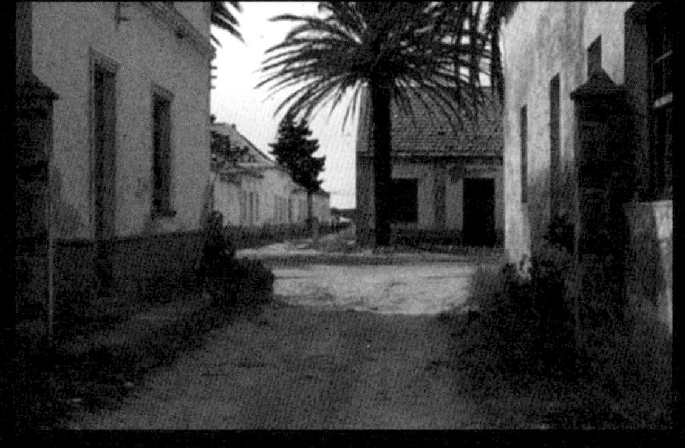

1   Sancti Petri

2   The Carretera de Sancti Petri leads into the village.

3   The Carretera de Sancti Petri is the only dry access
    to the peninsula.

4   There is marshland to the right of the Carretera
    de Sancti Petri.

5   There is a beach to the left of the Carretera de Sancti
    Petri.

6   The Carretera de Sancti Petri ends at the village.

7   The Avenida de Chiclana leads into the Plaza de la Iglesia.

8   There is a bend to the left at the end
    of the Carretera de Sancti Petri.

9   The Calle de la Cruz leads to the seafront.

10 All the residential buildings on the Calle de la Cruz have
    ceramic insignia on their facades.

11 –

12 –

13 –

14 –

15 –

16 –

17 Each of the residential buildings on the Calle de la Cruz
    has a front patio and contains three homes which each
    contain three habitable rooms.

18 The rest of the buildings on the Calle de la Cruz are
    dedicated to the processing of fish.

19 The factory.

20 The warehouse.

21 The generator.

22 At the sea-front the Calle de la Cruz turns to the right,
    around the large factory building.

23 The Calle de la Rivera continues
    all along the sea-front.

24 The Civil Guard's hut is on the left-hand side of the
    Calle de la Rivera.

25 The Quay is on the left-hand side
    of the Calle de la Rivera.

26 The main factory building is on the right-hand side
    of the Calle de la Rivera.

27 The Red Cross Centre is on the right-hand side of the
    Calle de la Rivera.

28 There are residential buildings on the right-hand side
    of the Calle de la Rivera.

29 Four parallel streets lead off the Calle de la Rivera,
    in a perpendicular orientation to it.

30 Calle del Reloj.

31 Calle Calleja.

32 Calle de San Pedro.

33 Calle del Carmen.

34 The Calle de la Rivera ends at the opposite extreme
of the peninsula.

35 The signal-master's house is located at the end of
the Calle de la Rivera.

36 An area of empty land extends to the right of the signal-
master's house and marks the end of the peninsula.

37 The area of empty land continues to the other side
of the peninsula.

38 Small boats are moored on this side
of the peninsula.

39 A path travels the length of this side of the peninsula.

40 Buildings back onto the path.

41 The path continues to the entrance to the village.

42 One end of the Calle del Mar gives on to the area of
empty land.

43 The Calle del Mar heads towards the centre of the village.

44 The Calle del Mar meets the Plaza de la Iglesia.

45 There is a series of transversal edifications on the
left-hand side of the Calle del Mar.

46 The transversal edifications form groups of one-storey
residences with hipped roofs.

47   Access to the residences is gained through alleys formed
     between each two rows of buildings.

48   The alleys close at their ends, forming areas of common
     services.

49   A factory block faces the transversal edifications.

50   The Plaza de la Iglesia is a square in the centre of
     the village.

51   There are palm trees, lamp-posts and benches on the
     Plaza de la Iglesia.

52   The village's mayoralty is a two-storey building with a
     chamfered corner, an arched portico on the ground floor
     and a balcony on the axis of the building on the first floor.
     It has a patio at the back and a flat roof.

53   The inscription on the facade of the mayoralty translates
     as follows: *Through the initiative and work of the most
     excellent gentleman Don Joaquin Perez Lila, president of
     the administrative council of the National Tuna Fishing
     Consortium, the homes and other dependencies of this village of
     Sancti Petri were built and the services of water and electricity
     were installed. Chiclana 1940-56*

54   The church and the school have similar facades, with
     variables in their front crests and points of access; they
     are bordered by lateral aisles and have pitched roofs.

55   –

56   –

57   At the back of the two buildings and accessible via the
     lateral aisles there are complementary dependencies
     for services.

58 The residences of the village's notables form a symmetrical
   building which is two storeys high at its lateral extremes.

59 The two lateral extremes are covered by hipped roofs
   with eaves.

60 The residences that are housed in the two lateral extremes
   are the only ones with complete bathrooms. The rest of
   the residences consist of four habitable rooms, a vestibule,
   stairs, a kitchen and a flat balcony above the arches of the
   ground-floor gallery.

61 Access to the ground-floor residences is located in the
   ground-floor gallery.

62 Access to the upper residences is located in the
   lateral aisles.

63 The Cuartelillo has a flat roof.

64 A residential building which consists of four terraced
   houses and has a pitched roof faces the church, the school,
   the residences of the village's notables and the Cuartelillo.

65 The Avenida de Chiclana leads away from the Plaza de
   la Iglesia.

66 The Avenida de Chiclana heads towards the Carretera
   de Sancti Petri at the entrance to the village.

67 There are blocks of housing in rows on the right hand
   side of the Avenida de Chiclana.

68 Each residence has a single bay which is parallel to
   the facade and two habitable rooms.

69 There are groups of terraced houses on the left-hand
   side of the Avenida de Chiclana.

70   Each house has a patio, a central gallery, a porch on the front, four symmetrical habitable rooms and a kitchen and bathroom accessible through one of the back rooms.

71   Four parallel streets lead away from the Plaza de la Iglesia, in a perpendicular orientation to it.

72   Calle del Reloj.

73   Calle Calleja.

74   Calle de San Pedro.

75   Calle del Carmen.

76   The four streets are comprised entirely of residential buildings.

77   –

78   –

79   –

80   –

James

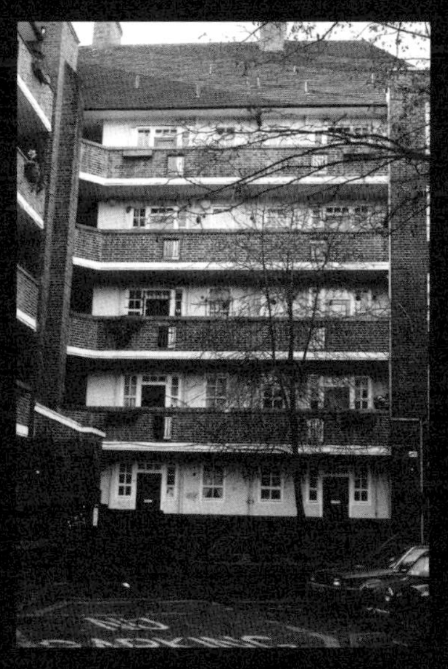

Grey Doors

CHARACTERS
JAMES, a young man
a PAINTER, in his fifties

*A block of flats in a 1930s housing estate in east London.
The block is five storeys high and access to the entrances
of each of the flats is gained via exterior walkways.
All of the flats' front doors are painted a matt grey colour.
Mid-afternoon.*

SCENE I

The PAINTER, *dressed in a paint-splattered overall, knocks
at one of the grey front doors on the first floor of the block;*
JAMES *opens the door.*

PAINTER. I've come to put the gloss on.

JAMES. What?

PAINTER. The gloss, I'm the painter.

JAMES. Oh yes, of course, I forgot. Is there anything I need
to do?

PAINTER. No, nothing at all, only it would be good if you were
going to be in this evening so that you can leave the
door open while it dries.

JAMES. Yeah, sure, I'll be in.

PAINTER. I'll just go and get my things then.

JAMES.   Right. [*Goes back into the flat as the* PAINTER *goes down to the courtyard to collect his paint and brushes which he returns with immediately.*]

PAINTER.   [*Knocking on the doorframe.*] I'm back; I'll get started.

JAMES.   [*Emerges from the flat.*] Great, would you like a cup of tea?

PAINTER.   No thank you, I'll just get on with it.
            [*Prises the lid off a pot of paint.*]

JAMES.   Is that the colour we're having?

PAINTER.   You chose it.

JAMES.   Yes I know but it looks different in the pot to the way it does in the samples.

PAINTER.   And it will look different again when I paint it on the door.

JAMES.   Why's that?

PAINTER.   It's to do with the way it dries, it just changes a bit, couldn't really say how. You've also got to bear in mind that when you see it on the sample or in the pot you're looking at a very small surface, the door's a lot bigger and the colour just looks a bit different, it's not a drastic change, though, I wouldn't worry about it.

JAMES.   Oh I'm not worried. If it was down to me I'd leave all the doors in the block as they are now, in that grey you painted them. It's a nice grey, so neutral, neither dark nor light, and I like its texture too, sort of matt and porous.

PAINTER.   I suppose they might look all right like that, but they can't stay like that, they're not finished. I mean the grey's just an undercoat, it's drab, it's not meant to be looked at.

JAMES.   What would happen if they were left like that?

PAINTER.   They'd get very dirty, for a start; it'll pick up anything, this paint. The wood of the door wouldn't be protected, either, it would rot eventually. The undercoat's just a base. It covers up marks and gives a surface with a bit of tooth to paint onto.

JAMES.   Does it only come in grey?

PAINTER.   Oh no, you can get it in just about any colour. If you were painting just one door or lots of doors in the same colour you'd choose an undercoat that was closer to the colour you were going to paint the doors. On a job like this, though, where there are over a hundred doors to paint in seven different colours, it makes more sense to bulk buy the undercoat in a neutral colour that you can paint any other colour over.

JAMES.   Yes of course, I suppose it's cheaper.

PAINTER.   A lot cheaper.

JAMES.   How many coats of the undercoat do you need to paint?

PAINTER.   Two. You could probably get away with just doing one if the door was already in relatively good shape but two's always surer and since it dries fairly quickly it's easy to do.

JAMES.   I really think that it's a lovely paint, can you get it anywhere?

PAINTER.   [*Looking eager to get started.*] Oh yes, any decorating
            shop.

JAMES.   [*Noticing the* PAINTER'*s impatience.*] Right, I'll leave
            you to it. You sure you wouldn't like a cup of tea
            before you get started?

PAINTER.   No thank you, I'm fine.

JAMES.   OK. then, I'll be in if you need anything. [*Goes back
            inside as the* PAINTER *starts to paint the door.*]

SCENE II

It is half an hour later and the PAINTER *is painting the last
touches on the door. The voice of* JAMES *is heard coming from
within the flat, on the other side of the half open door.*

JAMES.   Is it all right if I come out?

PAINTER.   Oh yes, I'm just about finished.

JAMES.   [*Emerging from the flat with a cup of tea in his hand
            and looking at the freshly painted door.*] Gosh, that
            was quick!

PAINTER.   [*standing back to contemplate his work and smiling*]
            I've had quite a lot of practice.

JAMES.   Have you been doing it for a long time, painting
            I mean, as a job?

PAINTER.   Only thirty-five years.

JAMES.   Thirty-five years!

PAINTER.   That's right. I started my apprenticeship at sixteen
            and I'm fifty-one now so that's what, [*thinks*] yes,
            thirty-five years exactly.

JAMES.   That's a long time.

PAINTER.   Probably longer than you've been alive.

JAMES.   Yeah, it is.

PAINTER.   You can tell that I've been painting for a long time
            if you look at my right arm. See how much bigger it
            is than my left, more developed, years and years of
            painting. I call it my Popeye arm! [JAMES *chuckles*]
            I'm not complaining, though. It is hard work but the
            money's good and I can take my holidays whenever I
            want. I spend nine months of the year painting – day
            in, day out, and all the hours there are – but then I
            spend the other three months, the autumn, usually,
            on holiday.

JAMES.   That's a long holiday, where do you go?

PAINTER.   I've been going to Thailand for the past ten years
            and I'll carry on going there I think, no point in
            changing if you like a place.

JAMES.   Oh, I agree completely. Sounds like a nice thing to
            do, going away like that for a good period of time.
            I met someone else who did that actually, he was
            an artist, a painter.

PAINTER.   Different sort of painter.

JAMES.   Well yes, I suppose so. Anyway, this guy, I can't
            remember his name, he would spend six months
            here in spring and summer teaching or doing
            whatever work he could get and then he would
            spend the autumn and winter months in Jamaica

where it's still sunny at that time of year – like in
Thailand, I imagine. His life there sounded idyllic.
He would live in this wooden hut on the beach and
make paintings outside by stretching a huge sheet
of canvas between two palm trees and then painting
on it.

PAINTER.   What did he do, portraits, still-life?

JAMES.   Well that was the other good bit. Every morning a
local boy brought him everything he needed for the
day: some fresh fish, a bottle of rum and some grass.
He would lay these out on a tree stump and paint a
huge picture of them before consuming them and
making himself unable to even think of painting
anything else!

PAINTER.   I don't do that sort of painting.

JAMES.   Just as well really, I saw his pictures and they were
pretty horrible. I prefer your grey doors, actually.

PAINTER.   But I can't really take the credit for those.

JAMES.   Why not? You painted them.

PAINTER.   Well yes, that's true, I painted them, but I didn't
decide what to paint and it's not as if it needed
inspiration or anything like that. I'm not saying that
it's not a skilful job, though. It might look simple
but it's quite tricky if you want to do it properly
without dribbles or build-ups of paint, and you
also have to prepare it properly to make sure that
the paint doesn't peel off soon after it dries. I do a
quick and economical job that will last, but it's not
as if anybody's going to put a door up on their wall,
especially not one that's grey and unfinished like
the ones you like!

JAMES.   I suppose not. [*Pauses*] So what do you do in
           Thailand? Three months is quite a long time
           for a holiday.

PAINTER.   I play a lot of golf.

JAMES.   Oh right, are there nice courses over there?

PAINTER.   Well they're good enough for me. I mean I'm not
           a great player, I just enjoy it. I suppose they're not
           championship courses but they do look nice. The
           weather's fantastic in the autumn when I go, as well,
           not too hot and not too cold, just perfect. Sometimes
           it rains for a bit and it's rain like you've never seen
           before, huge droplets that soak you whole, but it only
           lasts for five minutes and then the sun comes out
           again so you don't mind the rain so much, in fact
           it's quite nice.

JAMES.   And who do you play with?

PAINTER.   Expats, people on holiday, friends, whoever's around
           really, foreigners mainly, the locals don't really play.

JAMES.   No, I suppose it's quite expensive for them. But
           what about for you, how do prices compare to here?

PAINTER.   It's dead cheap. It has gone up a bit in the last few
           years with increasing tourism and that, but it's still
           not comparable to over here, particularly if you know
           it a bit and you don't go to the tourist places. You can
           find yourself paying four times the price for the same
           meal if you don't know your way around. But they
           don't try to con me; they know my face by now.

JAMES.   I think I had Thai food once in Amsterdam. I wish
           I could remember. Satay, that's it, bits of chicken and
           a spicy peanut sauce, is that right?

PAINTER.   Yes that's right.

JAMES.   I thought so, it was nice, we had other things as well
but I can't quite remember what they were. Don't
remember much about the whole evening actually.
We'd gone to one of those coffee shops you see,
and eaten some hash brownies. The first one didn't
seem to have any effect so we ordered more and still
nothing until an hour after we left the place and
then it hit us, wallop! We were completely wrecked,
couldn't even remember where our hotel was, and
then when we did find it we couldn't stop laughing,
we were in such hysterics that we couldn't even ask
for our room key. That was some time ago actually.
Now that I think about it, though, someone told
me recently about a Thai restaurant which had just
opened, quite good apparently.

PAINTER.   Is that the one in Shepherd's Bush?

JAMES.   No, I think it's near Holborn. As I say, I haven't
been there but I hear its quite good, what about
the one in Shepherd's Bush?

PAINTER.   It's fantastic. I've been to a few Thais in London
and that's definitely the best. Not that I've been to
all of them, tend to wait 'til I'm out there where I
get all the food first hand, fresher and a lot cheaper.
They do tend to rip you off here, a kind of exotic
tax. But you should go to this place some time, for
a special occasion, with a lady; you know what I
mean, if you want a 'good' night. [*Winks at* JAMES]

JAMES.   [*Smiling uncomfortably*] Right, yeah, I'll try that.
It's always quite hard to know what to order in
these places, though, especially if you don't know
the food.

PAINTER.   Yes, I suppose you do put yourself in their hands, and it's not cheap, either. You just have to risk it, really. That's what I like about being in Thailand, everything's much cheaper and once the people know you they don't try to rip you off. They're very nice, once they realise they can't get one over on you.

JAMES.   Do you own a house there, I mean where do you stay?

PAINTER.   I rent a house, it's pretty basic but it's got everything I need, and I pay next to nothing for it. The cost of living is so low out there, it's ridiculous, I can get a girl to live with me for twenty pounds a month.

JAMES.   [*Incredulous*] Right. [*A voice calls from the courtyard, which the* PAINTER *acknowledges.*]

PAINTER.   That's the other guy, I'll be going then, nice talking to you. As I said, it would be best if you could leave the door open for at least four hours so that it can dry properly.

JAMES.   Yeah, sure, I'm not going out.

PAINTER.   [*Packing his things up*] All right, good-bye then.

JAMES.   'Bye. [*Watches the* PAINTER *walk away and then enters the flat, leaving the door open.*]

END

Woodyard

A woodyard in east London. The yard covers quite a large plot of land, which is separated from a busy road by a wall. Access to the yard is gained via one of two large openings in the wall; one of the openings is designed for vehicles to enter and the other for them to exit – signs indicate this purpose. Adjacent to the second opening is located the yard's office – a small, house-like building with a hipped roof and windows looking onto the yard and the road.

The yard itself is tarmacked and slopes down from the road towards another wall, behind which is a canal. Most of the timber kept in the yard is stored on blue metal racks – large modern units that, by virtue of storing the timber sideways, allow fork-lift trucks to have access to it. These racks articulate the space of the yard – forming a broad avenue which is cluttered by stray loads of timber and disorderly vehicles, and which slopes gently down from the road towards the canal side of the yard.

Spanning the breadth of this side of the yard, and almost entirely obscuring the canal, is a massive wooden structure in which timber is also kept. Said structure is the equivalent of three storeys high and forms what is essentially a three-dimensional grid in which timber is classified and stored. The structure is topped by a corrugated iron roof that slopes down towards the canal. Since the back of the structure is clad roughly with sheets of board, glints of light are visible through cracks from the front of the structure, the intensity of the glints dependent both on the size of the cracks in the cladding and on the volume of timber held in each compartment. There is a narrow and fragile-looking set of stairs on the extreme left of the front of the structure. The yard workers who climb up these stairs proceed to

*clamber across the structure in order to get to the particular type
of timber that they require. The whole operation looks rather
precarious and the men, many of whom are stripped to the waist,
resemble monkeys exercising themselves on a piece of apparatus in
their enclosure.*

*The structure appears like an enormous sculpture on which
various actions are being played out: the men clambering about
it; customers looking at it; vans and lorries parking in front of it;
large amounts of timber being loaded on to and off it... It is as if the
structure had been constructed to serve the precise purpose of acting as
a stage within which to view these various activities; to those who are
not involved with the structure – those who are neither workers nor
customers – this view overwhelms the structure's principal purpose
of storing timber. This shift in emphasis is occasioned both by the
structure's dramatic presence and by the simple yet pervasive – to the
extent of seeming symbolic – curiosity of witnessing a structure made
of timber that also stores timber.*

*Although the access to the yard is always open, there is a definite
sense of the yard being a private place; a particular code of conduct
is required within it – one that respects the established hierarchies.*

SCENE I

JAMES *walks into the yard, looks around – not failing to notice the
large wooden structure and all its associations – and then enters the
office which is small and doubles up in part as a shop, stocking nails,
screws etc. A counter divides the area where customers wait to be
attended to from that in which the administrative staff carry out their
duties. It is a typical office of its kind, with cheaply veneered desks,
a dirty carpet and yellow-stained walls on which trade calendars
with images of naked women hang.* JAMES *looks towards the various
people behind the counter for about a minute until one walks towards
him and stands staring contemptuously through him.*

JAMES.   Do you stock joinery quality timber?

ATTENDANT.   What you after, mate?

JAMES.   Well, I needed some two by two and another
                yard told me that you had some that wasn't
                warped – that was true – I need it for quite a
                precise job.

ATTENDANT.   Don't know about joinery quality, we stock
                softwoods, you know, pine and that. I mean,
                I have got some two b' two and some of it's
                straighter than others, you know what I mean,
                mate, it's a question of finding the right piece…
                What you using it for?

JAMES.   [*thinking quickly*] Oh, um, I'm making some
                frames, for paintings, so I need it to be really
                straight. Would it be all right then, just to go
                down and choose some pieces.

ATTENDANT.   Yeah, sure… How much do you need?

JAMES.   About four metres.

ATTENDANT.   You'll get that out of one piece, just go down
                and pick it out, if you need help just ask one of
                the lads.

JAMES.   Where is it, the two by two I mean?

ATTENDANT.   [*Deliberately*] Just ask one of the lads.

JAMES.   OK. I'll just go down and have a look, thank-you
                very much.

ATTENDANT.   Yeah, sure, cheers. [JAMES *walks out of the office.*]

SCENE II

In the yard, JAMES *begins to look around for the timber he requires. One of the workers, who has noticed that he looks rather lost, approaches him with a generous sort of contempt.*

WORKER.   What you looking for, mate?

JAMES.   Oh, um, two by two… the guy in the office said it was all right if I chose some, I need a really straight piece, you see.

WORKER.   Yeah, right, follow me. [JAMES *follows him down to the wooden structure where the* WORKER *indicates a rack, which is at ground level.*] How much do you need?

JAMES.   About four or five metres

WORKER.   [*Pulls a length of timber out of the rack*] There you are.

JAMES.   Can I just check how straight it is, I'm sorry to be so fussy but I need it for quite a precise job.

WORKER.   [*Raises the end of the timber to his eye and looks down its length*] Well, it's got a bit of a warp at the end, like. [*Puts it back and pulls out another which he looks down again*] This one's worse, if anything. [*Puts it back and pulls out a third, which he inspects*] This one's better.

JAMES.   [*Rather shyly*] Can I see? [*The* WORKER *hands it to him begrudgingly and* JAMES *emulates him by looking down the length of the timber.*] It's a bit bent at the end, see.

WORKER.   [*Laughing yet annoyed*] You're never going to get something that's perfectly straight. I mean it's just luck, some lots are better than others.

JAMES.   But is this lot particularly bad?

WORKER.   No, not really, it's a building material: as I say, some
            lots are straighter than others but most bits will be
            a little warped. These ain't even what you'd call
            warped, though.

JAMES.   Yeah, I see what you mean, it's just that, well, I
            do need it to be quite straight. Would you mind if
            I looked through them, see if I can find the
            straightest one.

WORKER.   You help yourself, mate, but as I say it's in its nature
            not to be perfect.

JAMES.   So when do you get your next lot in?

WORKER.   [*Cross*] I'm telling you it won't be any different.
            We get deliveries every couple of days but you'll
            have the same problem every time.

JAMES.   Right, I'll just look through what you've got
            here then.

WORKER.   All right, you just give one of us a shout if you
            need something.

JAMES.   Oh, thanks [*The* WORKER *walks away, leaving* JAMES
            looking through the timber.]

SCENE III

JAMES, *after some time spent searching, finally finds a piece of timber
that he considers suitable. He looks around somewhat triumphantly
in order to know how to proceed with his purchase. His expression
changes as he notices that most of the yard workers are having a
joke at his expense – laughing at the fussiness of a person who wants*

to buy a single piece of timber. JAMES *continues to look around –
attempting not to show his increasing embarrassment.*

A BOY *who works in the yard notices that* JAMES *wants
something and approaches him. The* BOY *is about thirteen years
old and is crowned with a shock of dry, blond hair. He is dressed
just like the other workers in dusty, faded jeans and scuffed boots;
a leather belt with holster-like compartments for his tools is slung
low round his hips.*

There is a disquieting aspect to the BOY*'s appearance; though he
still carries with him a certain innocence particular to childhood there
is something about him that has matured too quickly – he displays
an odd sort of officiousness and sense of duty. However, the daily
working routine that he performs has not quite ingrained itself into
him, in the way it has into some of his older colleagues, and so a large
part of his mind is constantly taken up with a concentration on his
tasks. This has the effect of making the* BOY *appear blinkered – as if
he were unreceptive and even a bit stupid.*

BOY.   You all right, mister?

JAMES.   Oh yes, thank you, I just wondered what I have to
          do to pay for this. [*The* BOY *nods and picks up the
          piece of wood.*] That's all right, I can carry it if you
          like. [*The* BOY *has already walked off with the length
          of timber by the time that* JAMES *has had a chance to
          say this and is holding it up to the structure in order to
          measure it against some painted markings; he notes the
          length of the piece and, taking a pencil out from behind
          his ear, writes it down on a scrap of paper. He takes
          the length of timber onto his shoulder with a deliberate
          technique that is stilted yet strangely graceful and,
          beckoning* JAMES *to follow him with a gentle nod of the
          head, starts walking slowly towards the office – regularly
          equilibrating his gait to cope with his cumbersome load.*

JAMES.   [*Resigned to the embarrassment of being served by a
          child, follows the* BOY *towards the office. Having arrived
          at the door the* BOY *carefully leans the timber up against*

the wall and walks in. JAMES *follows and stares at him, performing the following actions: The* BOY *leans over the counter, stretches for a calculator which he places on the desk before him and slowly begins to calculate the price of the timber, looking in a manual for the price per foot of the particular sort that* JAMES *has chosen. His performance on the calculator is again characterised by a deliberate and meticulous concentration – as if the* BOY *were desperate to recall the order of a series of actions that had not yet become ingrained in his memory. He presses each of the calculator keys with such apparent fear that it looks as if he is defusing a bomb. When he finally arrives at a price he writes it down in pencil and then goes through the whole calculation again; the subsequent result he again notes and, confirming that it is the same as the first, writes it onto a piece of paper that he finds on the counter. He then looks up expectantly and manages to catch the attention of a kind face: that of a* WOMAN *in her thirties – the only female presence that* JAMES *has encountered in the yard. He finds it strange and a little embarrassing that she should be here amongst the calendars bearing images of naked women. She however, shows no signs of being distressed by her environment – seeming instead to be perfectly at home, and even in a position of power, within it.*]

WOMAN.   [*Smiling at the* BOY *and leaning over the counter in a feigned flirtatious manner*] Is this the gentleman's order?

BOY.   [*Eagerly but a bit shy*] Yeah.

WOMAN.   All right, I'll take care of it. [*The* BOY, *as if surprised at the ease with which he has been able to offload his customer, walks out of the office rather furtively, as if he had just managed to get away with something.*]
Do you need an invoice, love?

JAMES.   No, not really.

WOMAN.   All right then, that'll be seven pounds forty-seven.

JAMES.   OK [*He pays her and receives his change*]

WOMAN.   Thank you very much.

JAMES.   Thank you, goodbye.

WOMAN.   See you [JAMES *walks out of the office*]

SCENE IV

In the yard, JAMES *looks at his length of timber; he attempts to pick it up but realises that it will be too cumbersome to carry away. The* WORKER *who first helped him walks past.*

JAMES.   Excuse me, sorry… hello, sorry, can you help me?

WORKER.   [*sternly*] What?

JAMES.   I just wondered if it would be possible to borrow a saw for a minute – it's just that this bit of wood's too long to carry, and if I could cut it in half it would be easier.

WORKER.   You need a saw?

JAMES.   Yes please [*The* WORKER *walks away saying nothing but he returns quite promptly with a saw which he hands to* JAMES.] That's very kind of you, thank you. [*The* WORKER *nods and makes to walk away.*] Oh, sorry, where should I put it when I'm finished with it?

WORKER.   [*Nods towards the office*] Just leave it there.

JAMES.   OK, thanks very much. [*The* WORKER *walks away slowly.* JAMES *puts his length of timber down, measures it with a tape measure that he has in his pocket and saws it roughly down the middle. He then takes a roll of packing tape that is lying around and binds the two lengths of timber together; he puts the bundle down, returns the saw to the office and, after exchanging a few gruff pleasantries, reemerges, picks up his purchase and walks out of the yard, carrying it on his shoulder.*]

END

The Golden Heart

CHARACTERS
JAMES, a young man
a WOMAN
a MAN
various other customers of the pub

A pub in east London. Though the pub is actually quite old, the features are designed to make it seem even more antique: wood panelling, dark stained tables and chairs, items made of brass on the walls, etc. Those parts of the wall that are not clad in panelling are covered with a now nicotine-stained wallpaper of broad vertical golden stripes. The desire to make the pub look old-fashioned has not, however, ruled out the presence of a modern fruit machine and a jukebox which both emit bright coloured lights that reflect dully in the dark varnished wood.

The only person in the pub is a woman who sits with quite some concentration at one of the tables working over some papers while she smokes a cigarette. She is in her mid-fifties but her appearance is carefully contrived to make her look younger: Her hair is suspended in a nest-like arrangement which keeps it clear of a face that is densely coated in powder; she wears a tight two-piece suit over a white blouse garnished with a gold chain. She has high-heeled shoes on.

SCENE I

JAMES *walks into the pub and goes to the bar; it is obvious from the way in which he is looking around that he has never been here before. The* WOMAN *notices him and, leaving her paperwork, stands up calmly and walks behind the bar.*

WOMAN.   [*with a professional smile*] What can I get you, darling?

JAMES.   Half a lager please.

WOMAN.   [*she pours it*] That'll be ninety-seven pence please
my love

JAMES.   Thanks [*Having paid her and taken his change* JAMES
*goes to a table at the furthest corner of the pub at which
he sits down; he takes a pen and a newspaper from his
bag and begins to do the crossword. The* WOMAN *returns
to her table where she continues with her paperwork.*]

SCENE II

A MAN *walks into the pub: he is dressed in dusty clothes and
wears a large tool-laden belt on his hips. The landlady notices him,
smiles and walks behind the bar.*

WOMAN.   What can I get you, darling? [JAMES *looks somewhat
startled as he hears the* WOMAN's *voice; he has not
noticed the man walking in. He quickly returns to
his crossword.*]

MAN.   I'll have a pint of lager, please.

WOMAN.   Sure thing, darling. [*She pours his drink whilst he
looks around the pub, the look on his face becoming
increasingly mischievous.*] One ninety-four please,
my love.

MAN.   [*as he pays her*] It's a bit quiet in here.

WOMAN.   Some of us like it like that. [*Once she has taken
his money she returns to her table to continue with
her paperwork. He sits at a table in silence for about
thirty seconds*]

MAN.   [*suddenly, to the* WOMAN] Mind if I put the jukebox
on? [JAMES *raises his gaze; the jukebox is right next to
him and he assumes that the question is directed at him.
He looks down straight away when he realises that it*

isn't – relieved that he won't have to engage in any kind of exchange.]

WOMAN.   [*Without raising her eyes*] It's your money.

MAN.   Yeah, but I thought you might not want me to disturb this deadly quiet. [*He waits for her to rise to his comment but she doesn't. He chuckles and gets up from his seat to make for the jukebox. As he passes* JAMES *he looks at him and gives him a conspiratorial look of assumed camaraderie which also acts as a kind of threat.* JAMES *smiles in a nervous and noncommittal manner. The* MAN *scans the list of songs and keys in his selections, he then saunters back to his seat as* Rebel Rebel *by David Bowie starts to play.*]

SCENE III

The MAN, *having been sitting at his table for a couple of minutes, swaggers over to the bar and leans on it confidently. He lights a cigarette, hobbles a bit, mouths some words and then looks over to the* WOMAN *who is still at her table, trying to concentrate on her papers.*

MAN.   We haven't really got off to a good start, have we? It's just that I've just finished a long day's work and I just feel like being friendly and I like to relax by chatting – you know, the way people do. [*She doesn't respond and he looks downwards, smirks and shakes his head. Whilst he is doing this she looks up and smiles – her mood and attitude towards him seemingly changed. She then gets up, walks behind the bar and surprises him with a question which she delivers in a chirpy and friendly tone which has a hint of seductiveness that is habitual rather than intended.*]

WOMAN.   You local then? never seen you in here before

MAN.   [*pleasantly surprised*] No, from Wales actually, but I
        live out in Romford, my wife's from Stratford but we
        moved out there, couldn't stand to live in the city,
        it's nicer there – do you know Stratford?

WOMAN.   Yeah, it's not far, don't have much call to go
        there really.

MAN.   You from around here yourself?

WOMAN.   Oh yeah, East End born and bred me. I'd never
        live anywhere else, I love it here, the people,
        everything… it's a really nice community, you know,
        everybody helps each other. I'd never move from
        here, couldn't.

MAN.   Yeah well, as I said, my wife's from the East End.

WOMAN.   I don't class Stratford as the East End.

MAN.   [*surprisingly maintaining good humour despite the
        obvious slight*] I didn't think you would, still,
        she likes to think of herself as an East End girl.
        She works for the Tokai Japanese Bank in Europe,
        top job, done well for an East End girl. [JAMES
        *raises his eyes sporadically throughout the conversation.
        He is obviously listening in and his face betrays a certain
        interest in what is being spoken.*]

WOMAN.   I don't know, it doesn't matter where you're
        from as long as you're bright – I've got a daughter,
        she's very bright.

MAN.   Well I've got a daughter, she works in Covent
        Garden.

WOMAN. [*Looking into the air wistfully as if the mention of the place had flooded her mind with memories.*] Ooh, I like it there, but it's changed.

MAN. [*Softening in response to his realisation that she has been affected by her memories.*] All of London's changed.

WOMAN. [*Wistfully, expressing the growing camaraderie that is developing between the two.*] Yeah.

MAN. Everything's changed – look at me, a humble builder, who'd 'ave though I'd 'ave married my wife who works for a top bank – but the way I see it, someone's got to build the places for these people to work in.

WOMAN. You're right.

MAN. When I go on holiday with my wife, abroad like, her friends look down on me because I'm a builder, but my story is: If there weren't people like me building the buildings there'd be nowhere for these people to work. [*Throughout this statement her concentration has been waning and her attention shifting away from the man's speech. She has evidently come out of the trance that was set in train by her memories and is now aware again of the more boorish qualities of the* MAN *at the bar – she makes a point of ignoring him by resuming her work whilst he is in mid-sentence. He is so content with what he is saying that he doesn't notice the snub immediately; when he does he covers up his embarrassment by smiling condescendingly towards her.*] You're taking your job very seriously; you're obviously a very conscientious person… I suppose you're the landlady.

WOMAN. No.

MAN. You're not?

WOMAN.   Just a worker.

MAN.   [*with an impertinent yet strangely seductive tone*]
So how come you don't own your own pub?

WOMAN.   Don't want to, happy here.

MAN.   I think it's best to be self-employed.

WOMAN.   Do you?

MAN.   Yeah [*He shakes his head and smirks in what seems
like an overly rehearsed manner.* JAMES, *who is by
now engrossed in the conversation panics as he sees that
the* MAN *is walking towards him. He looks deep down
into his newspaper. The man walks past him and to the
telephone into which he inserts some coins and dials a
number.* Don't You Want Me Baby *by The Human
League starts playing on the jukebox.*] Oh hello, I'm
not calling you on my mobile 'cause it's costing me
too much money. [*he laughs*] How's Cassandra?
Oh good… Yeah, she's fine, doing well in Covent
Garden. I'm in a pub, not unusual for me. [*He
cups his hand over his mouth and the receiver as if he
doesn't want anybody to hear him but simultaneously
and quite deliberately raises his voice so to make it more
intelligible.*] I'm in this pub, right, and the landlady,
right, if looks could kill I'd be lying on the ground
with, like, hundreds of tomahawks in me. [*He laughs.
The* WOMAN, *who is evidently rather taken aback by the
MAN's conversation, climbs onto a stool behind the bar
so that only her legs are visible and begins to wipe dust
off glasses and replace empty bottles.*] Yeah, anyway,
give her my number, or yours, whichever's easiest.
All right then, Tally ho, that's what you've got to say
around here so they won't think you're scum, yeah
that's right mate, toodle pip. [*He hangs up the receiver
and struts back towards his seat.* JAMES *has been looking
increasingly nervous and amazed as the* MAN's *telephone*

conversation progressed. He looks even more surprised as the MAN, *instead of retaking his seat, stops at the bar and addresses the* WOMAN *– who is still standing on the stool – in a brash, confident and evidently self-satisfied voice*] Still working then?

WOMAN.   [*trying to sound unmoved but just slightly betraying her hurt and anger with her voice*] Some of us have to.

MAN.   Tell me about it, I started the job I've been on today at three o'clock this morning, that's the middle of the night, still, the money's worth it, four times what I'd earn if I was employed, nothing to what my wife's on though, stock exchange and that. [*She doesn't respond and he simply stands, looking towards her*] Why don't you come down from there and be friendly'

WOMAN.   [*betraying a little fear this time*] Why should I?

MAN.   [*in a sneering, insulting tone*] 'cause I'd rather look at your face than your legs [*she remains on her stool, he waits a little and then arrogantly*] Could I have some service please. [*very calmly she gets down to serve him*] Oh, thank you, I'll have the same again please.

WOMAN.   [*Having obviously regained her composure she musters an effortless and confident tone that manages to convey her compete disdain for the* MAN.] What was it? [JAMES *braces himself as he notices that her cool makes the* MAN *angry.*]

MAN.   [*Obviously angered and resigned to the fact that he will have to point to if not speak the name of the drink he wants. He points at it with a smile that he manages to forge in order to reassure himself that he has not lost the upper hand. She begins to pour the drink.*] Why are you so unfriendly? [*no answer*] Rude as well.

WOMAN.   [*Calmly puts the drink on the bar and speaks mechanically, almost jovially.*] That's one pound ninety-six.

MAN.   [*Puts the money on the counter and gets his change returned in the same fashion. He speaks, trying to sound like the wounded voice of reason.*] I come into a pub after a long and hard day's work and all I want is to relax and have some friendly conversation and all you do is be rude to me.

WOMAN.   [*has busied herself again – polishing glasses etc.*] I'm not rude, I'm busy.

MAN.   [*Showing his growing drunkenness and shocking* james *in the process.*] You look down on me, don't you, think I'm scum, well my wife probably earns what you do in a year in a day.

WOMAN.   Good for her

MAN.   [*desperate and aggressive*] Yeah, she's done well for an East End girl, oh sorry, you don't think of her as from the East End, do you, just as well I suppose. [*She smiles at him and he looks somewhat angered. He walks over to the phone, dials and begins a conversation in a loud voice, without making any attempt to pretend to muffle the words he is speaking. He carries out the conversation in such a way that it might well be considered that there is no one on the other end of the line. Certainly his words seem directed more towards the* WOMAN *than they are towards his interlocutor. During the conversation the* WOMAN *makes eye contact with* james *who reassures her that he is aware of the situation and tries to imply that he is not worried by the threat that the presence of the* MAN *implies.*] Hello darling, it's only me, how's the stock exchange? Oh, that's good. Yeah I'm calling from a pub and I'll be on my way to see Darren soon, none too soon with the reception that I've had here. The landlady thinks I'm scum, yeah, funny isn't it, I've told her about how you probably earn more than her in a day than what she does in a year. Yeah, they see you as a builder and think you're scum, her problem and does she have a problem! All right darling, see you later: if I make it out of here alive, that is! [*He puts down the phone and walks over to the bar with what seems like restored confidence but without having lost his anger. The* WOMAN *keeps up a stern appearance, as if unaffected by his vitriol, which seems to further fuel his anger and he makes his final address to her attempting a kind of nobility but betraying the first signs of reeling drunkenness.* JAMES *attempts to look concerned and ready for action. It is going through his mind that he should be ready to step in and help the* WOMAN *in his own kind of gallant way should it be necessary. He puts down the newspaper.*] I'm leaving now but before I do I just want to say that you are the rudest and most unfriendly pain that it has ever been my pleasure to meet. [JAMES, *who is flabbergasted at this outburst, watches the* MAN *walk out and turning back notices the* WOMAN *looking at him.*]

WOMAN.   Can you believe that man! I'm just glad my husband wasn't here or he'd have torn him apart, talking to me like that and calling me rude on top of it.

JAMES.   Yeah, it was er, amazing, really rude. [*Faltering, obviously embarrassed at the fact that he said nothing to confront the* MAN *about his rudeness.*]

WOMAN.   [*has come out from behind the bar and gone to look out of the door to make sure that the* MAN *has really gone*] My husband would have made mincemeat out of him. I'm glad he wasn't here 'cause that man wasn't worth the trouble, and my god, would there have been trouble!

JAMES.   Yeah, it's probably best, I'm sorry, I felt I should
            have maybe said something, but it would have only
            been rising to him, he was probably just looking for
            something like that to happen.

WOMAN.   [*In a not unkind but slightly patronising tone that
            suggests that she thinks* JAMES *to be quite sensible but
            not a real man.*] Oh you're right darling, trouble's
            not worth it for the likes of him. [*A man and two
            women walk into the pub. It is obvious that they are
            local and that she knows them quite well for as soon as
            she sees them she breaks off her conversation with* JAMES
            and addresses them.] You would not believe the man
            we just had in here. [*She looks towards* JAMES *for
            confirmation of the story and he assents by shaking his
            head incredulously*] He was the rudest man I've ever
            seen – I mean you should 'ave heard him, insulting
            me, I couldn't believe it, [*looking towards* JAMES]
            isn't that right, darling?

JAMES.   [*Shaking his head again and trying hard to express an
            affronted incredulity.*] Yeah it was amazing, so rude,
            I mean, I thought he might get violent. [*More people
            enter the pub who also seem familiar to her and each is
            greeted by her telling them about the* MAN. JAMES *sits
            smiling uncomfortably and looking at his watch, nodding
            with assent and fake surprise and incredulity when it is
            required of him. His phone rings in his bag, he takes it
            out and puts it to his ear.*] Hello… Yes…[JAMES *looks
            angry and, without appearing to end the conversation,
            he puts the phone back into his bag, quickly finishes his
            drink and, after gathering his things, walks out of the
            pub saying gruff good-byes that no-one really notices, so
            attentive are they to the* WOMAN*'s story.*]

                              END

That That Which

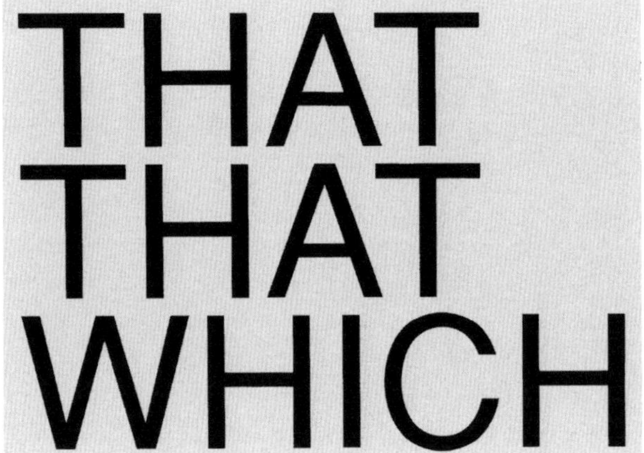

Lock and Quarry

Lock

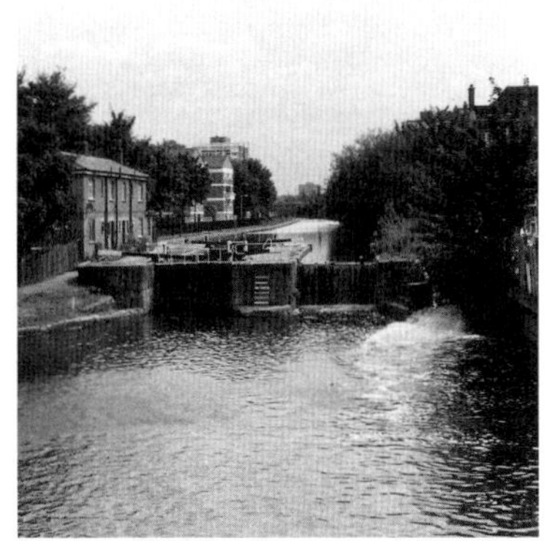

James, a young man
a Man in his early fifties
a Woman in her late forties

The action takes place in a pub in East London

A room in a pub in east London. The room is narrow and long, and fashioned to look like the interior of a narrowboat. The walls taper up towards the ceiling and are clad with dark, varnished planks of timber. Windows on the right-hand side of the room give onto a canal, while those on the left onto a small and rather affluent residential street. The ceiling is also clad with timber, and has three skylights along it, the furthest of which is covered up by a tattered old film poster that has begun to peel off. Also on the ceiling are a number of bulbous lamps that are unnecessarily turned on, emitting a nasty yellow glow. Contrasting with the canal theme, a richly patterned carpet covers the floor. A number of old converted sewing-machine bases serve as tables that are neatly ranged along both sides of the room, each with four chairs at them. This gives the impression that the room is one that the pub uses to serve food during meal times. This impression might be furthered by one of the tables bearing a number of sets of cutlery wrapped up in red paper table napkins, together with an array of savoury sauces and sachets of salt and pepper. A constant stream of music plays through two speakers that are attached to the wall at either end of the room. The range of songs that can be heard suggests that they are selections from a jukebox that must be located in some other part of the pub. The volume of the music seems too loud for the predominantly empty surroundings; it is a level that would be more fitting if the pub were full with bodies on a busy evening, absorbing the volume. As it is the room is almost empty, with bright sunlight illuminating it and making the music seem rather stark.

Spotted around the inclined timber-clad walls are a number of framed antique photographs of subjects around the canal: they picture long narrowboats navigating the canal; their passengers manning them; children looking on from the tow path; locks being operated by their keepers while the boats wait to continue their journey… Also framed on the wall is a small map of the waterways around the area in which the pub is located. On the far wall, filling the entire wall and therefore being cropped by the walls and ceiling, and framed by the room itself, is a huge black-and-white photograph of a lock in a canal. It has a kind of sepia tone to it – probably caused by years of nicotine staining – that gives it an aged look, as if it were harking back to times gone by. The image is taken from a vantage point on top of the lock, looking straight along the lock and onwards to the lower section of the canal which flows away to the left of the image. There are a number of houses that give onto the tow-path either side of the lock, and a narrowboat in the lock's enclosure that is at an intermediate level; there is no indication as to whether it is being raised or lowered. Because the image is taken looking straight down the lock it has a dramatic perspective to it, the lock almost becoming a squat pyramid. Since the image fills the entire wall, the perspective seems optically to continue that of the room itself. This has the effect of accentuating the perspective and therefore the depth of the room, much like the kind of effect that might be witnessed on the stage of a theatre. Directly beneath the image is a long padded bench clad in a diamond-patterned fabric that is built into the wall and which also spans its entire breadth.

A lock changes the level of a canal. The purpose of this is to allow the canal to follow the contours of the land along which it travels. The lock is a break in a journey that is there to allow its continuation.

A narrowboat that wishes to descend to a lower level sails into the enclosure. Formerly, almost certainly at the time that the photograph was taken, a lock-keeper, for the price of a toll, would have undertaken the service of closing the sluice gates behind the barge and then opening a valve to allow water to flow out of the enclosure. Many canals no longer employ lock-keepers, and it is up to the people travelling on the narrowboat – often people who have hired the boat for the day or for a week's holiday – to perform this task. Once the level of the water in the lock has descended to that of the lower section of the canal, and the narrowboat has consequently floated down to this new height, the other set of sluice gates are opened and the narrowboat is able to continue on its journey downstream. For narrowboats that wish to travel upstream a similar procedure takes place, but in reverse order: the lock is filled with water, thereby raising the level of the narrowboat that has sailed into it.

JAMES walks into the room with a drink – half a pint of lager – that he has just bought at the bar. *And It Stoned Me* by Van Morrison is playing on the speakers. He sees a MAN and a WOMAN sitting together at the far end of the room and decides to sit facing them at a table at the opposite end of the room, next to the entrance. It's not that he wants to watch them; his decision on where to sit is based on wanting to maintain a decorous distance from them and not to be so rude as to turn his back on them. However, his position is unwittingly akin to that of an audience that might be looking at the two people as performers on a stage. Having settled himself, taking a sip of his drink and perhaps lighting a cigarette, he takes out a note pad and pen from his bag. He begins to read some notes from his pad but his attention soon shifts to the MAN and the WOMAN, whom he notices are having quite an involved conversation. They are sitting on the padded bench that runs the entire length of the far wall, directly beneath the image of the lock. This has the effect of making them appear framed by the image, as if the photograph were a backdrop to their conversation. As they speak, JAMES writes notes in his pad, as if he could be transcribing elements of the conversation that the two people are having. It is, however, quite difficult to hear the conversation since the loud music drowns out the two voices. The couple indeed have to lean over towards each other to make themselves understood.

They are both in late middle age, though he is probably the older of the two. He has quite a drab appearance; if one were being polite one could describe it as a studied dishevelment but truly, if this is the intention, it is not very well achieved. He looks soft rather than fat and has a balding grey head of unkempt frizzy hair. He is wearing a patterned woollen jumper over a white shirt gone grey, the collars of which frame his stubbly neck unevenly. He gives the impression that he lives alone and that he is rather proud of his messy appearance; in his mind he is an absent-minded intellectual. It must be said that despite the generally unappealing demeanour of the MAN, he does have a glint in his surprisingly beautiful pale blue eyes.

She has rather a more affluent appearance and wears what could be described as the uniform of a professional person: a navy-blue two-piece skirt and jacket suit over a white blouse that is adorned with a gold chain. Her plump powdered face is complemented by a pair of large round plastic-rimmed glasses and her hair is dark, permed and set. She really is quite fat, and seems a little uncomfortable with her bulk as her suit stretches itself into strange contortions over her flesh. Apart from this she has the contended and resigned aspect of someone who probably has a family.

It is as if the two are fairly recent acquaintances who have quickly become soulmates. There is however a strange lack of intimacy between them and a very definite power relationship in which he is dominant. She hangs on his every word and admires everything he says while he takes advantage of this adulation. She is obviously the more affluent of the two, but his down-at-heel appearance serves actually to affirm what is an intellectual and moral superiority that he actively and even wilfully projects to her and to anybody who might have the misfortune of being in the same room as him. They are sharing a bottle of white wine which is half empty, indicating that their conversation has been going on for a little time already. As JAMES walks in the WOMAN is replenishing both their large glasses, emptying the bottle as the MAN speaks.

MAN: [Gesticulating as he speaks and barely looking at his companion.] Why do you sympathise with the Travolta or Samuel Jackson characters in *Pulp Fiction* who are morally beyond the pale? Because you know what they're going to do, it's a classic ploy, like in *King Lear*. Do you know the play?

WOMAN: [nodding thoughtlessly as she drinks] Yes, yes, sure.

MAN: Well Desmond there

WOMAN: [interrupts, slightly embarrassed] Oh I don't know
          it so well

MAN: [Smiling in an understanding manner and
          continuing seamlessly.] Well Desmond there, he's
          the bastard son, he comes on stage and says 'See
          that guy over there, I'm going to kill him' and
          then you're hooked because you are now tied to
          his destiny. Even though you might find him and
          his actions despicable you nevertheless want to
          know the outcome. And since he is your link to the
          story, the person through whom you perceive the
          events that are taking place, you somehow forge
          an alliance with him. It's a bit like when there's an
          operation on telly or when you see an accident on
          the motorway and you know its horrible but you
          still have to look. [As he is speaking *Is This Love*
          by Bob Marley starts to play. She looks truly taken
          and impressed by his comments and nods sagely
          and appreciatively, so much so that she gives the
          impression that she has not understood a word of
          what he has said. He is looking very pleased with
          himself and is smiling at himself, gloating at the
          fact that despite his lucidity she has not been able
          to penetrate his superior intellect. She makes her
          excuses and gets up to go to the toilet. He smiles
          and when she has turned leans back on his chair
          and takes a draught of his drink with supreme self-
          satisfaction; the appreciation which he has received
          from the WOMAN pleases him. His face turns
          almost dribbly, like a cat being stroked on the
          chin and behind the ears. His pleasure increases
          as he plays the situation back to himself in his
          head; erratic smiles appear on his face. He sees
          her returning and acknowledges her presence but

before she reaches the table she looks at their bottle of wine which, to her feigned surprise, is empty. He notices her noticing and they give each other quite an endearing naughty sort of look of camaraderie.]

WOMAN: Would you like another drink?

MAN: Well yes, that would be nice, but just a glass.
[He puts his hand into his pocket rather pathetically, as if he expects her to stop him.]

WOMAN: [obligingly] Oh, don't worry, I'll get these.

MAN: [faltering in a mannered fashion] But, well, you got the last ones.

WOMAN: [confidently, trying to put him at ease and also claiming some superiority of her own] Don't you worry [She heads towards the bar and he continues with his self-satisfied gesticulations which have if anything increased. He is obviously not embarrassed at being bought so many drinks but rather delights in the status which this confers upon him. She returns holding a bottle of white wine in her hand and shrugging her shoulders in a 'why not' sort of way. He smiles back at her.] It's not really worth getting two glasses; the price is almost the same as a bottle.

MAN: [smiling, almost winking] Fair enough [She settles herself down and fills their glasses as *West End Girls* by the Pet Shop Boys starts to play.]

MAN: So, how's your script going? [He asks this smiling, as if it is a question that is expected of him. It seems indeed as if this is the whole point of their meeting, or as if he were fulfilling his part of the bargain for having been bought so many drinks.]

WOMAN:	[pleased that he has asked but nervous] Well I'm still working on this idea about a gang of kids, they're bad boys, joyriders, only that they're not so bad really, more victims of their circumstances. They're all from this poor estate and the things they do are more out of boredom than real malice.

MAN:	[Assimilating what she has said quickly and without thought, and going on to comment in a way that he seems to have done countless times before.] I suppose the first thing you have to establish is why these characters are there in the first place, to give some reason for their presence. This is what you might think of as the beginning of the plot. You see it's not enough simply to examine who the characters are, that's something that comes out of the plot, but it shouldn't be seen as the purpose of the plot. You see, plot can be defined as the characters' journey through time, but to make it convincing you have to be very clear about stipulating what that time might be – from what point to what point is your plot taking the characters.

WOMAN:	Mmm, that's the difficult bit. I had thought of looking at the characters through the eyes of someone else, another character who witnesses them ram-raiding a jewellery store, But I don't know, I'd really just though of that as an aside, and I don't know whether it's too complicated. [She pauses to think and light a cigarette.] I really just wanted to have the thing be about a day in their lives. They're hanging around the estate and out of boredom really they steal a car. Then it all escalates and they get this sense of reckless adventure, that's when they ram-raid the jewellery store. And then it's about how they get away and how some of them get caught. The idea of the other character, the one who witnesses the robbery, is just really to change the tone a bit, to see this event through someone else's eyes. I just thought that the robbery is the moment when the kids really transgress and perform the kind of action that could have severe consequences. I was thinking that they might even unwittingly kill someone. But I don't know, I don't know whether the idea of this other character's too complicated, I don't know. [Throughout, the MAN has been nodding complacently, with an annoying smile.]

MAN: Well, not necessarily, that could be useful as a device. But you have to remember that everything you need is there, in the characters and in the way that their actions unfold.

WOMAN: [perplexed] Right, yeah, I think I see what you mean.

MAN: Think of it like this: When a sculptor is sculpting a bust out of a block of marble he isn't actually adding anything to the marble but simply finding the form he wants from within the marble by taking parts of it away. He's uncovering the bust that was always there by concentrating the marble on it, by removing everything that is extraneous. Well it's the same with writing a script, your characters journey from A to B, from the start to the finish of the script is already there and it is the plot that describes it by drawing from it just what you might consider essential to describe that journey. Do you see what I mean? [He looks very pleased with the lucidity of his last statement and rewards himself with a long draught from his wine.]

WOMAN: [attentively] Hmm, yes, yes, I think so.

MAN: A lot of people make the mistake of thinking that writing a script is simply a question of transcribing reality, and that's a big mistake. It would be like

the sculptor saying that the block of marble was his
sculpture. It's simply not enough, or too much perhaps.
You have to remove everything that's irrelevant in order
to come up with something that's pointed and relevant
and entertaining. It's not just about representing or
giving a version of reality but about editing it so that
you can arrive at some meaning through it. Otherwise
it becomes like Borges' map and that's ridiculous. [As
he is speaking the WOMAN's mobile phone rings from
her bag. He doesn't notice and continues talking as she
takes it out, looks at the display and switches it off.]

WOMAN: [Rather confused, as she replaces the phone in
           her bag.] Borges' map, sorry, I don't understand,
           what's that?

MAN: Borges? He's a writer, Spanish, fabulous writer.
           There's a short story he wrote, I can't remember the
           title. It's about this king who wants a perfect map
           of the world, but he wants it to be so perfect that he
           ends up remaking the world on top of the world, in
           real scale. I can't remember exactly the details but
           that's the gist of it. It's kind of about the absurdity
           of attempting to reproduce reality. You simply end
           up with the same thing again and what's the point in
           that? No, you have to carve away everything that's
           extraneous, remember that it's fiction you're making.
           [She nods as she looks away, obviously confused by
           his explanations. There begin to appear on her face
           the signs of tedium, as if she is starting to get a little
           irritated with his self-assured countenance. The music
           stops and she looks towards JAMES, who she realises
           has possibly been listening in to the conversation and
           gives him a non-committal expression of camaraderie,
           as if she felt the need to tell someone that she wasn't
           being taken in by the MAN's words. JAMES feels
           slightly embarrassed that his eavesdropping has been
           discovered and he doesn't respond to the WOMAN's
           acknowledgement, instead he buries himself deeper in

the notes he is scribbling. She turns back to the MAN and resumes her submissive role.]

WOMAN: Gosh, there's so much to think about. You'd think it would be simple, telling a story. I've been writing stories since I was a kid, but when you want to do it properly there are all these things to think about, god! [laughs nervously] It's hard enough just finding the time to write, with the kids and that, and my husband's not exactly supportive. Not that he minds me doing this writing, but you know, when you've been together that long a new interest is like a kind of threat. It does just take so much time.

MAN: But you mustn't let all that stuff put you off. I mean, the most important thing is your imagination, and that can't be taught. It is important to learn the ways in which to channel things so that they make sense. It's a kind of professionalism, the difference between a story that is personally meaningful and one that is able to resonate more broadly, to mean something to other people and to fit the formats that I'm afraid all stories have to fit into. It might seem difficult now, but with time it will come naturally. Of course there are some sacrifices involved, and I'm not saying it's not hard work. I've been writing for a long time and it has stopped me doing certain things, but that's the price to pay and I don't complain. [For the first time in the conversation he seems sincere, if still full of self-adulation. She smiles at him with equal adulation.] Don't worry. I'm looking forward to reading your script, I'm sure it'll be great.

WOMAN: Oh god, I do hope so. [An awkward silence ensues that coincides with JAMES finishing his drink. He gathers his things away into his bag and leaves, watched by the MAN and the WOMAN.]

END

Quarry

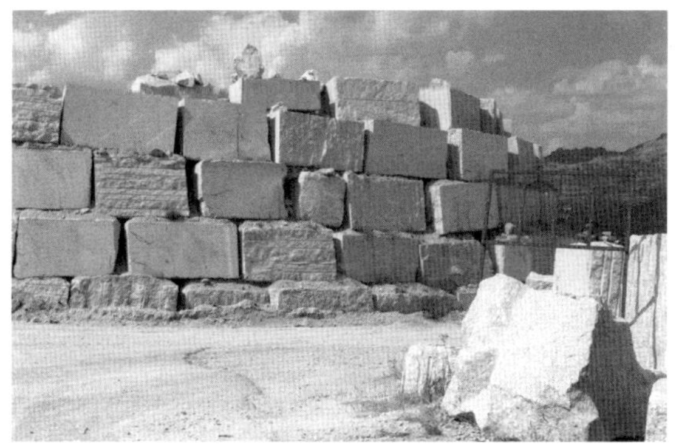

James, a young man
a Man in his late fifties
Various other workers and attendants

The action takes place in a masonry yard in east London.

A masonry yard in east London. The yard consists of a workshop, and in front of it a courtyard which is separated from the small street on which the masonry yard is located by a wire-mesh fence. The courtyard is full of various colours and varieties of marble and granite slabs stacked vertically and roughly sorted according to type. The slabs lean on each other like stumbling dominoes caught in suspended animation. They are supported by roughly hewn but sturdy wooden structures that criss-cross the courtyard. Although the arrangement of these structures seems somewhat haphazard, it is nevertheless noticeable that they are all located in either a vertical or horizontal orientation to the rectangular courtyard. Access to the courtyard is gained via a large gate in the fence that would appear to be designed for lorries to load and unload their merchandise. Parallel to the fence and delimiting the extent of the courtyard is the large industrial workshop built out of dirty orange brick. Directly opposite the gate is the entrance to the workshop, again a large opening designed for the loading and unloading of merchandise. This entrance is wide open and a mist of marble dust flows steadily out into the courtyard. Since the day is bright and sunny the mist sparkles, the crystalline marble dust reflecting the sun. The noise of rumbling machinery also tumbles out of the workshop. It is possible to see this machinery through the entrance but the luminous dust makes it seem distant and, together with the noise, somewhat forbidding.

The area between the gate and the entrance to the workshop forms a short driveway, and to the right of this driveway, if one were walking into the yard, is a large, old and somewhat dilapidated wooden shed, of the kind that one might expect to find in a back garden. Although the shed is evidently freestanding the back of it is strangely truncated by the building, suggesting that the two structures are internally connected. The door to the shed is ajar.

JAMES walks along the street towards the yard's entry gate. He notices a yellow New York taxi that is parked directly opposite the gate, ponders it for a few seconds and then walks into the yard. He stands on the driveway for a while taking in the scene that has just been described. He can see no-one through the entrance to the workshop and looks to be somewhat intimated at the prospect of walking into the factory setting. He looks towards the more accommodating wooden shed, and seeing that the door is ajar decides to take his chances there.

JAMES pushes the door open trepidatiously and peers in somewhat blindly, since it is quite dark. His eyes adjust quickly. He walks into a corridor that leads through the hut into the workshop. Alongside the corridor a room is built into the hut with windows and a door giving onto the corridor. Through the windows JAMES can see a MAN who is working at a desk in the room. The MAN has not noticed him and JAMES knocks on the door. The MAN looks up, a little startled.

MAN: [He looks to be in his late fifties with grey balding
            hair combed forward over his temples and a small
            overly groomed grey moustache. He is small and
            comfortably, but not obesely, fat. His skin is tanned
            and leathery, his hands rough and hard from a life
            of work. A fine layer of dust covers him and his old
            work clothes.] Yes.

JAMES: [Pushing the door open and poking his head around
            it] Hello, we spoke on the phone earlier, about that
            slab of statuary.

MAN: [officiously] Oh yes, come in, come in [JAMES
            looks around the room which he notices is quite an
            ordinary shabby little office of its type with cheap
            furniture and stacks of disorganised papers. Hung

on the walls of the room are various panoramic colour images of different quarries. They picture mountainsides that have been carved into neatly and in large steps. The immense scale of these steps is hinted at in some of the images by pick-up trucks and lorries that are parked along dusty tracks that wind their way around the mountain. Because the marble that is being quarried in most of the images is white, there is an amazingly stark brightness that comes from them despite the fact that they are small and faded. The images have a real majesty about them; they give a sense of the heroic nature of heavy quarrying operations that seems at odds with the drab environment of the dingy office.] Did you close the door after you?

JAMES: It was open when I arrived, I left it like that.

MAN: [Getting up and walking towards the door, slightly irritated]. You never know, can't be too careful round here. [He closes the door and returns to JAMES who makes slightly pathetic gestures of apology.] Statuary, wasn't it? I haven't made any enquiries yet.

JAMES: But you said you had some that was slightly thinner, three centimetres?

MAN: [bluntly] Yes

JAMES: Could I see it, just to get an idea of that width on that scale?

MAN: [surprisingly courteous] Oh yes, sure, come this way. [JAMES follows the MAN into the workshop. As in the courtyard, various types of marble are stacked on wooden structures. There are also many large machines for working the stone, that give off a constant drone. As well as the unworked slabs there are also scattered around various pieces of worked stone: tombstones, fireplaces, sinks and various other objects that have evidently been fashioned but are nevertheless not immediately recognisable. There is also a mezzanine floor in the yard, propped up on sturdy wooden stilts and into which it is not possible to look. A heavy layer of dust covers everything, giving the impression of activity taking place and simultaneously of great stillness. JAMES looks around in wonder as he follows the MAN through the stone and the machinery, obviously impressed at the scale of the operation. They arrive at a stack of large slabs of white statuary marble. Statuary marble is white with prominent grey veining and the odd brownish streak in it.] Here it is. [JAMES looks at the marble in the stack while the MAN tries to push over half of the stack in order to show JAMES the piece he has in mind. He is unable to do this on his own and so he calls over one of the yard's workers, who have until now been strangely absent, to help him. The worker goes over and with some effort he and the MAN push over a number of slabs to reveal the beautiful surface of a large slab of statuary marble.] There you go, nice piece of statuary that. It's got some veining in it of course, but you can't control that, it's a natural material. The quarry in Italy just cut into the seam, and they have to take what's there at any stage, that's the beauty of it. [He leans casually on the stack of marble that he has just pushed over.]

JAMES: [Feeling the surface and the edge of the stone, quite excited] Yes I can see that, it is a really nice piece, it's just the thickness, I really was after four centimetres.

MAN: What you using it for? A table, is it?

JAMES: [Uncomfortably, as if he realises that the MAN is

about to try to persuade him of something.] Yeah, kind of. [For the next period of conversation JAMES and the MAN shuffle around each. It is as if they don't want to make eye contact and are reticent to engage in conversation. They do, however, as they continue talking, develop a greater camaraderie. It is as if the MAN's boredom is slowly eroded away, as is JAMES' reticence.]

MAN:		Well three centimetres is thick enough, and I'll tell you something else, it's much lighter, that extra centimetre's going to add a lot of weight.

JAMES:		Yes, I can see that, a third on top of what's there again.

MAN:		[almost impressed] That's right, and that's a lot of weight. My guys, they carry marble around all the time, and it is heavy stuff, you've got to know what you're doing if you're going to move it anywhere. You've got to treat it kindly 'cause one knock at a strategic spot and it's liable to crack.

JAMES:		Oh I see, that's interesting. Actually I need to, well the guy I'm making it for wants it up a flight of stairs. If I were to get it from you, do your people do that, I mean would they transport it for me and carry it up some stairs?

MAN:		Oh yes, there'd be a charge for that, of course.

JAMES:		Sure, I realise that. But would it be possible to carry a four-centimetre thick block, if one were to turn up, up a flight of stairs?

MAN:		[smirking knowingly] Anything's possible, it just isn't easy. The three-centimetre would still be heavy but it would also be considerably easier to carry than the four-centimetre, you've just got to decide what you really want and what compromises you're prepared to make. I'll tell you something, as well, when I make a table I always put the marble on a base of twelve-millimetre plyboard.

JAMES: Oh, right.

MAN: Yes, you see, marble is a material that can crack, it's a natural material and it's got faults that, even though you might not be able to see them, are there all right. I've seen it happen, piece of marble is intact for years and then one day for no rhyme or reason, bang, [Claps his hands for emphasis] it snaps in half. Now, if you've got no support underneath it other that your table legs, that slab is going to come crashing down, and that's quite some weight. Now, you might be able to get your parquet floor mended, but what if there was a little kid playing underneath it?

JAMES: I see what you mean, it's a horrible thought.

MAN: Doesn't bear thinking about. And that's why I put the ply underneath, so that if it were to crack there'd be something there to support it. But what's more that ply could give you that extra thickness you're after. [He smiles, as if he had hit on the perfect solution.]

JAMES: [a little dismissive] Yeah, I suppose that is a possibility. But ideally I would really need that thickness, it's part of the design. Do you think it would just be impossible to get a piece like that?

MAN: No, it's not impossible, by any means, I just haven't got anything like that here. It would have to be ordered specially. You see, I tend to keep the marble I have for myself, to make things with, so I order just what I need in bulk and that keeps me going for a while. You know, I mean I just had a container of

Carrara arrive last week so I've got a lot of it, but just not in the thickness you want. I mean, to order one piece means it being packed up and paying for its space in someone else's container, which really isn't very economical.

JAMES: So do you mean that it just wouldn't be in your interests to order such a piece?

MAN: Basically, no.

JAMES: [nodding] I understand, I see what you mean. Are there any other marbles that are white and which you might have in that thickness? You mentioned something about a Turkish marble on the phone.

MAN.   Well yes, but again that hasn't got the thickness.

JAMES: What's it like, the Turkish marble?

MAN: It's all right, not as good as the Italian, though; it just hasn't got the quality.

JAMES: Is that where the statuary and the Carrara are from, Italy?

MAN: [with genuine enthusiasm] Yes, that's where the best marble comes from, at least the most popular. It's the marble people want; white marble's very popular. This Carrara's [Beckoning JAMES to follow him a few yards along the stacks of marble to the place where the Carrara is stacked. Carrara marble is a milky grey colour with regular spots, dapples and tiny veins of a darker grey.] the best marble in the world, regular, you can rely on it. It's dappled, not veined like other marbles, best material in the world this, this won't crack on you like these Turkish marbles, it's got no veins you see, which is where the marbles crack.

JAMES: Is it stronger than the statuary then?

MAN: Oh no, not really, the statuary's good too, but
          dearer, depends what you want to use it for.
          [He smiles wryly, as if he were enjoying imparting
          his expertise.]

JAMES: What are they normally used for?

MAN: Well Carrara's a funerary marble, for tombstone
          and memorial use, you know. [He adopts a sad look,
          which he snaps out of quickly.] The statuary's used
          for all sorts of things… flooring, whatever. We're
          building a staircase at the moment for this fella out
          in Romford, using four-centimetre thickness for
          that, but of course, the pieces are smaller than
          what you want. What exactly was the size you
          wanted again?

JAMES: About six foot square.

MAN: That's quite big, and it's for a table you say, what
          size base you using, I mean does it go right up to
          the edge or you got some sort of overhang?

JAMES: There is an overhang; the top's larger than the base.
          I think the base is four foot square, so that's what, a
          foot overhang on all sides, do you think that would
          be all right? [He seems to be becoming impressed
          with the MAN's knowledge.

MAN: Yes, I think that that ought to be fine, but I'd still
          recommend putting that sheet of ply underneath
          it, can't be too careful can you, as we said earlier,
          you could avoid a nasty accident. But as far as the
          base goes that sounds fine, as long as it can hold the
          weight, of course, what's it made of?

JAMES: Oh it's quite strong, four-centimetre section square stainless steel tubes welded together. The guy who made it for me seemed to know what he was doing and he assured me that it could take the weight.

MAN: [Surprised at JAMES' precision.] You'll be fine, then. In my opinion a base like that, with an overhang, is far better than one that supports the slab at either end. Come here, look at this. [He walks to another area of the workshop, near the main entrance, that is full of off-cuts and broken pieces of marble and granite. JAMES follows.] See that big broken slab, [He points at a cracked slab of emerald green marble with distinct veining and striations.] that was a tabletop that was supported at both ends on two stands. Now the stands were easily strong enough to hold the weight but the marble wasn't. What I mean to say is, that if the marble has some length you put a hell of a lot of pressure on its middle by just supporting it either end, makes it liable to snap, not immediately, but give it enough time under such strain and bang, and if there are little ones happening to be playing underneath at the time, well I'm afraid they're goners. I have to say that this isn't a particularly good marble, it's from Spain you see, and although they do produce very beautiful marbles, they're not too noble, full of pretty treacherous faults. But even the best marble can surprise you. You can see the veins all right but it's not until you cut them that you can see how dodgy they are. Now that marble in particular we can repair, because it's so busy and veined, use a special cement and if you do it properly you can barely notice it. Other marbles though, like Carrara for example, that are plainer and don't have any veins, well, they can't be fixed so easily. For one, if they snap it's not along a vein, so the cut's likely to be that much more irregular. Also you can't disguise the join as a vein and it looks terrible. You run into all sorts of problems, might as well get an entirely new piece, really. That's one of the advantages of these Spanish marbles, they're so busy and full of incident that it really is quite simple to conceal the joins when you repair them, but then again if the marble was a bit better quality it wouldn't snap so often. Not that it's the only marble that snaps, or that it's all bad quality, but on the whole I tend to prefer to go for the Italians, unless of course I've got a client who especially wants that richer kind of colour, and there's those who do.

JAMES: Is there much marble produced in Spain?

MAN: Fair amount; I don't deal with them very much personally though, 'cause as I say the price to quality relation isn't brilliant. But they are quite big producers. I import all my Spanish marble, had some in yesterday as it happens, from… oh what's their name… can't remember, big company in the Basque land. They're not a quarry, mind, they're dealers and exporters, and you could buy Italian Carrara from them just as well as any Spanish marble. Huge company, though, and they know their stuff, but if you ain't got the raw material then there's very little you can do. I had a Basque guy working here for a while, good little mason he was, but he went back. Had an English wife and child you see and they had problems… Very sad. [He shakes his head sullenly but again snaps out of the emotion quickly.] Most of the marble in Spain comes from around Valencia; do you know that part of the world at all?

JAMES: No, I've never been to Spain.

MAN: Oh, it's beautiful round there. I go to Javea, which isn't far from Valencia, every year.

JAMES: That must be nice. Do you have a house there?

MAN: No, we looked at a villa last summer, my wife and me. Nice it was, on top of a hill. But it needed a lot of work doing to it, and you know, Spanish builders. Would be nice to have a place there, plan to retire there. It's beautiful, the landscape, the climate.

JAMES: Hmm, I can imagine. Difficult to have builders doing things there though I imagine. Even here, you've got to be right on top of them or it can go on forever.

MAN: Well, one day it'll happen.

JAMES: [Though JAMES seems to be enjoying the conversation, not to mention his satisfaction at having endeared himself to the MAN, he seems to realise that he should probably get on his way.] Uhm, I was wondering whether you might have any small samples of Carrara and statuary that I could take away with me.

MAN: Yeah, I probably have [He walks towards a large plastic box and JAMES follows him. The box is full of a jumble of small pieces of marble, which are a bit like small books – paperback novels – in size and shape. The MAN dangles himself on his large gut into the box and fumbles about with the marble. He comes up – as if for air – and hands JAMES a piece of marble] Here's a piece of the statuary. [He re-submerges] Can't see any Carrara though; [Back up] hang on, there might be some over there. [He walks across the room and repeats the operation, this time with a little less vigour.] No I can't find any Carrara Bianco, I'm afraid. Bianco means white, you know, although Carrara's not really white, more of a grey marble actually. The people in the quarry in Italy say to me, they say Carrara being called Bianco is the worst thing that's ever happened to us, because it's not really white and people have unrealistic expectations of it. Not that not being white means it's a worse material or anything, but that from the name people expect it to be white and they're sometimes disappointed. The statuary's a white marble, pure white.

JAMES: Yes, you can see that in this piece, it's beautiful, glows when you put it up against the light, look. [JAMES draws the MAN towards the large opening onto the courtyard, holding the marble up to the light as if it were some kind of talisman or a spoil of victory.]

MAN: [With genuine admiration and wonder for the material] Yeah, that's right. [They both spend quite a few seconds here on the threshold of the workshop side by side looking at the raised stone and twisting it around, admiring the play of the light and looking moved at its intricacies. JAMES lowers the stone and they move simultaneously out into the sunlight. They spend a few seconds squinting, and as they do this they get themselves into a position where they are standing and facing each other at a distance of about a metre, sideways on to, and directly in front of, the entrance to the workshop. The glinting marble dust seems to transform the scene, giving it a certain nobility and exoticism. The MAN, with his short grey hair combed over his temples, could be a Roman senator and JAMES his young protégé. The drive on which they are standing could then seem like the floor of the forum, and the slabs of marble classical edifications. The yellow New York taxi is still parked outside the gate.]

JAMES: [breaking the charm] Well, thank you very much for all your time and help. As I said it was really that four-centimetre depth that I was after, but I seem

to be having so much trouble finding it that I might
have to change my plans. If I did would you be able
to cut me some of the three-centimetre statuary?

MAN: Oh yeah, no problem, you think about it and let me
know. [JAMES seems as if is about to say goodbye
when the MAN stops him] Something else: how
would you want the marble cut?

JAMES: I wasn't sure about that. I know I want it polished
top and bottom, but the edges, well initially I
wanted them simply to be cut, but then I heard that
if they were just cut, and not polished, that they
were liable to chip because of the sharpness of them.

MAN: That's right. It's best to take the edge off. You see, if
the edge is sharp and you knock it with something,
a glass or a plate or something like that, it will
chip. But if the edges are rounded and polished
any impact, unless you whack it with a hammer of
course, will just bruise it. You'll see there's been an
impact but it won't cause bits to chip off. Look at
this. [He picks up a piece of marble from a nearby
pile of off-cuts and shows it to JAMES. The piece is
small, book-sized again. Its bottom edge is sawn off
straight but the top edge is rounded off all the way
down to the bottom.] See, if you round the top edge
off like this it makes the marble look thicker, it's not
thicker, it just looks it, it's an optical thing. That's
what called a bulldogged edge. If it's the other way
round, with the bottom edge rounded [he turns the
piece upside down] it makes the piece look thinner.
That could be your solution, rounding the top edge
to make the three-centimetre look thicker. It would
make the marble stronger as well, less liable to chip,
as I was saying.

JAMES: [Dismissive, but trying to seem receptive] Right,
that's interesting, I'll bear it in mind.

MAN: You do that; you know where we are.

JAMES: OK, thanks a lot again. [He makes to leave but
            then suddenly remembers the piece of marble in his
            hand] Oh, do I owe you anything for this sample?
            [Disingenuously]

MAN: [Benignly, as if someone had told him that he looked
            like a Roman senator] No, no, no, that's all right,

JAMES: [Humbly, ever the protégé] Thank you very much,
            that's very kind, thanks for all your help, goodbye.

MAN: 'Bye. [The word hangs in the dust as JAMES walks
            out of the gate and along the pavement. The MAN's
            eyes follow him through the translucent mesh.]

END

Driving Back

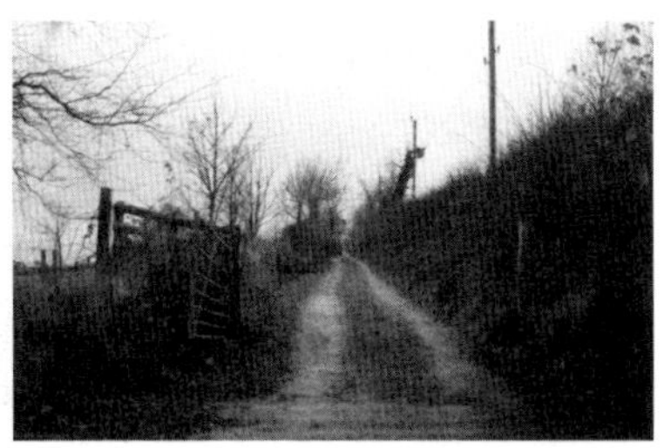

[1:1] A grey metal gate hinged on a wooden fence-post is open. Were it to be closed it would bar passage between a cemented courtyard and an earth track that ascends a shallow slope. The track is flanked on its right-hand side by a straggly hedge into which two telegraph poles are rooted. On its left-hand side a lower hedge from which there grow young trees separates the track from a field which descends on the back of a small hill. Wheels have worn the track on either side, but along its middle there remains a band of grass.

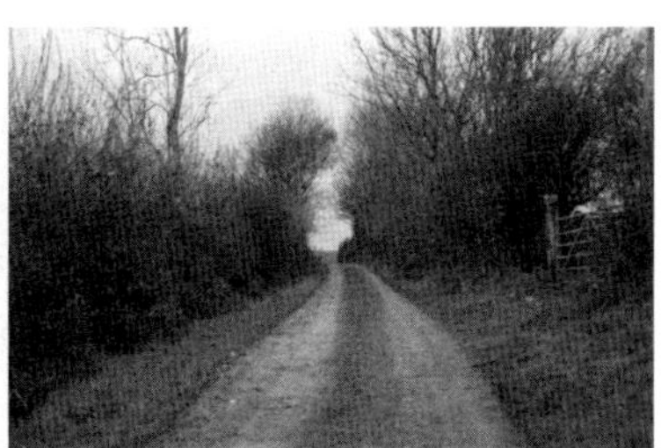

1:2] Edging gradually to the left the track ascends towards a very green field on which sheep are grazing. On either side of the track narrow grass verges precede straggly hedges from which increasing numbers of trees grow as the track approaches the field. Towards the end of the track's ascent the hedge on its right-hand side is interrupted by an opening that is barred by a grey metal gate.

That was great, it was a really nice few days. There's something so special about these times spent away. They let you forget who you are and what you do; they let you rest from that impulse always to define yourself.

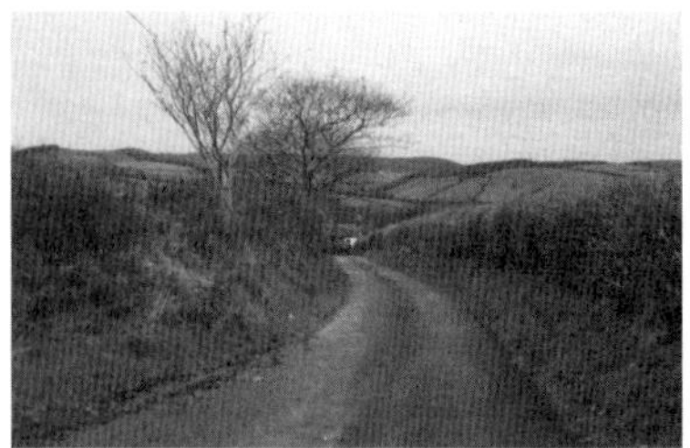

[2:1] A narrow tarmac road is flanked on either side by hedges. It bends left around three trees that grow from the hedge on its left-hand side and heads towards a small white house with a pitched slate roof and a chimney. Beyond this and in the distance is a hill populated by fields and woods.

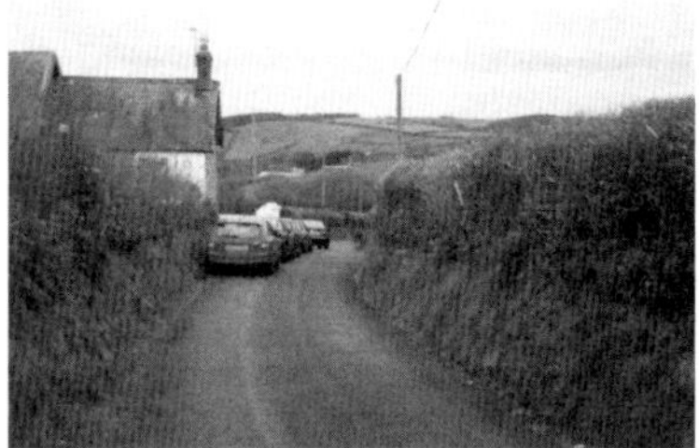

[2:2] A number of cars are parked outside the house, on the left-hand side of the road. As it passes the cars the road begins a shallow descent around a tall clipped hedge on its right-hand side and towards a few farm buildings that are visible on the hill beyond. Telegraph-poles are rooted to the hedges on either side of the road.

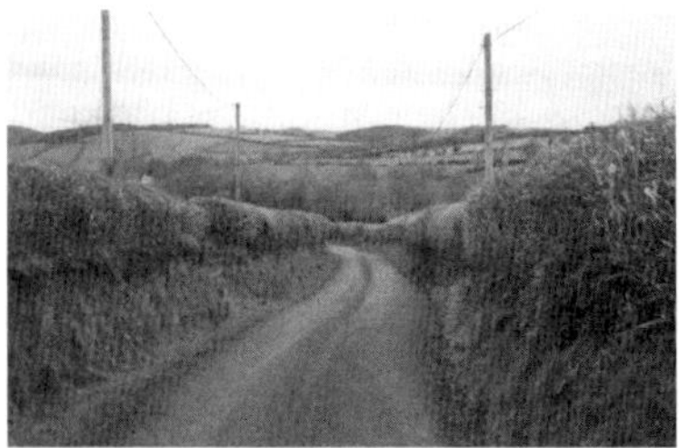

[2:3] The road continues its descent, bending to the left. Telegraph-poles are rooted to the hedges on either side of it.

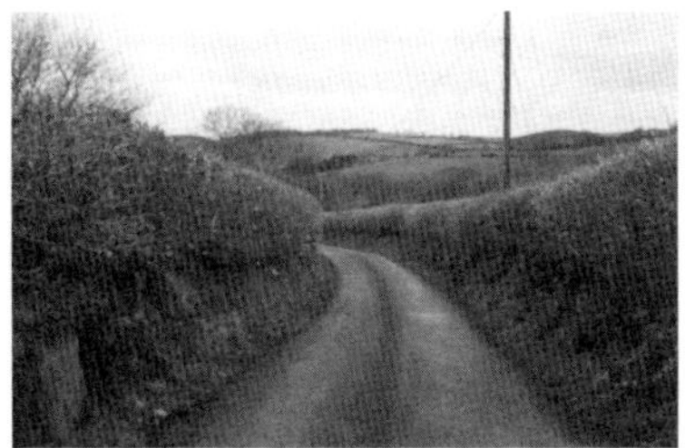

[2:4] The road continues its descent, bending to the left. Telegraph-poles are rooted to the hedge on its right-hand side.

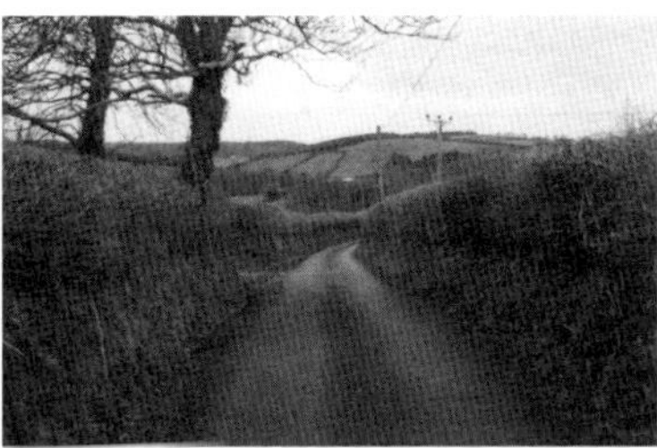

[2:5] Beneath two large trees with overhanging branches a track leads perpendicularly away from the left-hand side of the road. On meeting the track the road abandons its straight course and begins to veer right, around a telegraph-pole.

Every time we drive back I find that I never really realise when our journey starts. We always do the same things: load our bags, say our goodbyes and drive up the track, waving out of the window. And then we find ourselves on the road, on this route that we know so well.

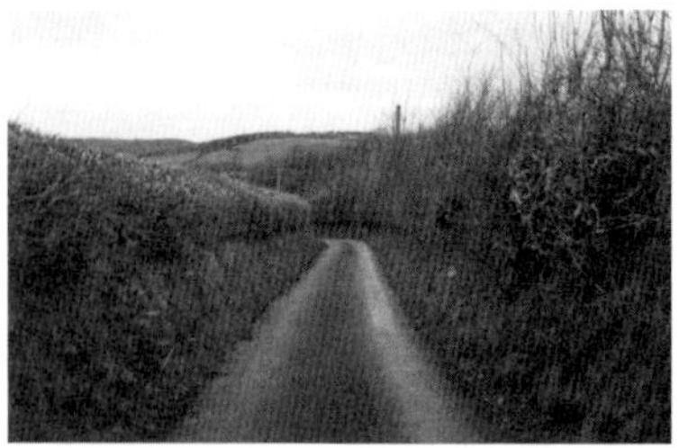

[2:6] Abandoning a straight course to veer left where a telegraph-pole is rooted to the cropped hedge on its left-hand side, the road continues to descend, its vantage on the hill beyond steadily diminishing.

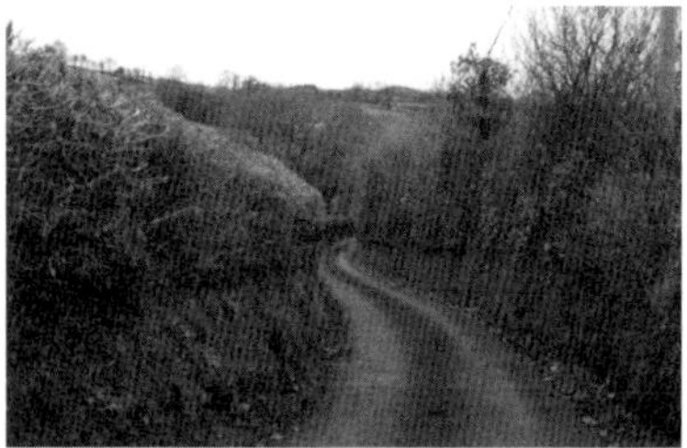

[2:7] The road S's first left and then right, descending towards large trees. The hill beyond is almost entirely obscured by these trees and by the tall hedges that flank the road on either side.

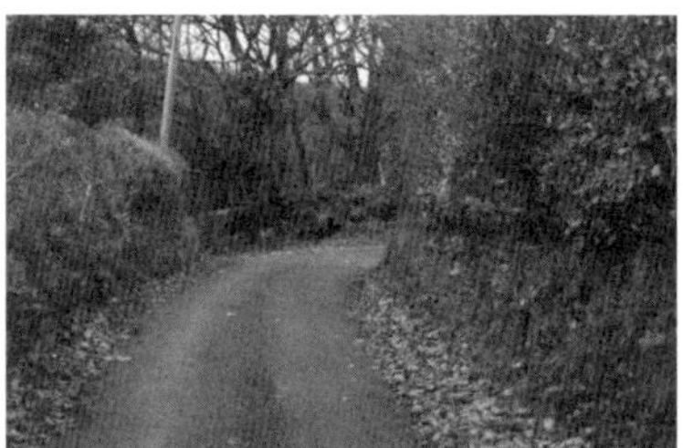

[2:8] Light brown leaves are scattered on either side of the road as it bends sharp right, veering away from the large trees. On the left-hand side of the road – at the sharpest point of the bend – a series of intermittent white lines on the tarmac indicate a junction.

We turn left here, don't we? It's funny how I still have to ask you that. I think I just want to delay that moment when I have to structure my thoughts.

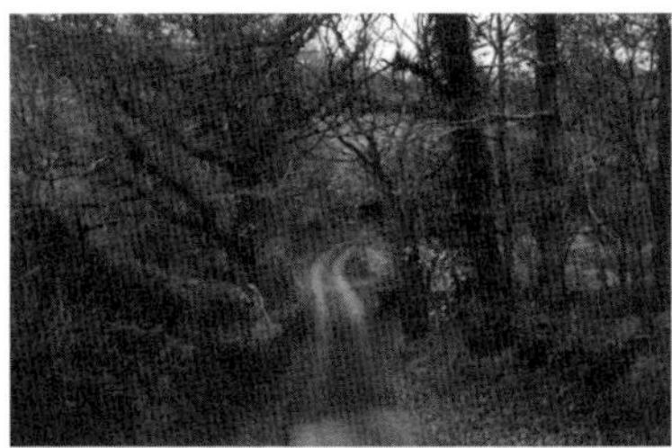

[3:1] A road descends through a small wood that is populated by large trees. Light brown leaves line either side of the road until it emerges from the wood and begins an ascent, bending to the right.

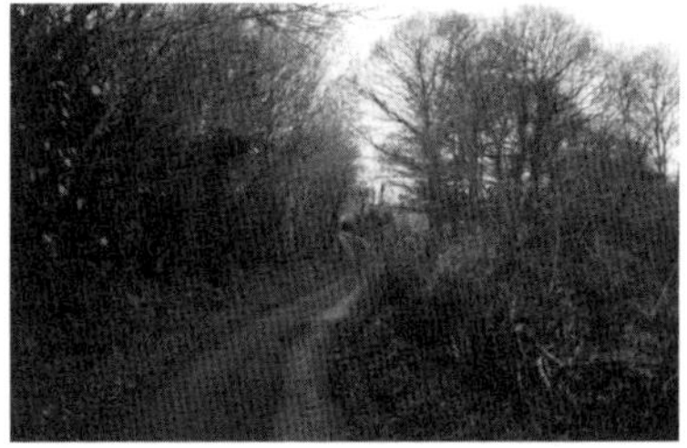

[3:2] Flanked by trees and straggly bushes the road continues to ascend, curving first right and then left.

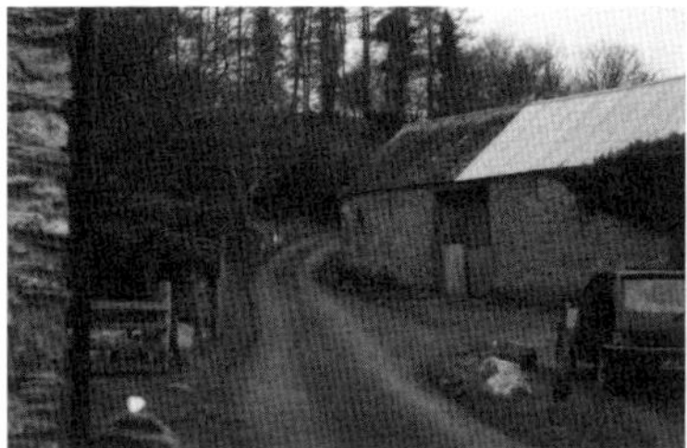

[3:3] A black car is parked on the right-hand side of the road. Between it and the road is a small patch of grass on which there lie three large rocks and into which is rooted a black post.

Beyond this is a large stone barn the roof of which is clad in two sections: one of slate and the other of corrugated iron. The beginnings of another stone building can be seen on the left-hand side of the road, and adjacent to this a wooden fence that runs alongside the road. Behind the fence is a garden in which a small white terrier chases its tail in quick pirouettes. Through all this the road continues its ascent, turning right behind the barn towards a line of tall trees that grow on the back of a hill.

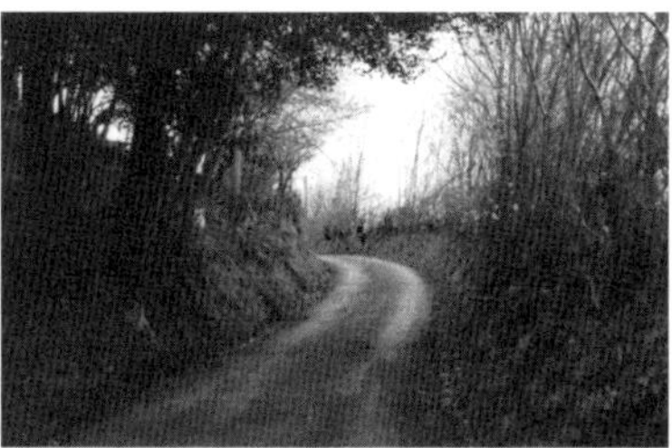

[3:4] Trees which grow from a grass bank on the left-hand side of the road form a canopy over it. Beyond them the road emerges into light and veers left.

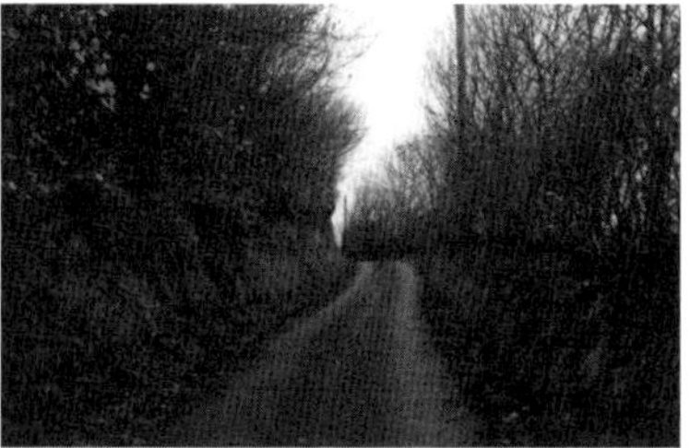

[3:5] The road ascends through straggly hedges and begins to turn left as it hits a ridge. Two telegraph-poles are almost camouflaged by the hedge on the right-hand side of the road.

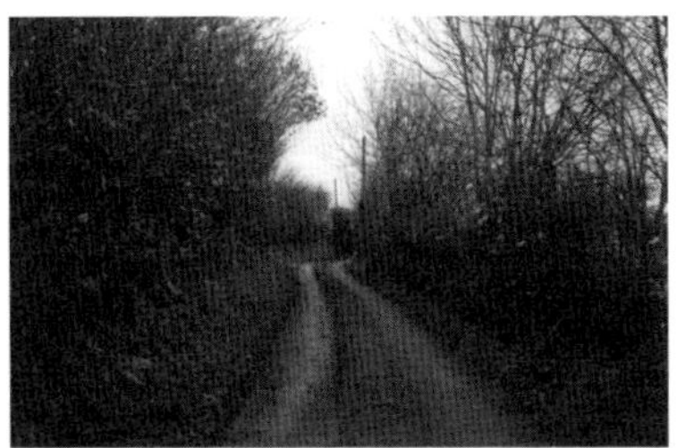

[3:6] Straggly hedges flank the road on either side as it bends left and then begins to curve towards the right. Telegraph-poles rooted to the hedges on either side of the road appear like slalom gates.

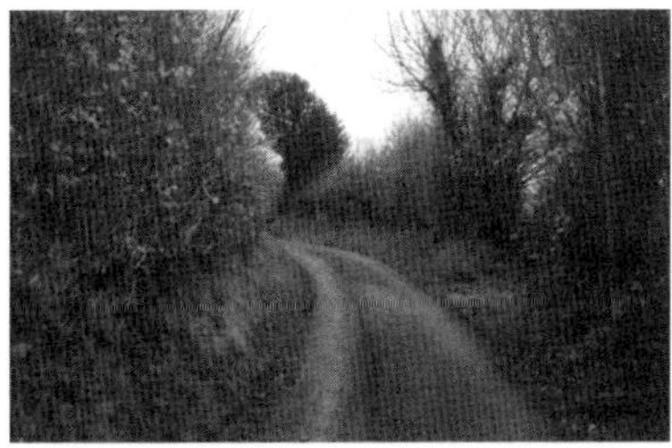

[3:7] The road makes a sweeping bend to the left, towards an unusually verdant tree.

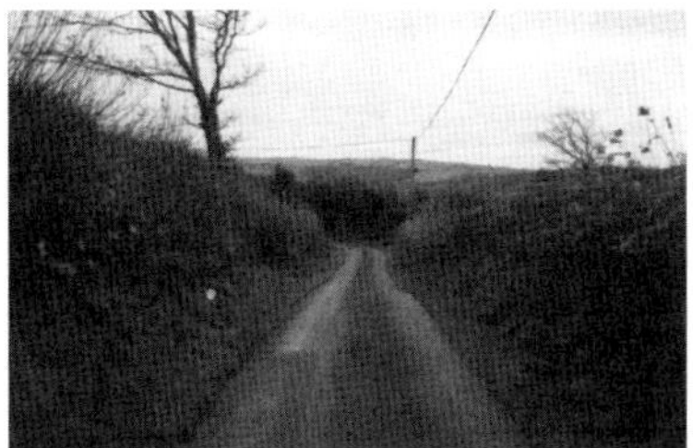

[3:8] Muddy tracks on the road veer away towards a grey metal gate on its left-hand side. The road curves in the opposite direction, towards the verdant tree.

It's like that concert that we saw. The guitarist walked alone onto the stage, sat down and began to tune his guitar and this seemed to take a long time and you wondered when he would finish tuning and start playing

whatever piece he was supposed to be playing. And then
you realised that he had begun playing that piece and
that the tuning had become the piece. But it was as if it
did not have a beginning but was rather an escalation of
things, the notes of the tuning acquiring a shape that
felt structured. And then when you realised the tune was
being played you begun to miss the tuning, to miss its
lack of finality or direction.

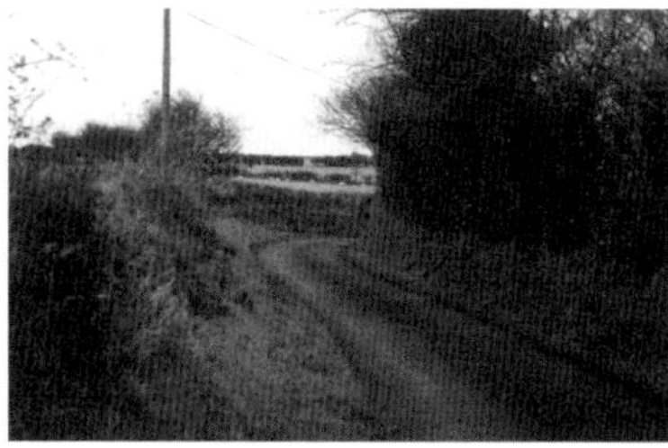

[3:9] As the road bends gradually right the straggly hedge that
flanks it on its left-hand side suddenly stops. It clears the way
for a tarmac lane that leads perpendicularly away from the road.

No, I know that you cannot pretend to maintain that
innocence indefinitely, but it is just part of the ritual of
our journey. It's almost as if we have a script. Not that
we say the same things every time, but that what we
talk about does not really seem to matter. It is just a way
of filling the time as we drive back along the road and
through the landscape. We might talk about fishing,
the books we have read, whatever, but the road and the
landscape are always the same.

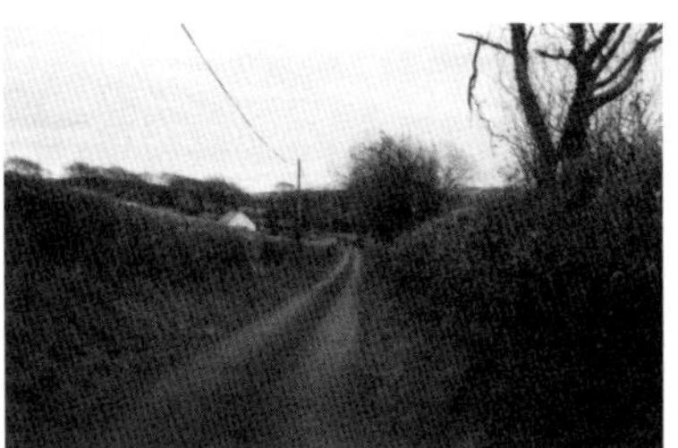

[3:10] Flanked by low hedges the road follows a flat course, bending to the left. Telegraph-poles rooted to the low hedges appear like slalom gates.

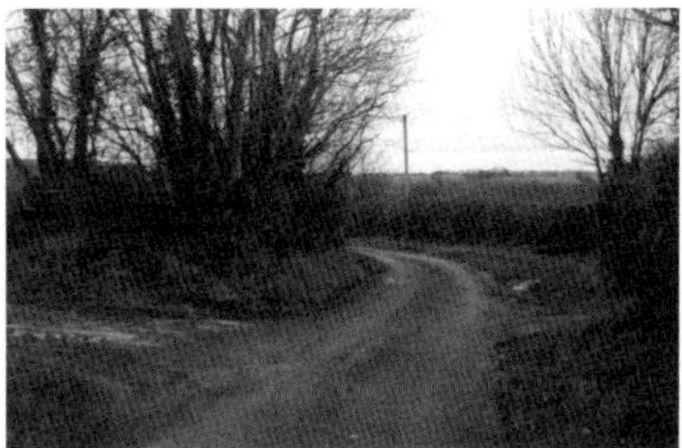

[3:11] The road continues its flat course, bending first slightly to the left and then more sharply to the right. Telegraph-poles on either side of the road support a cable diagonally across it.

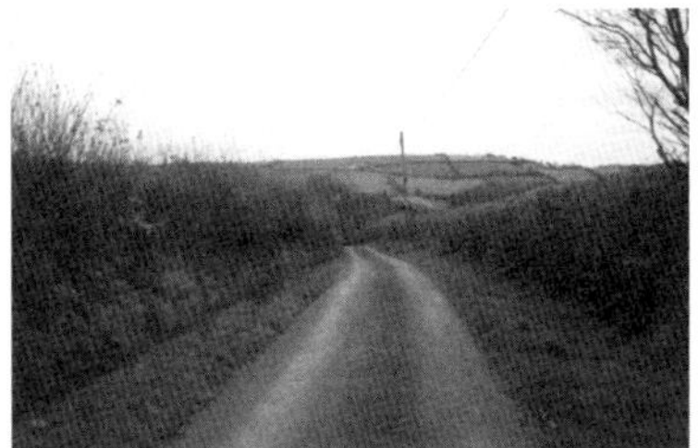

[3:12] Flanked on either side by tall straggly hedges that form a canopy over it, the road begins a shallow ascent. As it emerges from the canopy a patch of light illuminates the tarmac.

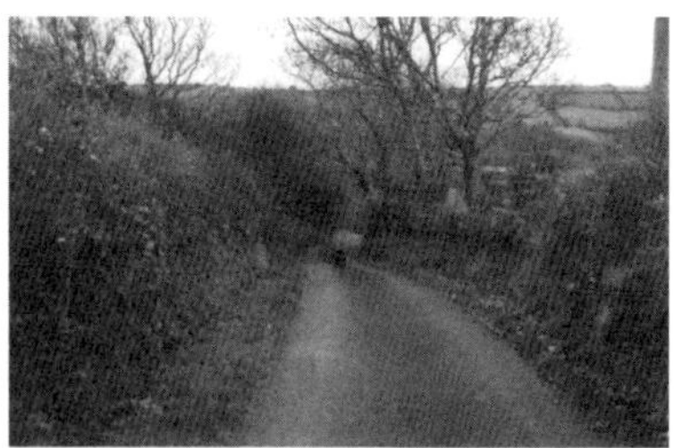

[3:13] A slack cable supported by three telegraph-poles accompanies the straight course of the road along a light descent through trimmed hedges. In the distance is a hill populated by fields and woods.

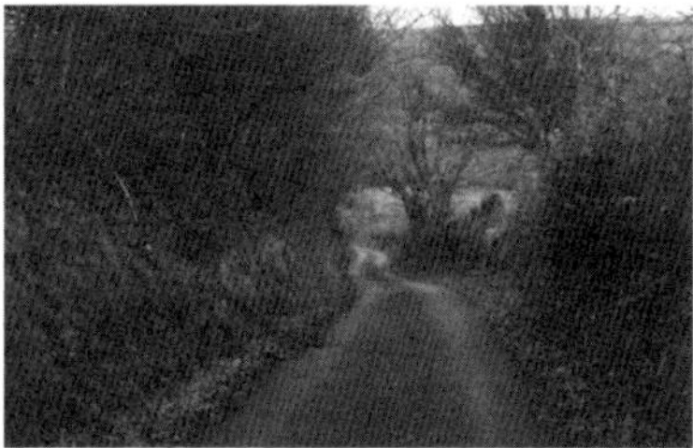

[3:14] Grey metal gates directly opposite each other on either side of the road bar entrances to fields. Between them there are muddy tracks across the tarmac. Beyond these the road continues straight, passing under a cable that is supported by telegraph-poles on either side of it.

And I do find it beautiful, this landscape I mean, with its hills and hedges and trees. Beautiful, but also like so many other landscapes. Maybe it is the road that makes it seem so generic, because it imposes a kind of forced perspective on it that frames it, that makes it seem like a picture that is constantly evolving.

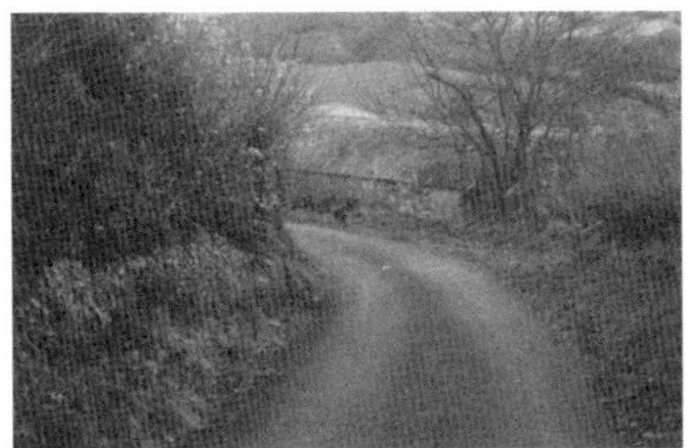

[3:15] The road begins a straight descent and then bends sharply left. This course is followed in an angular fashion by a cable supported at the outside edge of the bend by a telegraph-pole. Before this a spindly tree grows from the hedge on the left-hand side of the road.

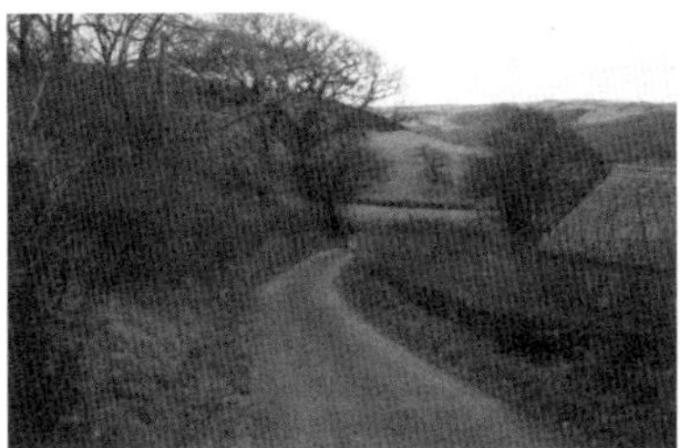

[3:16] There are sheep in the fields behind the trimmed hedge on the left-hand side of the road. On its right-hand side the road is flanked by a much more untamed hedge around which it makes a sharp bend. The cable continues to follow the road's course.

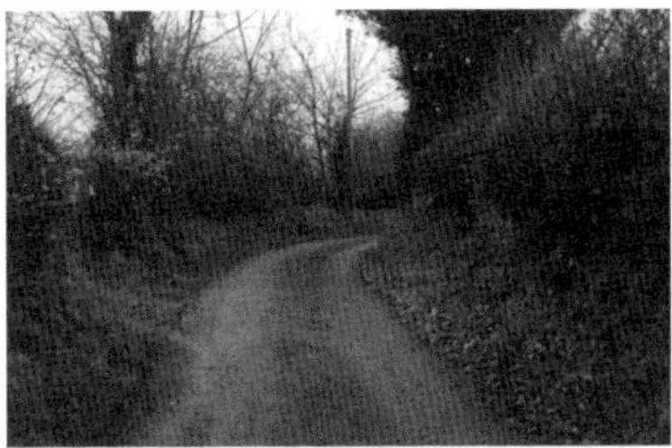

[3:17] The cable, supported by three telegraph-poles, continues to follow the road's course as it descends straight and then reaches a left bend where it flattens out. At the bend, on the left-hand side of the road, is a neat white house with a pitched slate roof. Behind the house is a straight line of tall trees.

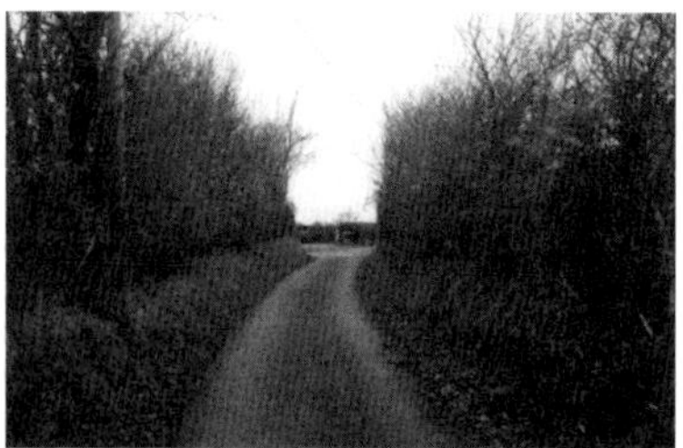

[3:18] A wet and muddy track stops at the left-hand side of the road. A few yards further along another similar track does the same on its right-hand side. Beyond them both the road bends left around a dense cluster of trees.

And it will be the same when we get back. Streets, buildings, rooms with floors, ceilings and walls with doors and windows. All these structures that frame things, that give points of reference.

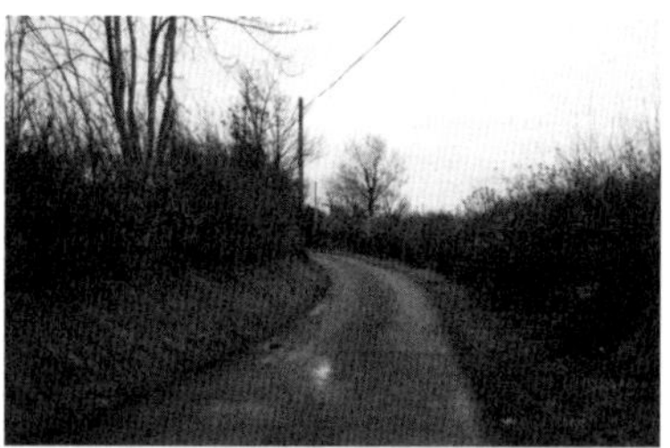

[3:19] The road descends through trimmed hedges, its course followed by a slack cable supported by a single telegraph-pole. Several fields populate the hill beyond.

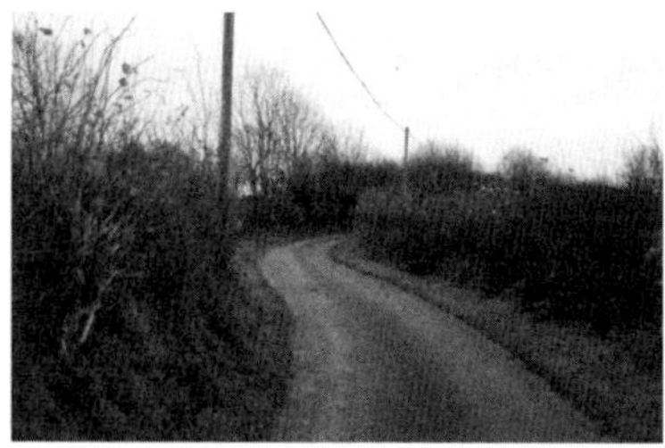

[3:20] The road veers gradually left and then right, continuing its descent through trimmed hedges. The trees that grow more and more numerous from these hedges increasingly obscure the hill beyond.

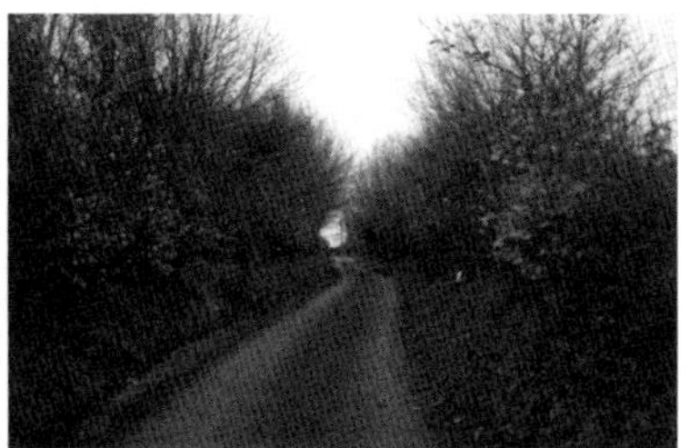

[3:21] The trees through which the road is descending by gentle curves almost entirely obscure the hill beyond.

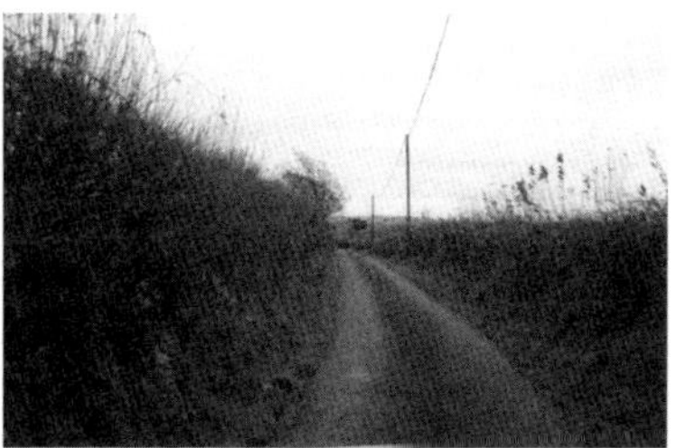

[3:22] The road continues its descent, turning left around a straggly hedge and past a large stone barn with a mossy, pitched slate roof. Behind the barn and at the bottom of the hill beyond is a large green field.

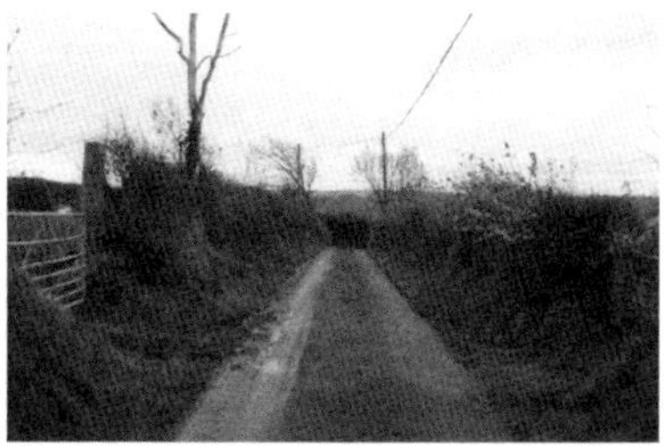

[3:23] Heading towards a flat area of green fields at the bottom of the hill beyond the road bends right around the barn and past tall trees on its left-hand side.

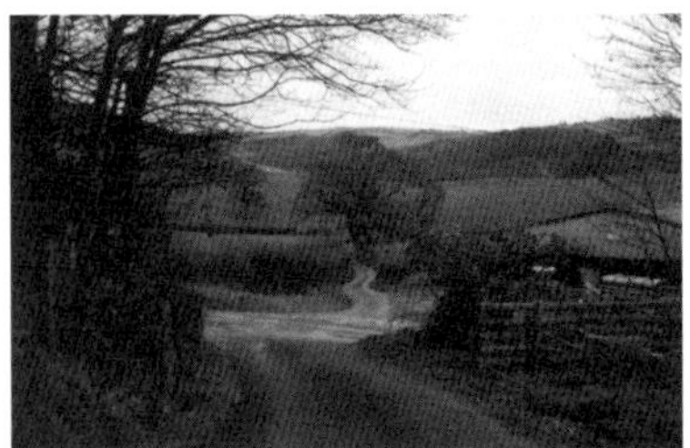

[4:1] A road emerges from the shade of a tree's overhanging branches to meet a crossroads that nestles among green fields. On the right-hand side of the road, just before it meets the crossroads, is a black metal gate which bars access to an enclosure delimited by a wooden fence. Opposite this, on the far side of the crossroads, is a large, corrugated iron farm building with a pitched roof, in front of which is parked a red tractor with a grey horse-box. The road continues past the farm building and ascends away from the crossroads making small curves through hedges and past trees. Very green fields flank the road on either side until it reaches a small summit beyond which there is a hill that is populated mainly by woodland.

I mean, it is like that stage on which the guitarist was playing. I suppose all stages are like that, the ultimate generic places, because they have the potential to become anywhere, to frame any event.

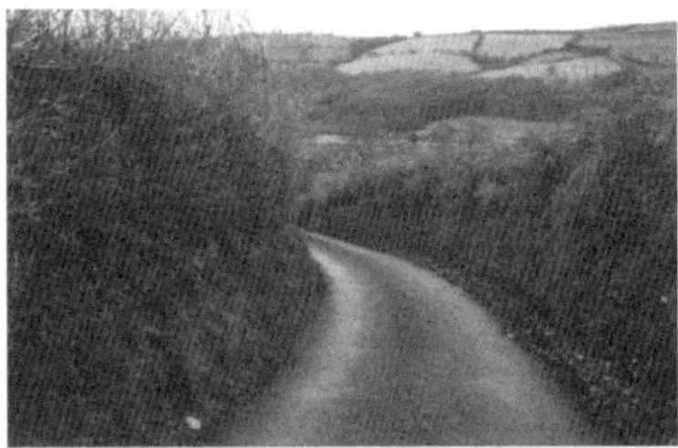

[4:2] Making a sweeping arc to the left the road begins a descent through straggly hedges. Woodland and fields populate the hill beyond.

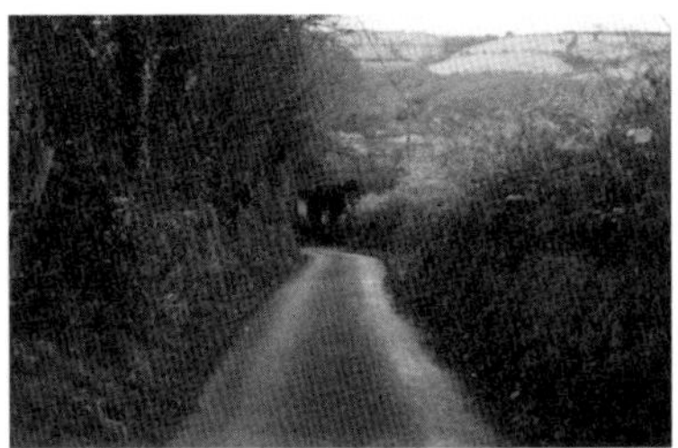

[4:3] Passing a grey metal gate on its left-hand side the road
continues its descent straight, until it reaches a point where
it shimmies first left and then right. A cable supported by
telegraph-poles on either side of the road traverses it diagonally.

**And the guitarist got on the stage, performed, and then
left the stage when he had finished. Just as we got on the
road and will depart it when we get to our destination.
And we ignore all these other possible turnings, all these
roads and tracks and gates that lead away from our
route, because we know where we are going.**

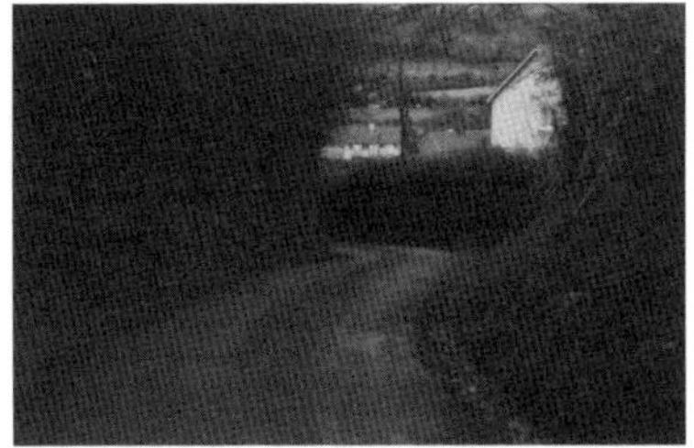

[4:4] Passing through an area that is darkened by overhanging
trees that grow from the hedges on either side of it, the road
begins to level out as it winds right and then turns sharply left.
Beyond the hedge on the outside edge of the sharp bend are a
number of houses with pitched slate roofs.

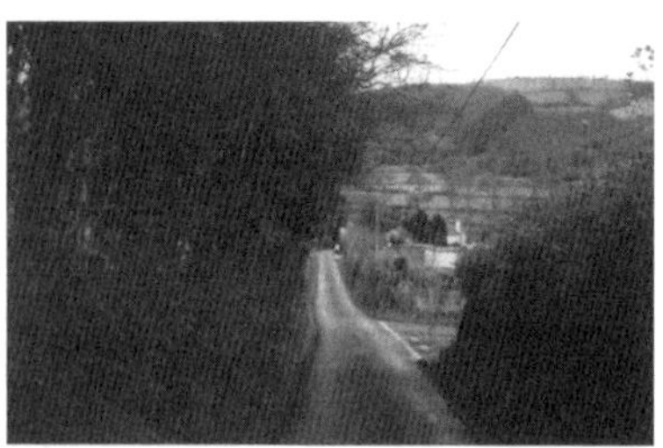

[4:5] The tall hedges on either side of the road gradually thin out and diminish as this descends towards the bottom of a hill that is populated by fields and woods. Openings in the hedge on the right-hand side of the road clear the way for junctions with two other roads. Between them a single telegraph-pole supports a slack cable that accompanies the road towards the bottom of the hill. Here there are more fields among which there nestle a number of white houses with pitched slate roofs.

I just like to entertain that possibility of not having a fixed purpose, of being here but not really thinking of where we are going. Like when he was tuning up, when you could enjoy the notes for what they were and not for what they were forming.

Meter

Meter

Art
Aptitude
Faculty
Ability
Competence
Fitness
Heartiness
Exercising
Use
Operation
Procedure
Course
Direction
Bearing
Manner
Method
Routine
Habitual
Periodic
Repeated
Frequent
Recurrent
Perpetual
Continual
Ceaseless
Incessant
Constant
Unchanging
Changeless
Enduring
Permanent
Stable
Fixed
Established
Entrenched
Secure
Safe

Protected

Guarded

Careful

Cautious

Observant

Attentive

Alert

Aware

Conscious

Known

Understood

Conceived

Instituted

Achieved

Completed

Finished

Full

Brimming

Teeming

Abundant

Ample

Extensive

Spacious

Roomy

Broad

Comprehensive

Capacious

Sweeping

Vast

Big

Large

Enormous

Gigantic

Immense

Huge

Massive

Tremendous
Colossal
Monstrous
Cracking
Breaking
Bursting
Exploding
Shattering
Snapping
Biting
Sharp
Pointed
Sarcastic
Acerbic
Austere
Harsh
Severe
Caustic
Mordant
Acicular
Acute
Spiked
Acuminate
Keen
Fine
Refined
Genteel
Polite
Civilised
Civil
Courteous
Fair
Impartial
Just
Equitable
Even

Level
Flat
Equal
Alike
Similar
Identical
Matching
Akin
Same
Corresponding
Comparative
Relative
Correspondent
Acquaintance
Friend
Companion
Associate
Comrade
Assistant
Aide
Adjunct
Addition
Summation
Accretion
Accumulation
Agglomeration
Collecting
Gathering
Assemblage
Entirety
Whole
Entire
Complete
Total
Absolute
Perfect

Ideal
Ultimate
Furthest
Farthest
Extreme
Greatest
Finest
Best
Excellent
Exceptional
Aberrant
Deviate
Vary
Change
Modification
Alteration
Shift
Transfer
Assignment
Duty
Obligation
Responsibility
Reliability
Trustworthiness
Goodness
Decency
Honesty
Integrity
Virtue
Morality
Righteousness
Rectitude
Right
Legitimate
Lawful
Legal

Sanctioned

Authorised

Official

Definite

Defined

Tangible

Touchable

Corporeal

Material

Palpable

Obvious

Apparent

Evident

Visible

Visual

Ocular

Viewed

Noticed

Received

Heard

Perceived

Caught

Entangled

Foul

Disgusting

Fetid

Gross

Aggregate

Added

Combined

Coupled

Connected

Joined

United

Linked

Attached

Familiar
Common
Communal
Community
Group
Assembly
Convention
Muster
Congregation
Collection
Variety
Diversity
Innovation
Feature
Characteristic
Typical
Representative
Specific
Particular
Especial
Individual
Single
Only
Alone
Separate
Apart
Separated
Distant
Removed
Transferred
Given
Granted
Presumed
Assumed
Accepted
Orthodox

Certified

Allowed

Affirmed

Endorsed

Signed

Settled

Determined

Resolute

Resolved

Insistent

Unrelenting

Cruel

Unkind

Fierce

Brutal

Barbarous

Furious

Frenzied

Demoniac

Diabolical

Devilish

Fiendish

Satanic

Santa Maria 5 O'Clock

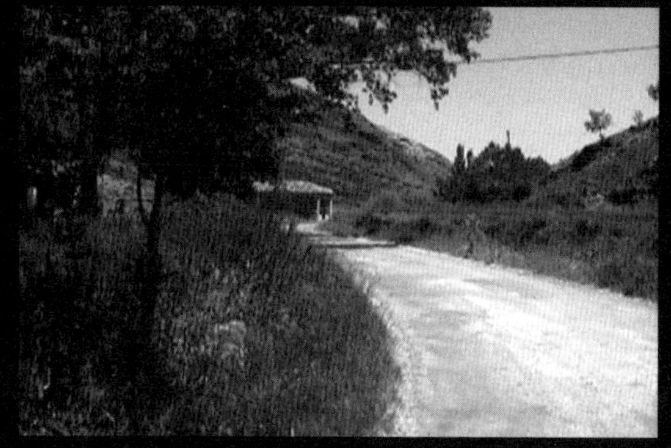

At five o'clock I'd leave the house and walk to a bar
in a neighbouring village. I was punctual because I
wanted to be there in time to get myself something
to drink and then sit at one of the tables outside to
watch the express train speed by. I did this every day
during the week I spent in the village.

Every day the express train would rush past the bar
at exactly the same time. So that I could get there in
time to see it, I always set off from the house at five
o'clock during the week that I spent in the village.

Because I was so taken by the sight of the express
train rushing past on the tracks in front of the bar, I
made sure to leave the house at five o'clock every day
during my week's stay in the village.

Since I had little else to do during the week that
I stayed in the village, I'd leave the house at five
o'clock each day so that I could walk to the bar in
the next village in time to get myself a drink and
then sit at one of the outside tables to watch the
express train rush by.

During the week that I spent in the village I'd leave
the house at five o'clock every day. This meant I
could reach the bar, buy a drink and then sit at one
of the tables outside in time to watch the express
train speed by.

In order to reach the bar in time to watch the express
train rushing past, I'd leave the house at five o'clock
each day during the week that I spent in the village.

Each day during the week I spent in the village I left
the house at five o'clock. This allowed me to get to
the bar in the neighbouring village in time to sit at
one of the outside tables and watch the express train
rush by.

Portrait of a Sculptor

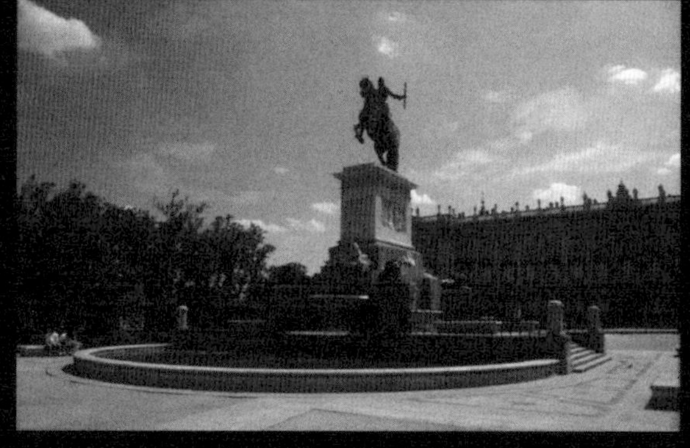

A

The copyist told me that there was no point in talking about the painting – that everything he could tell me about it was already written in the books. Well, not everything, because not everything could be written down, some things just had to be experienced. The only thing that would be of any use for me would be to film him copying the painting, right there in the museum. But neither of these things – the copying nor the filming – were allowed.

I first saw him as he was talking to another copyist who was in the same gallery making a copy of another painting by Velázquez, a copy that it was hard not to see as a caricature of the original. But he was a serious copyist; he had all the gear. On a grey blanket his heavy easel was placed at an angle such that he could see the original but not block the view of the museum visitors. Also on the blanket was his box of paints and brushes, and his stool: a folding aluminium structure with a stripy nylon fabric for the seat. A group of schoolgirls formed a crescent behind the blanket, watching the copyist trouble the surface of his canvas. It was almost as if it were his job to avert the gaze of museum visitors from the original.

My gaze had been averted more directly. I knew when I walked into the museum that I wouldn't be allowed to make any video of the painting, I don't know why I knew this – I suppose it's just common knowledge that you don't do such things. But I thought that if I feigned ignorance and came clean I might get away with something. So I showed my camera to the guard at the entrance and asked him if I could use it. When he told me I couldn't I said that I would only take still images with it. To my surprise he seemed convinced, and he allowed me to proceed.

I walked down the monumental central gallery without allowing myself to look at any of the paintings and found the gallery in which I knew the painting I had come to see would be hanging. Before stepping into the gallery I took my digital video camera from my pocket, switched it on and opened the viewing screen. Even before I had time to adjust the angle of the screen, a museum guard tapped me on the shoulder and told me that it was not permitted to make video. Yes, of course, but I wouldn't be making video, I would only be using my camera's facility to make still images. I said this as innocently as I could, but she knew the rules – and human nature – too well. She almost recited that no camera with a facility to make moving images was permitted to be used in the Prado museum, whether it was being used for that purpose or not.

I put the camera back in my pocket and went to look at the painting.

I've been to the Prado many times but only at some of those times have I had any kind of worthwhile experience with the paintings. I say the paintings, because the sculptures have never really done anything for me. I'm sure that one day I'll wake up to them and they'll seem quite wonderful, but that hasn't yet happened. Many of my experiences there were ruined by the pressure of being an art student and thinking that there must be something that I would learn from looking at the work. I'd stare and stare at an annunciation or a crucifixion and try to understand what it was, beyond the visual pleasure that the work might give me, that I could derive from it. Wincing my eyes I'd try to see the structure of the composition, to see those lines that I'd seen derived from pictures in books about painting. Trying to understand that it wasn't the subject matter, but the structure, that mattered – all to see if could learn something.

This visit was different: I hadn't come to learn anything, nor to browse around studiously, but to try to film one painting in particular – a painting that had fascinated for me for years.

The caption that currently accompanies the painting translates as follows:

Diego VELÁZQUEZ (Sevilla 1599 – Madrid 1660)

Juan Martínez Montañés (1635 – 1636)
Oil on canvas, 109 × 83.5 cm

Born in 1558 and died in 1649, Martínez Montañés is one
of the most important Andalucian sculptors of his time,
friend of Velázquez's father-in-law and teacher Francisco
Pacheco, to whom is attributed the polychromy of some of
his sculptures. It seems that he also maintains a cordial
relationship with Velázquez and this portrait shows him
in a relaxed pose, close to us, not at all contrived. In June
of 1635 he comes to the court to make a bust of the king
which – with a canvas by Velázquez – was to be sent to
Florence so that the sculptor, Pietro Tacca could cast an
equestrian portrait of the monarch, which today
can be found in the Plaza de Oriente of Madrid.
He appears modelling, in wax or in clay, said bust,
but he faces forwards, towards the model or the
spectator, expressing that this is an intellectual work,
not merely manual, that sculpture is art and not simply
artisanship. We find the same idea in *Las Meninas* [Cat.
1174], where Velázquez paints himself in a similar pose.
[Cat. 1194]

The first time I saw this painting, it hung in a small gloomy
room which served as a kind of antechamber to Gallery 12, the
grandest gallery in the museum, in which hangs *Las Meninas*,
along with many of Velázquez's other, better-known, paintings.
Although *Juan Martínez Montañés* or *The Sculptor Juan Martínez
Montañés* is and must have been the official title of the painting,
that first time I saw it I came away with the idea that it was
called *Portrait of a Sculptor.*

Besides this, the most striking memory I have of seeing the
painting for the first time – and the thing that has retained my
interest in it for so long – was the shock and pleasure of seeing
raw canvas in a painting of that period. Indeed, the joy of seeing
in a museum a material that I could think of as real. For what

the caption doesn't mention is that the bust, rather than having been painted by Velázquez, is represented by a patch of bare canvas onto which a few features are sketched. There are some texts about the painting that insist that it is unfinished, but I find this interpretation unconvincing. I maintain that, instead of depicting the bust, Velázquez finds an equivalent, in relation to painting, that indicates the unfinished state of the sculpture.

I'm sure my interest in this had something to do with my education: I studied painting with people who would encourage you to think as much of the sides of the paintings as you would the front, to think of the painting as a sculptural and material presence and not a pictorial vehicle. It sounds like a parody when I write it, but I have much respect for this way of thinking, and some empathy with it. So to see the raw canvas – or rather linen, perhaps – in the painting allowed me to engage with it in a way that had always been impossible for me with paintings of its type. I had of course looked at *Las Meninas* before, and considered the way in which that painting reveals the mechanics of its making. There is an edge of canvas at the back of the large stretcher that Velázquez depicts himself painting – but it isn't real, it's a painting of canvas and not canvas itself standing in for the real thing on what should be an illusory plane. That's what's so amazing about the portrait of Juan Martínez Montañés.

Partly because of the humble room in which the painting hung and also because there were no postcards of it in the museum shop, I assumed that it must be quite a minor work by the artist – the kind of work that would probably appeal to connoisseurs for its strangeness but which the public at large might not appreciate. Ultimately, it was just the fact that I'd never seen nor heard of the painting that made me think that it couldn't really be that well known. I felt vindicated in this judgement by several return visits to the museum when the painting wasn't exhibited in the galleries: a minor work that no one would miss. My judgement was further consolidated one evening when I had dinner in London with one of the Prado's curators: we had mutual friends and he had come over with them to authenticate a painting that hung in a stately home in Dorset. I mentioned my interest in the painting to him and he

expressed some delighted surprise. He complimented me, and
said that few people appreciated it but that scholars agreed it
was a deeply fascinating work.

So, given this affirmed rarity of interest, when I decided
that I would go to make a work about the painting I made sure
to call the museum first to check that it was on show before
flying to Madrid. Yes, it was, in Gallery 12. It annoyed me that
the painting had been re-hung in such a much more visible
place: I felt that my interest was no longer so particular. I also
speculated as to whether, had the painting been in the less
prestigious place where I'd previously seen it, I would have
been able to get away with filming it more easily. As it was it
had been promoted into the gallery for which it had previously
served as an introduction. I couldn't help wondering whether
my conversation with the curator, which had taken place about
a year before, had had anything to do with the painting's
relocation. I had thought before coming that I might contact
this man again to talk at greater depth about the painting, but
at this moment I decided I wouldn't. My conversation with
him had possibly already had too great an effect upon my
object of study.

2

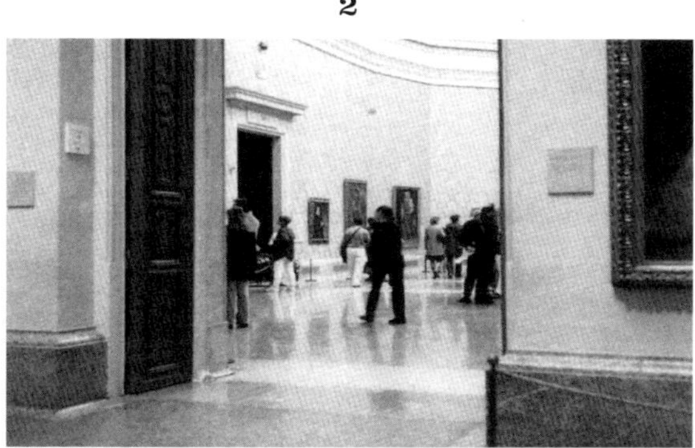

Since I couldn't take video of it, I looked at the painting. So
drawn had my attention been to the patch of bare canvas that
I'd never really looked at the rest of the image. Now, for a
while at least, I was able to look at it without purpose, and I
noticed things that had escaped me previously: the pink of the
sculptor's forehead and the way in which this changes as it is

covered by his soft, white hair. It gives such a strong sense of the clamminess of a brow and the relative dryness of the hair that partially covers it. The light in the image was much more golden than I remembered. Neither did I recall the implement that the sculptor holds poised in his right hand, nor indeed how badly drawn is his left hand, the hand that almost tenderly grasps around the back of the bust. I also noticed the difference in the size of the heads for the first time: the bust's is much bigger than the sculptor's...

3

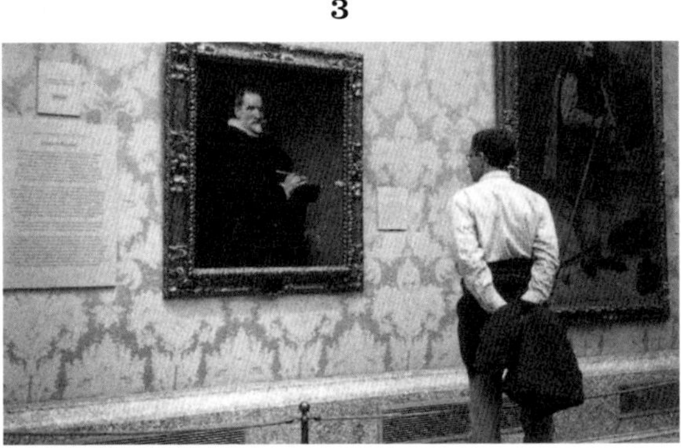

Much as I was enjoying this unfocused attention, I couldn't escape the purpose of my visit for very long. My thoughts grudgingly shifted from the painting to the piece that I had committed myself to making about the painting.

I remembered that early on in my thoughts about the piece I had considered paying one of the copyists to make me a copy of the painting. It's an idea that I put aside quite quickly because it seemed too obvious, too detached. But now seeing the copyist in action made me curious again about this possibility. I realised slowly, and a bit painfully, that he was in some measure engaged in a very similar activity to my own. Here was I looking at this painting and thinking about how I could make a work about it, thinking about how I could represent it or arrive at some sense of an equivalent. And there was he; I didn't know what he was trying to do, but I did fear that it was something similar to what I was trying to do. So I stood amongst the group of schoolgirls looking at the copy being made.

There's a kind of aura around anyone at work, and even more so if they are engaged in an activity that could broadly be termed as artistic. It was surprising, therefore, to see the copyist interrupted in the midst of his labours by a small and officious-looking man dressed in an impeccably cleaned and ironed grey suit: almost a shiny grey suit, one of those suits which should – and this one indeed did – have a small, ominous badge on its lapel. In other times I might have expected it to indicate allegiance to the Falangist league, but such associations are now no longer visibly tolerated, so I knew it would be something rather more anodyne on the breast of a man who turned out to be an authoritarian democrat. The badge identified him as a copyist, an official copyist of the museum. Of course, this is what gave him the right to interrupt the other copyist – colleagues may do this to each other. The interruption was brief, almost obligatory, and I didn't gather its subject, but I did determine that I would talk to the man.

I didn't consciously pretend to be interested in having a copy of the painting made, but I see how he might have received that impression when I asked whether it was possible to have a picture copied. Immediately he asked me which one I was interested in, and when I pointed it out he complimented me on my choice, told me it was a fine painting that he'd copied many times before. I told him about my interest in the painting, to which he listened politely, and then took out his diary and told me that he had a gap in May – would that suit me? He said there was no problem with booking museum time because it was not permitted to paint any of the paintings on this side of the gallery in situ anyway. The museum provided the copyist with a cibachrome instead and he painted the copy from this in his studio, but he assured me that there was no difference, that I would not be able to distinguish it from the original. There would of course be a small difference in size – the copyists were not permitted to make their copies of the exact size of the original – but unless I was to measure it every time I looked at it I wouldn't notice.

He'd painted every Velázquez in the museum, he told me, some several times and in different sizes. He'd painted all the Goyas too, and many of the Dutch school. But Velázquez was the one to which he was closest. No one could paint Velázquez like him, and he invited me to ask people about this. He'd painted Velázquez for palaces, embassies, for the wealthiest people in the world. This painting, the one I was interested in, he'd painted for the First Lady of the USA some years back. I was surprised at this, and I wasn't sure I believed him.

I tried to turn the conversation back to the work in hand by asking whether it was absolutely impossible to obtain permission to paint or video the painting there in the gallery. He said yes, that it was absolutely impossible, unless of course one were to have official permission, or maybe if one were to pay – that's what they did when they made documentaries, they paid. But they weren't allowed to copy directly from the paintings on this side of the gallery and he wouldn't break that rule unless it was for something official that would give him official permission to do so. I asked him whether it was therefore better to paint the things directly from the original rather than from a photograph, however detailed. He assured me again that I wouldn't be able to tell the difference.

I knew that he'd seen through me when he asked me what I did. It wasn't necessarily the question itself but the fact that he felt able to ask it that assured me he'd figured it out already. And when I told him I was an artist he said that he'd thought so all along. Was I a painter – no, I made installations and works with video, photographs and writing. I was really interested in filming the painting. I knew he would and he did ask me why, and I told him again about my interest in the painting, also about the statue in the Plaza de Oriente, a fairly nearby square. The head on this statue was the very one that the sculptor was sculpting in the painting. He looked unimpressed and repeated that one wasn't allowed to copy directly the paintings on this side of the gallery and that it was the press office I should speak to about video, but they probably wouldn't let me do this either. When he copied it he used a cibachrome that was as good as the original. Regarding video and documentaries, he had been in a few: they'd filmed him copying paintings, but not the ones on this side of the gallery, one was not allowed to copy these directly.

I needed to progress. I asked him how he went about copying this painting, and in particular how he dealt with the section of the bust. I was curious about whether he copied the sketched features as closely as he could manage or whether he undertook Velázquez's actions and made an equivalent quick sketch onto raw canvas. I was keen to know whether there could be some life left in this work. It certainly is a painting that establishes an open circuit, and to see a copyist copying a painting that is about making copies of things suggests that the circuit is still active. But the more I spoke to the copyist the more I thought that this circuit had probably extinguished itself. As if it had run out of energy and existed now merely as an indication of how it might once have worked. Not that the copyist was not concerned with process, but it was all to the end of achieving the surface. Process, he told me in answer to my question, was his secret. It was the way he prepared the canvas that was so important. He went about preparing the copy in the same way that Velázquez would have gone about preparing the original. He did admit though that in recent years he'd begun to use a slightly darker ground so that it wouldn't be so harsh on his retina. This wasn't really what I wanted to find out – I wanted to know what it meant for him to copy something, and whether this was at all like what it meant for me to be doing what I was doing.

4

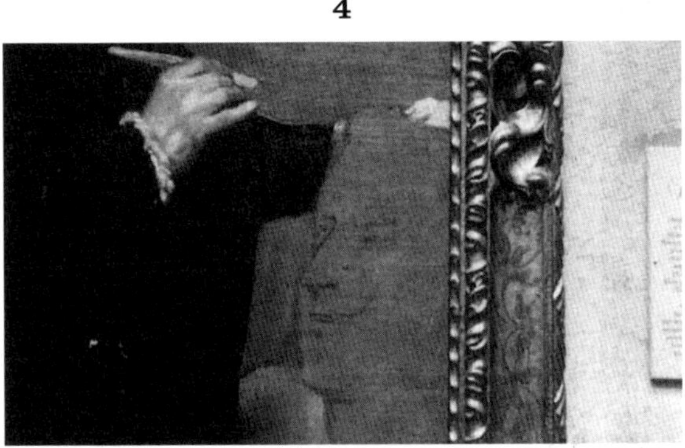

He told me that Velázquez was a genius, no, more than a genius. Goya was a genius, as were Titian and Caravaggio. Velázquez was paint, he'd assimilated everything that had gone

before him and had never been surpassed since – not even by
the Impressionists, who claimed to be closer to their medium
than any had been previously. The way the copyist got close
to it was through the process. His colleague – and he nodded
towards the man he had spoken to earlier – he wasn't bad, but
he simply didn't come close to his own standards. If I wanted to
see the way he painted I would have to return in the afternoon
when it would be his turn to be copying that painting – he
should have been doing so now, but his inferior colleague
had jumped the queue. It wasn't a problem because there
remained the afternoon. But it would be that painting and
not *Juan Martínez Montañés* that he would be painting, it was
not permitted to copy directly from the paintings on this side
of the gallery.

I didn't think I would be there in the afternoon and I asked
if I could get in touch with him on another day. He said that he
would be only too happy to have me over to his studio to talk
about the painting. He gave me his phone number and then told
me again the whole story of the painting and why he wasn't able
to paint from it directly. I tried to fan the pleasure in my own
connoisseurship by stating in an interrogative way that it wasn't
a very well known painting. Without blinking he told me that
it was one of Velázquez's most famous and then bluntly stated
that he wasn't able to talk to me right now since he had to go to
lunch so that he could paint in the afternoon.

★

The cafeteria at the Prado retains the antiquated look of a place that hasn't yet been turned into a franchise for an international café company. There's a bar where you have to stand and then a self-service eatery with tables arranged neatly like in a school canteen. I went to the bar to have a drink and gather some excited thoughts: I'd gone to the museum to film the painting but couldn't and met a man – the copyist – who made copies of the painting but who also couldn't do it there; he had to use the cibachromes with which the museum supplied him.

5

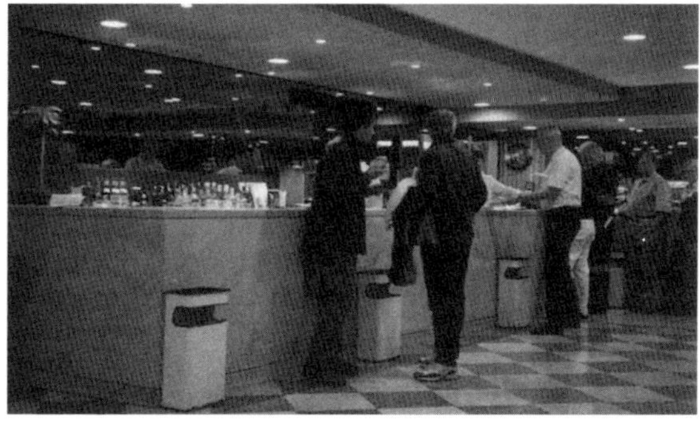

I had a beer. I was excited. The copyist seemed to me at the time such a perfect equivalent. I thought I'd contact him, try to speak to him again, even ask him whether I could tape him or film him while he talked about the painting and copied it. I drank, I smoked and rushed with a kind of excitement. This excitement was a bit conspicuous. For some reason it annoyed the surly bartenders and I was half-pleased when their manager appeared and admonished them for the messiness of the bar. I turned away, embarrassed to see the waiters humiliated.

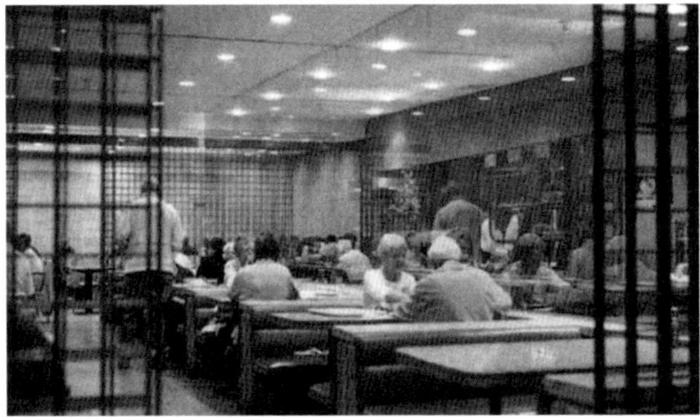

I looked through the iron grille that screens off the restaurant at the people eating. It seemed fateful to see an old man who looked like my copyist sitting alone at one of the tables at the far end. I walked closer to the grille and realised with the kind of desperation that is aroused by an overly pragmatic narrative that it was my copyist, who had come to lunch, fittingly, in the museum cafeteria. This was my chance: I could go and talk to him and declare my interest – implicate him in my work. I walked closer to the grille to make sure I'd recognised him. There was no doubt, it was he, and I wavered, began to doubt my intent: Surely it wasn't right to disturb someone while they had their lunch. But he was eating in a public place, so why be so ridiculously considerate about it ? I paced towards and away from the restaurant cursing myself under my breath, aware of the kind of lethargy that always precedes work. So catching myself between thoughts I launched towards the restaurant, took a limp turn around the self-service counter, another, and stood demurely next to his table. He'd noticed me a few steps back and was gracious with a minimal gesture that allowed me to sit with him. It was then I realised that I should have thought more carefully about what I was going to say to him. Although even if I had I probably wouldn't have been able to say it with any degree of fluency.

Without preamble, and stumbling over my words, I asked if he'd mind if we talked about the painting and I recorded our conversation. He was unfazed and clear, he had no problems with talking but not that, not being recorded. I continued to blunder by asking him whether I could some time invite him to lunch and then record him talking about the painting. This did irk him a bit and he told me that it wasn't a question of being invited to lunch. He'd told me before that he'd be delighted for me to visit his home and see him painting and talk about Velázquez. But there was nothing he could tell me that wasn't in the books.

Having said this he concentrated on his main course: breaded escalope with chips and salad. He cut up all his meat into bite-size pieces and ate them one by one. Then, after taking a piece of bread, he ate all his chips and – again after bread – the salad. A bit more bread and then he drank half his water. Now he could speak again.

Well, there were things he could tell me, but he'd have to know me better first. These were his secrets; the material secrets he'd learnt which allowed him to copy Velázquez so successfully. He didn't let his colleagues know any of these. He'd worked hard to achieve this knowledge, but it was no good to me. I could go to his house, see him painting there.

He proceeded to deal with the large yellow-green apple that was next to an orange on his tray. The peel of this he removed in one spiral strip. He then quartered it, cut out the core and sliced each quarter into three pieces. These he ate with a fork.

His colleagues, like the one who was upstairs earlier – in a slot which was, incidentally, allocated to him – were not bad painters, but the copies they made weren't like his, they had no life, no sense of the painting. His own had something more, a sensibility, a kind of tactility. I could see it for myself if I wanted, that very afternoon when he would be painting. But not the painting I was interested in: it would be the other painting that he'd be copying – the one his colleague had been copying in the morning. I should go and see for myself. He explained again why he could not paint *Juan Martínez Montañés* in situ, not unless it was for something official – it had been decreed like that by the minister of culture at the time, and he would not go against such a fine man. Others might, but not him, not unless it was ordered officially. I realised then that he liked to think himself as a court artist, just like those whose work he copied.

He peeled the orange, also in a complete spiral, and then, just as I was expecting him to split the segments, he cut it into

indiscriminate quarters with his small, blunt dessert knife,
showing utter disregard for the orange's natural divisions.
He then sliced the quarters and consumed them in the same
way as he had the apple. He followed the orange with the small
piece of bread that remained and then finished off his water.

He had to go, it was time to paint and he did what he could
to make his feeble frame hurry through the tables.

I left very soon after him. I wasn't sure that I wanted to see
his copy, or him painting the thing, and so I wandered through
some back corridors of the museum. I was half looking for a
maquette of the equestrian statue of Felipe IV that a friend
of my father's had told me about. The actual statue, which is
sited in the Plaza de Oriente, is the one for which the sculptor
Juan Martínez Montañés is sculpting the bust in Velázquez's
painting.

I couldn't find the maquette, and so I went to the museum
bookshop to see if there might be a reference to it in the
museum catalogue: there wasn't. I wasn't really concerned,
I was on my way to see the real thing now anyway, and I was
sure that was in place. While in the bookshop I looked for
postcards of the painting, but there were still none there.

7

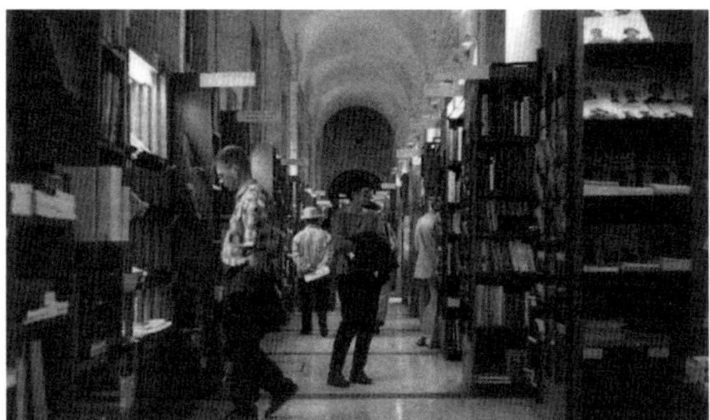

As I was leaving, I walked through Gallery 12 again. I noticed
that another copyist's gear had been set up in front of the other
painting, the one that was being copied in the morning. I'd
forgotten, or put from my mind, that my copyist had told me
he would be here presently. I was pleased he hadn't arrived yet,
and without stopping I looked at his copy. It was about half

done: there remained much unpainted but terracotta-primed canvas – to ease the strain on his retina.

★

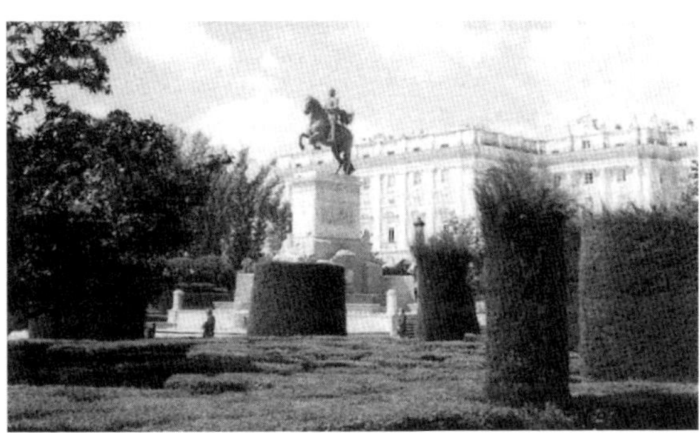

C

I took a taxi from the museum to the Plaza de Oriente to see the equestrian statue of Felipe IV. I'd been looking forward to this moment and naturally I feared disappointment. This fear was exacerbated by the course of action denied to me in the Prado; the statue now had to carry quite a lot for me. So I skirted around the edges of the plaza, distracting myself by watching people take photographs of each other.

8

But inevitably I was drawn in. I looked at the head from various angles trying to find a way of picturing it; trying to find some way of relating it back to the painting; trying to make it do something for me. I thought it would be helpful to jot down all the inscriptions. The inscription on the plinth of the statue translates as follows:

FOR GLORY OF ARTS
AND ADORNMENT OF THE CAPITAL
ERECTED ISABEL II
THIS MONUMENT

In front of the statue is a small pedestal with an inscription that translates as follows:

THE EQUESTRIAN STATUE OF FELIPE IV
WORK OF THE SCULPTOR PEDRO DE TACCA,
CAST IN FLORENCE IN 1640
WITH THE ADVICE OF GALILEO,
WAS DONATED BY THE GREAT DUKES OF TUSCANY
INSTALLED INITIALLY IN THE GARDENS
OF THE PALACIO DEL BUEN RETIRO,

IN 1844,
UNDER THE RULE OF ISABEL II,
IT WAS MOVED
TO THE PLAZA DE ORIENTE

Postscript

Matt's Gallery secured funds for my exhibition from the Henry Moore Foundation and Goldsmiths College, and I flew back to Madrid. In preparation I looked at all the material I'd gathered on my first visit and spoke to Robin K. about the way it might constitute an exhibition. I determined that I would repeat my itinerary – taking a taxi from the airport to the Prado to take some photographs and then on to the Plaza de Oriente to take a video of the statue. However, as I landed at Madrid Barajas airport I noticed that it wasn't raining, as the forecast had told me it would be, and so I changed my plans.

I took a taxi from the airport straight to the Plaza de Oriente and made a video of the journey. (It's one of a series of videos I've been making between the airport and the city whenever I fly anywhere.) When I got to the Plaza de Oriente I set up in the appropriate spot: after my first visit I'd decided that I would take an hour-long video of the head from the same perspective as it appears in the painting.

As the hour passed the day became increasingly overcast, and though I didn't stop taking the video I did reckon something was wrong. There's an all-over blueness that I associate with the Madrid sky, and I realised then that I wanted it in the video. So I returned two days later when the sky was characteristically blue and repeated the exercise. Since I'd flown out on a Friday, it was late Sunday morning when I took the second hour of footage (I'd discovered morning to be the best time to take the video because the sun was then behind me.) Families strolled contentedly, and a puppeteer handled a marionette of an opera singer, making it mimic the actions of a diva to recorded music. Towards the end of the hour a military band started to play.

In between the two days, on the Saturday, I went to the Prado and took photographs of the painting as well as of the cafeteria and the bookshop. I took these with an old Rollei medium-format camera with a very fast film and no tripod – tripods are not permitted in the Prado museum. A museum guard approached me at one point and before she could say anything I told her that I was only taking photographs, that this was not a video camera. She told me she thought it was a beautiful camera – just like the one her father used to have.

When I returned to London I set about trying to make an exhibition at Matt's Gallery that would relate to my experiences around the painting.

THE WINDOWS IN GALLERY II
HAVE BEEN OBSCURED SINCE A WALL
WAS BUILT FOR TONY BEVAN'S EXHIBITION
OF A SINGLE PAINTING *Head*,
4 SEPTEMBER – 3 NOVEMBER 1996.

THE FOYER HAS SERVED
AS THE GALLERY BOOKSHOP AND
READING AREA SINCE
MATTHEW TICKLE'S EXHIBITION
Idyll, 1999

APPLICATION FOR PLANNING PERMIT

FLINDERS STREET STATION

Designed by JW Fawcett and HPC Ashworth and built between 1901 and 1911 in the Federation Free Classical style with strong French influences. Australia's first steam train ran from this site to Sandbridge (Port Melbourne) in 1854. The station is the centre of Melbourne's rail system and it boasts Australia's longest platform, at 707.1 metres

All the stations in Spain have a plaque on their main platform that states their height above sea level.

The village station, which only has one platform, is 872.9 metres above sea level. I find it almost impossible to think of stations being at any height at all. I've never been on a train and felt that it was either climbing or descending. Railways seem to be constantly on the level: parallel, straight, neat. That's how they keep their perspective so intact.

This station doesn't feel as if it's as high as the sign declares it to be. Ben Nevis, the tallest mountain in the British Isles, is only 1344 metres high, and if you were on its summit you'd certainly know that you were at some altitude. But not here. Everything around is tremendously flat. There are some rocky hills – the foothills of a mountain range that starts just north of here – but the rest of the terrain is flat. This increases the further south you get and the more distance you put between yourself and the foothills.

The reason for what is not a rare combination of relative altitude and flatness is that the village is on the Meseta Castellana, a flat, almost lunar, plateau on which Old Castile sits. If the geography of a territory has some bearing on shaping the attitudes of the people that inhabit it, then one could form an argument to say that the entrenched right-wing, monotheistic attitude for which this part of Spain is known might in large measure be due to the severe, arid flatness of its terrain. A story is told of a man who upon his visit to Old Castile encountered a shepherd, and after much trivial conversation asked him some fundamental questions: What constituted the horizontal in Castile? The answer was immediate: it was the horizon, which was always as it should be – straight, horizontal and true. And what about the vertical, then? The answer was equally resolute, stating that in

Castile the vertical was defined by the rows of earnestly upright pine trees that line the roads and rivers. The third question was a logical, or at least geometrically logical, progression, and it concerned the nature of the diagonal in Castile. The shepherd looked taken aback and replied, with the voice of someone delivering a meaningful punch-line, that there was no diagonal in Old Castile.

Such stories are often used to give a measure of pride to the severe, entrenched attitudes of the region, as if to say: look at the land, look at what this is, and then understand why I am like I am and why my forefathers were the way they were. And this is quite convincing. Views which one might think intolerable in people living with some degree of comfort can be understood a bit more amongst those who live under harsh conditions that seem, aesthetically at least, to generate these attitudes.

Strangely, it is archaeology that gives the lie to this geographical determinacy. The first question archaeologists have to ask themselves every time they encounter the ruins of what usually turns out to have been a place of worship is whether it was originally a synagogue, a mosque or a church. And there are often occasions when this is impossible to determine. In such cases the ruins are often taken over by entrepreneurs who transform them into large and usually medieval-themed restaurants. It might be the case that these modern-day transformations are just the latest in a long line of transformations that the buildings have suffered. Before they became ruins, many of the buildings will have gone through periods of allegiance to the three faiths – Judaism, Islam and Christianity – changing as the controlling interest in the region changed. One only has to think of the extraordinary – and this is a rare accurate usage of the word – cathedral in Córdoba, where all the internal and hierarchical structures of a Catholic cathedral are wedged into the grid-based arrangement of columns that constitute the mosque that was previously there.

It is easy to reach the conclusion that these problems in identification indicate a lost age of multiculturalism in the region: an age in which various races, peoples and religions co-existed in spiritual and mercantile union. The picture develops in the mind like a virtual-reality simulation of a village square, with people of all races milling about together and buying each other's strangely shaped vegetables. In truth, though, there is no evidence of there ever having occurred this kind of co-existence here. It is more likely that those in power at any given time would have subjugated those of other races and faiths and taken over their buildings just as they would have their other assets. Since the claim was always to the land, and since each of the contesting groups had a valid claim to the land, they could each use its character and attributes to defend their respective actions. When you owned the land you could claim to be a victim of the land.

BLOCK ARCADE

The Block Arcade, which runs between Collins Street and Elizabeth Street, was built in 1891 and is an intact nineteenth-century shopping arcade. Its design was inspired by the Galeria Vittorio in Milan and features intricate mosaic tiled floors, marble columns, Victorian window surrounds and detailed plasterwork. The arcade has been fully restored and houses a variety of specialist shops.

The village is too small to have its own shops. Many of the inhabitants survive largely on the produce from their gardens and eggs and milk that are traded with those that have them. If shops are required, then there are many in a larger neighbouring village, where there is also a market every other day. However, this village is not really walking distance away, especially for the largely aged population who, on the whole, do not have cars, and so combi-vans stocked with produce come to the village on a regular basis. Combi-vans are especially popular in Spain – I'm not sure why, but you see a much higher proportion of them there than in any other place I know, and I really don't know why. The Castilians are not the kind of especially practical people who might see the benefits of having a vehicle with some of the loading capacity of a van and the road handling of a car – I'm sure they appreciate this, but no more than anybody else. Of course the producers of combi-vans have noticed this allegiance to their product, and have attempted to capitalise on it by launching a number of variations on the basic theme onto the market. You can get vans with windows in the back, and even a row of seats – so that you can turn your combi-van into a car. The people in this part of the world fall for all the novelties that they are offered by the manufacturers.

All the vans that come to sell their produce in the village have no windows in the back. Their owners need that space to write their name and address and what it is they sell. They alert people to their presence by playing loud military marches from roof-mounted horn-speakers. As the din of the music is heard women finish putting on their make-up and arranging the clothes that they have prepared in anticipation of the coming of the van. This is not the kind of dressing-up that would precede a date or a visit to the cinema, but the kind that aims at projecting a proud and well-kept appearance: the kind of dignified appearance that might make the act of haggling seem more like a plea for reason than a desperate attempt to make money stretch far enough to buy food for the week. The financial desperation is a fact of life and so it comes to be addressed with a degree of dignity.

There's one van that sells fish, another meat, and a third general provisions – these all come to the village once a week. Then there's a van selling bread that comes every other day and of course the post van that comes when it needs to deliver.

Those whose first stay it is in the village are initially shocked as they are awoken early by the blaring horns of the vans. They've come here to enjoy the peace and tranquillity that they had led themselves to expect the village would offer them. Military marches played badly, as if from an electioneering bandwagon, were certainly not expected. But they're awake, and they're on holiday – so they can catch up on sleep later, so why not go down to see what the noise is about. And then how wonderful to be able to shop with the villagers. To let them feel how much a part of their community they want to be they wait in line with the locals. Except that they have just pulled on yesterday's clothes and have not washed or brushed their hair, and make the spruced-up villagers look ridiculously precious. But this is no reason to be put off attending: they don't mind, it's probably nice for the locals to feel that they're dressed better than those who they know to be so much more sophisticated than they. What does put people off getting up so early to join in with the local habits is the poor quality of the produce that the vans offer. This is often the beginning of a disenchantment when visitors are reminded of what it means to be close to people whose economic situation is so much worse than theirs: it means they eat worse, live poorer lives, live shorter lives. They stop shopping from the vans and they begin to be a little more distant, stop trying to fit in and instead try to prolong their idyll by finding ways of dealing with the superiority for which they now feel responsible.

STATUE OF JOAN OF ARC

Near the State Library, corner of Swanston Street and
Little Lonsdale Street.
Sculptor: Emmanuel Fremiet
Acquired by the Gallery of Victoria 1906;
erected 4 February 1907

She always thought she was a bit special, and by all accounts she was. At school she was good at sports and chased by the boys. It was only among the more intelligent and existentially minded girls that she wasn't so popular. But she put this down to jealousy – a disclaimer of others' sentiments that she would employ often in her life.

Unburdened with the seriousness or concentration that would make her good at academic subjects, she did very well in drama and art. So well in the former that in her final year the drama department selected the school play around her. She would play Joan of Arc in the play by Anouilh. Her openness, vivaciousness and – for the time – outrageousness were only part of the reason for this casting. Her hairstyle also came into play because, like Joan, she had short hair, and though their locks had been shorn for very different reasons the style nonetheless gave the impression of disquieting purity of spirit and certitude of mind.

Whether it was because she enjoyed playing St. Joan or because she liked being an actress she didn't know, but she did know that she was having the time of her life. And since being an actress was more viable an option than leading armies on horseback, she decided that acting was the career she wished to pursue. Her parents were horrified when she told them. Even if there had existed such things as drama schools then in Spain they would still have refused her request. As it was, an actress was considered to be little different to a showgirl, and the profession one that attracted people of that same pedigree. So not only was her request refused outright, it also made her parents embark on a programme of remedial social education for her benefit. They blamed themselves for failing to have instilled in her the values befitting a young girl of her age and geographical and social position.

A large part of this programme concentrated on pairing her off with a decent partner. They were not intransigent about who it should be; they realised that were they to be successful they would have to entertain some kind of compromise. All they asked was that the young man was from a good family and had decent career prospects. As to his personal qualities, they were quite happy to allow their daughter to determine whether these were to her liking. In this respect they could convince themselves of how equitable they were being, unlike other parents who would go so far as to offer opinions on the character of their daughters' suitors. These opinions would often purport to be spoken by experienced voices belonging to those who had seen before how harsh could be the winters that followed the most beautiful summers.

Within a year she was married to a smiley young man who liked to have sex with her often. When this wasn't possible, because of a lack of time or the will on her part, he would ask for permission just to be inside her – because he loved her so much.

Whether through action or procrastination a son was born to them as quickly as was legitimately possible. Life was tolerable: she loved the child and was provided for quite comfortably by her husband, who had a good and secure job in his father's company. They lived in a nice flat in the centre of town and she would spend her days pushing her son around in his buggy, visiting her old school friends and meeting new ones.

One day, just as she was feeding the ten-month-old child his dinner, her husband arrived home from work. It was more or less his usual time but his bearing was considerably more cheerful than usual. He hadn't gone to work, he told her, he'd been in that nice little village they'd visited a couple of weekends ago. Did she remember that beautiful house they'd been looking at in the main square? Well, he'd bought it and arranged for it to be fixed up: it would be habitable within three months. She was pleased.

Though they weren't her own favourites, the rustic villages that her husband liked to visit at weekends had grown on her. She had recently even begun to be able to make her own observations about the beauty of certain churches, to point out unusual crests above doors. The idea of having a house in one of these villages to visit at weekends pleased her. It was as she was entertaining thoughts of what they might do there that her husband dropped the leaden line that they would put their flat on the market immediately, that he was even looking forward to the hour-long drive he would take to work every day. She needn't worry, because shop vans came to the village most days. He wouldn't entertain her objections.

Their son is now at university. He returns in the summer months and takes a job looking after the refuge at the top of a hill near the village. Because he is a student he always takes work with him. He has a black-and-white photograph of her playing St. Joan that he uses as a bookmark. She's kneeling in a double genuflection with her palms together in an attitude of prayer. She looks ahead blankly, her eyes slightly raised.

STATE LIBRARY

The State Library, with its Classical Revival facade facing Swanston Street, was built in various stages from 1854. When it was completed in 1913, the reinforced concrete dome over the octagonal reading room was the largest of its kind in the world.

Many visitors are drawn to the village because of its location. It's at the base of the foothills of a dramatic mountain range that continues to the north. Further south the Castilian plateau seems to go on forever: arid, flat and so harsh. So the land around the village takes the best of both sides and fashions a pleasant environment of hills and rivers and meadows. When they are there people often think that they would like to walk in the hills and when they ask the villagers for advice on a relatively challenging and picturesque route they are routinely told to follow the route up the tallest hill that neighbours the village and then go down the other side to the convent. It is then possible to hitch-hike back to the village along the main road.

The hill in question is high enough to merit a small refuge at its summit: a solid structure of bricks, stones and cement that is able to withstand the harsh conditions that can sometimes buffet this land. Because of its construction it is also able to retain a good measure of coolness inside, even in the hottest days of summer. It's a young man who's there – a student lining his pockets during the summer holiday. He checks the meteorological instruments when he arrives and also when he leaves, and for the rest of the time sits in the shelter or in its shade reading a book. He always brings two books with him for the day. One always reflects the nature of his studies in art history, a subject he chose to read at university as the result of a compromise between his sensitivity and his sensibleness. It was a subject that would allow him to indulge his keenness for beauty and for other ways of thinking about living and the world while maintaining his viable engagement to the economy within which his parents had told him he would need to operate. It was a happy compromise: so happy, in fact, that it was probably not a compromise at all, but an inevitability. What else could he have done? As a very young child he'd wanted to be a laboratory chemist because of all the colours he thought he would be able to produce in shiny test-tubes. His father had approved of this, but told him casually one day that the best profession he could think of was that of an artist, because it hurt no-one and resulted in the production of beauty. The child, however, still wanted to be a chemist – he found it easier to conceive of colours being contained in test-tubes than in the black lines of his colouring books. He hated colouring books, and this hatred later developed into a habit of biting his nails – getting rid of the edges within which he was not able to be contained. A bit later on his professional plans changed and he decided he would be a diplomat or a lawyer because he thought that this would allow him to have a large office, be gracious to people and spend a long time on the telephone, just like he saw his father doing during the long summer holidays when he was sometimes responsible for looking after him.

More or less tacitly, and mainly in the minds of his parents, this remained the state of affairs until the time came for him to leave school and make his decision count. They were surprised when he told them that he wanted to be an artist: he had, after all, never displayed any talent in this area, he was by his own admission unable to draw; he had famously always been unable to draw. He pointed out that contemporary art wasn't based on skills such as drawing; he knew they knew this and he also knew what their response would be: that though the art didn't display it, it was through an understanding and mastering of these skills that progress in the arts occurred. If one could not master traditions, then how could one hope to go beyond them? They said that all the best artists had mastered the traditions of their time before they progressed to make their best and most groundbreaking work.

These arguments were less convincing than those that pointed out the uncertain financial future that he might face were he to be an artist. There were members of the family on both sides who were artists and who both struggled not to survive but to be able to be able to afford luxuries like holidays in the sun and fast cars. Would their son really be prepared to sacrifice the way of life to which he was accustomed? Could he not perhaps turn his thoughts to being an architect or a designer? That way he could train his visual and material skills but also develop a profession.

But visuality and skill had little to do with his interest in being an artist. He was concerned with meaning, with the way in which in art, things were said to mean more than they were. And so it was that he settled on art history. If he could not be a practitioner in the field of making meanings he could at least learn as much as he could about the process, and how it had played out in history.

His parents were delighted that he had agreed to the benefits of an academic discipline and they imagined him turning his hand to business after he had completed his degree. They told him that when he was older and had perhaps earned a secure living for himself he could then maybe devote himself to being an artist. It was something he could keep doing anyway, as a hobby, as something he enjoyed. To make his parents happy he pretended that he agreed with them about this. To make himself happy he assured them of how sure he was that he had taken the right decision. But he knew that he'd surrendered something extremely important.

The art-history book rarely changes, because he takes such a long time to plough through it. The other book, which is usually a work of fiction by a known and esteemed writer, changes daily or every two days. There is little else to do on the mountain-top but read. Last summer his art-history tome was Erwin Panofsky's *Meaning in the Visual Arts*, a large volume that he lugged with him daily to the top of the mountain. He read very little of it, choosing instead to concentrate on his novels. However, such a constant part of his apparel was Panofsky's book that he came to be associated with the work.

OLD MAGISTRATES COURT

The Former Magistrates' Court was designed by GHB Austin and built in 1911 in the Federation Romanesque style. It has detailed ornamentation, turret forms, parapets, an octagonal dome with a lantern, and rock-faced masonry. The building was active as a court until the early 1990s, before being taken over by RMIT University.

The crossroads is quite smart now. If driving, you have to perform a kind of loop to turn left, which is the direction you'd usually take from there as it leads to the nearest small town with a decent market and shops: the town where the biscuit factories are. You'd be heading north in that direction. That's certain because the road runs exactly north-south – one of those roads that's so satisfying when looking for directions on a map; a road you could imagine being in place before someone thought of building the landscape around it. That's not so far fetched: there are shopping centres that develop around roundabouts; parks constructed over bridges; depositories built to house records before there were any records to house. But this place is more real, and the road has changed: it wasn't always as glistening and straight and black as it is now. If you were to turn right and head south it would take about an hour by car to get to the first city and you would notice the greenery of these small hills change to endless flat yellow fields. If you turned left, the changes would happen in reverse. That would be heading towards the sea, which is also about an hour from here, and the hills would grow to mountains before descending to the rich green meadows of the coast. It must be quite an ancient route. The tract between the city and the village follows the course of a canal which was dug long before the road was laid. It's not navigable any more, and during the larger part of most years is completely dry, but it's traceable through almost the entire length of its course. There are plans to make it navigable again, so that it might add charm and activity to the region's recently discovered touristic potential. But they're those kind of plans of which the origin is unclear, the kind of plans that everyone knows about but for which no-one is responsible. There are an awful lot of plans like that. The road improvement was one of them. For years people had complained about the dips and bends, about having to slow down to go through villages. They didn't actually complain, they moaned – for there was no purpose or direction towards which they pointed their dissatisfaction. Everyone knew it was a bad road and it made everyone feel better to agree about that. The first roadworks were met generally with surprise, as if someone in a position of authority had been offended on discovering the criticism which they had been dishing out secretly and over-reacted with this radical solution of doing something about it. So gradually, amidst complaints of misjudgement and slowness, the road was widened, straightened and levelled.

Since they had moved to the village he had travelled to and from work along the road every day, but it was before this that he had first noticed the church. He remembered it from his childhood, and he loved showing it to his son like his father had shown it to him. It's a perfect small Romanesque church with beautifully matched, rough-hewn stone blocks of considerable size. It demonstrates the achievement of a perfect ordinance in its particular style. The eye travels over the classic eastern end, rising from the apses up over the transept walls, almost imperceptibly to the cupola squinches and finally to the lantern. The decorative features are all there – billets outlining the windows, engaged columns and cornices with carved modillions. But these were not the details that interested him about the church. Indeed, neither he, nor his father, nor his son, had ever spent very long studying the church itself, what was so fantastic about it was the way in which it appeared from the road. Literally it appeared, rising up slowly from the otherwise barren terrain as he drove back from the city to the village. And gradually it disappeared, as if slowly sinking down into its foundations. Some moments later it slowly appeared again and then slid back down into the ground. In total, the church would perform its trick seven times, and he always made sure to count that it was seven times it was doing it. There was something quite reassuring about knowing that it would happen seven times, the kind of reassuring self-confidence that is bred with familiarity. When he passed the village that the church served he would always take in the scene of the church in its stable setting and would marvel at how normal it looked, at how oblivious those who used it for serious acts were of its frivolity.

His had been one of the loudest voices at the meetings convened to discuss the shocking state of the road. Every day he had to use it, and every day he put himself in danger. Neither was the period during which the repairs were carried out a happy one. The endless diversions and reduced speed limits meant that it was not unusual for his journey time to be doubled. Four hours a day in the car and not even the reward of driving through places for which he had a real affection – he was quite an emotional man, and he was excited like a child on the afternoon they reopened the road. So special did he consider this day that he insisted his son take the afternoon off school and come by train to join him so that they could drive back together.

They drove through some of the same old villages, the names of which they could both recite in the right order; they noted those villages that the road no longer traversed. They grumbled about sharp bends that remained and marvelled at the long straits that would save them so much time. The father had his favourite CD playing – Al Stewart's *Year of the Cat* – and though his son didn't particularly like the music he did have to admit that it suited the landscape well, with its tragi-heroic melodies and winging, sexy guitars. They chuckled at each other about the huge red-brick brothel that had been built a couple of years previously and right in front of which, conveniently, the new road passed. The corruption in local politics was one of the father's favourite subjects to rant about, and his son was now old enough that he'd talk his politics with him at the kitchen table while the mother washed up after dinner.

The father spotted it first but said nothing; he was waiting for his son to see it and he smiled, waiting to be pleased. His son had seen it but he wasn't sure it was the one; he was less familiar with the road and he would have to wait for it to sink down into the ground before he could be certain. This it wasn't doing, and they both stared harder and harder, trying to lose sight of it. Very soon the new road was taking them past the village and their heads turned in unison following the church. It was the father who, for the sake of safety, peeled his eyes from the church first.

WORLD TRADE CENTRE

The World Trade Centre is a twelve-storey office complex on the north bank of the Yarra River. It was completed in 1983 and in 1994 Melbourne's first casino opened there.

Having walked over the mountain and through the burnt-out village, the reward of the cakes at the convent is enticing and deserved. If it's been a while since your last visit then memory begins to fail you, and you begin to think that you might find the equivalent of a tea-room where they might serve coffee or hot chocolate along with samples of their cakes. This is indeed a failure of memory, for the nunnery – open as it is to commerce – provides nothing as wasteful or distracting as a public space. And this is not to do with the nuns' purity: with the ostensible challenge to the vows of taciturnness, and even chastity, that such a space might suppose. No, there is no such space because it would not be viable economically.

This is a tiny convent, but not insignificant. It was founded in the second half of the twelfth century (1190) by Doña Mencía, and its plan is Cistercian. The church maintains a nave with a transept and three apses, as well as a beautiful cloister with semi-circular arches on paired columns. Also worthy of note is the Chapter House. Bernardine nuns, followers of St. Bernard of Clairvaux, live in the convent. St. Bernard was a French theologian and reformer who entered the Cistercian monastery of Cîteaux in 1113 and became the first abbot of the newly founded monastery of Clairvaux, Champagne, in 1115. This fast ascent was the result of his studious and ascetic life and his stirring eloquence, qualities that made him the oracle of Christendom. He founded more than seventy monasteries and is described by the Catholic Church as the last of the Fathers of the Church. His writings comprise more than 400 epistles, 340 sermons, a life of St. Malachy and distinct theological treatises. He was canonised in 1174. The monks of his reformed branch of the Cistercians are often called Bernardines, as are the nuns.

If you want to buy cakes, or indeed see any of the convent, you have to knock on a small opening in the wall during the severely restricted opening hours. And then you have to know what you want, for only a few of the nuns are allowed to speak, and the others are unable therefore to tell you what they have available. When you finally receive your box of cakes the packaging looks familiar. This is because the nuns market their cakes in supermarkets throughout Spain. If they have not yet found an international market it is because their produce has a national identity that is too typical, and would be difficult to sell abroad.

They make assorted *pastas de té*, which are fatty, shortbread-like assorted biscuits, some with nuts, some with a bit of chocolate. They also make *raquelitos*, which have the light, flaky texture of fat cheese straws but with a sweet flavour and a heavy dusting of sugar. The variety doesn't stop there, but I can't remember the names of any of their other sweet produce. Another of the nuns' money-making ventures is the tours which they offer around the monastery. They are generally conducted by an older nun who, it would seem, has been divinely excused from her vow not to speak. She bids you follow her and recites the academic text-book spiel about the convent. At the end of the tour she goes through the various products that one can buy from the shop. As well as the cakes, these include small plaster replicas of the corkscrew columns from the famous cloister, as well as key-rings and coasters with similar motifs.

The convent is also well known in specific circles for its codex. This is known as one of the last great illustrated codices, with an enormous number of miniature paintings. Its style is not dissimilar to that of the output of some of the miniaturists from San Pedro de Cardeña, and the possibility exists that it may have been realised in this monastery in Burgos. Of special note is the fact that for the first and last time, some of the miniatures in the codex incorporate foreign iconographic symbols in illustrations created within the high medieval Hispanic tradition. There is nothing that would announce the presence of anything much post-1200; that is to say, nothing exists that could be called Gothic. Because of this, amongst other things, it is understood that the codex must have been copied no later than around 1210–1220.

Silver and gold are used quite freely in the codex, clearly indicating the luxurious and important status of the work. For many years the codex remained housed in the convent, almost as its raison d'être. It was certainly its most valuable asset. However, in 1882 the asset became too valuable for even the devoted nuns to be able to resist selling it to the Bibliothèque Nationale de France.

MELBOURNE MUSEUM

The New Melbourne Museum is located directly opposite the old Royal Exhibition Building in Carlton Gardens. The $550 million museum houses an impressive collection and the complex includes an Aboriginal Centre, a children's museum, a living forest gallery, major exhibition galleries (covering Australian society, indigenous cultures, wonders of the human mind and body and science and technology), a touring exhibition hall, a 3D interactive theatre, a study centre, a two-level retail outlet and three themed restaurants/cafés.

Such is the wealth of Romanesque art and architecture that there are plans to establish a centre for the study of the Romanesque in the largest village of the region. Various committees have been established to try to ascertain what the best way of doing this might be. There are those who call for a panel of international experts to be appointed as a steering group that would become a board of trustees. A director could be selected from the board and the centre would thereby ensure that there was a person of international standing at its helm. Though no-one doubts the value of attracting prestigious figures to the project, some believe strongly that the directorship should be given immediately to someone local – someone who might understand the peculiar politics of the region and be able to steer the venture. The local person they mean is Jeremias.

Jeremias lives in a smaller neighbouring village. He supports himself by teaching history in a local school. This constitutes social support, because financially Jeremias has no need to work.

His father was a wealthy lawyer and Jeremias an only child who inherited money and land on which he'd never set foot but which gave him rents large enough for him to easily maintain himself and a family in the utmost luxury. He had no family; he spent his money instead on prostitutes in the new brothel that had been established on the road into the main town. This is a brothel that has little to envy any in Spain. It's sited in a red-brick building that is more akin to an office block or an airport hotel than to a house of sin. Locals have indeed given it the nickname 'the hotel'. It is there that they tell their wives that they are going to meet their friends. The immediate entrance continues the ruse and presents a reception manned by a smart concierge. Few of the regular visitors stop to talk to him; his role is to subtly disabuse holidaying families from England and Germany who wander in looking for a meal or a room for the night. The regular visitors walk through a gilt-framed door and into a room of polystyrene classical elegance illuminated by a soft purple light that barely reveals the tired faces of the attendant whores. Most of the women are African, often lured to Spain with false promises of nannying or cleaning jobs and then forced into prostitution by mafias who hold their passports hostage. Jeremias often finds himself thinking with his historian's head about those times so many hundreds of years ago when Africans ruled this land.

What Jeremias does in the brothel is his own business – often it doesn't involve sex, though he does like this. But the way in which he excuses his visits there to himself is by defining it as a kind of forum where he might meet other local men and exchange stories. In the brothel he will be as compromised as any of the other customers he might meet. They will share a secret about each other which each with his visible presence makes a tacit promise not to divulge. And sharing a secret with someone is a great bonding act – one that often allows further indiscretions. It is this that interests Jeremiah, for though he studied history, and is a very learned and well-regarded historian, his real interest is in local gossip. It was this interest that made him such a fantastic student, because he would invest historical fact with the enjoyment of stories. He was not so concerned with what happened on a grand scale, but with what people did privately when they returned home in the evening after accomplishing historical deeds.

This gave him an unusual insight into the affairs of the world. He had become an expert in the Romanesque because it was the most important branch of local history of which there remained some material evidence. And it was very important to him that whatever he did should be local: he could not possibly leave this place, of which he had become the semi-official narrator.

So the reasons for which they wanted Jeremias to be the director of the new centre were as much to do to with his more than intimate knowledge of local affairs as they were based on his acumen as a historian – undisputed as this was. They felt it would be useful to have someone in charge who knew about the idiosyncrasies of the local powers that be: the councillor who had the Buddhist shrine in his house. He had been bitten by the flowery bug of redemptive Eastern philosophy and had wanted to manifest this as a material presence in his house. The shrine was small, but quite ornate; it stood out markedly against the austere Castilian decorative order that his wife had achieved. She hated the shrine, but to demonstrate her tolerance of his interest said little about it. With her he was arrogant and proud about his interest, claiming intellectual and spiritual superiority. He claimed that she could say nothing to dissuade him, for how could a path be denied? The very fact that she would not join him in meditation just revealed her pride, and showed how far from enlightenment she really was. Often in the middle of these discussions her mother, who lived next door, would call round. This would send him into the panic of trying to conceal the shrine before she could see it: to facilitate this task he had fitted casters to its base.

The judge who would not leave his house until he had come up with some kind of catchphrase with which he felt he might amuse people and be thought of as witty and interesting. Some years before, when there were still river crabs in the local river, he had emerged from his home after a fortnight in hiding and gone to his local bar. He was served his beer, and when asked whether he might like something with it he asked, with a triumphant smile, to be given some oceanic monsters. The barman looked bemused, and the order was repeated with a nonchalant turn of the head; repeated again more directly and a fourth time with clear anxiety in the voice. It had happened again, the concealed sniggers, the pitying looks. Jeremias was the first to commiserate.

FEDERATION SQUARE

Federation Square covers the railway lines leading from Flinders Street to the eastern suburbs, allowing more direct access to sections of the Yarra and to some of Melbourne's premier sporting and concert venues. It was designed by the architects Donald Bates and Peter Davidson, and it incorporates a massive civic plaza, a new museum of Australian art, a screening and national multimedia centre, restaurants and cafes, and an outdoor auditorium. It is also the home of the national television broadcaster, SBS.

In the main square is the shell of a building. Its grand proportions betray the mighty ambition which once lay behind it. All that is there is the structure. The internal walls were never rendered, nor the floors laid. Doors and windows were never put in. The external walls are coloured black, as if the building had been alight once and was now charred. But there is no evidence of burning. The black colour is probably that of some kind of protective paint that the bare and once orange bricks need as a protection from the weather. There are neatly ordered piles of onions, potatoes, horseshoes and old doors throughout the ground floor of the building, the villagers having begun to use the building as a kind of warehouse. This is quite understandable because the openings for doors and windows give directly onto the square, and this makes the building feel like a covered extension: what would be a shelter in a more civic-minded place, but which is subject here to the practicalities of the villagers' existence.

The building was to have been a rehabilitation centre for young drug addicts. A man who was quite a prominent cartoonist in a national newspaper set its construction in train some years ago as a charitable deed. It was quite easy for him to find and buy the plot for very little money. He quickly obtained a grant to begin its construction but then lost heart when he realised the mountain of work he would have to undertake in order to secure funding for the completion and subsequently the running of the centre. He never showed his face in the village after that, and when asked by people of the city what had happened to that project he used to talk about so much he said that he had been forced to back down because of the stubbornness that the insensitive and reactionary villagers had shown towards his plans. He told his city friends that the villagers were scared that the recovering addicts would rob them and ruin the tranquillity of their community.

The village had not been tranquil for many years. It was silent enough, and peaceful, but this was because its potentially active population had left it many years previously as a result of late industrialisation. Some of the people in the village still worked, but this tended to be on smallholdings or looking after family herds. The flour factory, which lay on the railway some four kilometres away, had been quite a major employer but it required many fewer labourers now and could in no way keep the community in employment. It used to supply the biscuit factories in a local town that had grown to become large national interests, with names that were famous throughout the country. It seems they became too large, for all but one of the three large companies had been bought in recent years by large multinationals. The reason for the biscuit industry having taken root here was the supply of raw materials that existed in the area: eggs, wheat and honey, the same materials that the nuns in a local convent have used to make their cakes for hundreds of years. It is, however, now too expensive for the multinationals to obtain these ingredients from small-scale local production, and it is in fact beginning to be too expensive to keep the biscuit factories themselves open, production being cheaper to maintain at their bigger factories in the cities. The smell of biscuits does still hang in the air as you approach the town, and it gets stronger when you're there. A sweet, rich, warm, comforting smell that's been mixing with the air that people there have been breathing for at least two generations; almost certainly this has contributed to their good nature.

It was through the biscuit factory that the cartoonist had come to hear about the town and then the village. It started as a detour which the Michelin *Green Guide* had indicated with two stars was worth taking. Not three stars, which would urge one to visit the place for its own merits, nor merely one, which would simply declare the place to be interesting; two stars – worth a detour. He'd looked the place up because he'd recognised the name from the biscuit packet – he was recently divorced and had taken to eating these biscuits for breakfast. He realised, as he smelt the factory, what a solace these biscuits were to him, how good they made him feel. He was unfamiliar with the area but had, before becoming a cartoonist, studied art history at university and was therefore aware of the wealth of Romanesque architecture that the region had to offer. This gave him a way in to this place that had so touched him. The architecture became the focus of his return visits, which got more and more frequent as he began to contemplate buying a house in which he might spend more time in the region. He found one in the village.

For some years he enjoyed life in the village, spending increasing amounts of time there until at times it seemed that he lived there. He mixed both with the traditional inhabitants of the village and with those few families who had more recently escaped the city and made the village their home. He always struggled with the extent to which he was prepared to allow himself to be subsumed by the village. His instinct was to become 'one of them' and to be not a visitor but another villager. But he feared that he knew that what really appealed to him about being here was his vanity, and this was exercised by two things: he found the village exotic, and he knew the villagers found him exotic. To erode this exoticism was obviously desirable, and inevitable, but he had accepted that to maintain his reverie it would have to remain. The idea of establishing a rehabilitation centre came to him as he was looking to resolve this conflict. It seemed to him that such an idea struck the perfect balance by being both an act of local civic spirit and one that defined him as someone special in the community.

CROWN ENTERTAINMENT COMPLEX

South of the Yarra River. The complex includes the Luxury Crown Towers Hotel and the Crown Casino, with over 300 tables and 2500 gambling machines open round the clock. There are waterfalls, jets of fire, a giant cinema complex, a variety of nightclubs, a 900-seat showroom, a multitude of bars and restaurants, and a designer clothing and specialist shopping complex.

The cultural centre looks like a long bungalow; it has a few swings and a climbing frame for the children outside and inside a bar that stretches the length of the building. One image hangs behind the bar, that of a football team standing huddled in front of a dry, earthen pitch wearing white shorts and maroon shirts. The cartoonist had spent many Saturday evenings in the cultural centre – Saturday being the only day on which it was open – looking at the photograph and trying to ascertain something from the players' expressions. This seemed a good way of achieving some calm in the noisy atmosphere that was created there by whatever was playing on the television that was perched at a clumsy angle on the wall, and by the clattering of dominoes from all the tables.

During the first few weekends and, if he could manage it, longer periods that he'd spent in the village, the idea of being a part of the community had appealed to him immensely; he felt that in this environment he'd found something of which he'd always been aware but which he'd never been able to grasp. The place was a revelation, like those moments when something very obvious seems to acquire huge weight and import, when the passing of time is triggered by something to feel different, more purposeful. He felt a different person when he arrived at the village and he'd rush out to celebrate this with those he'd met there. Drinks at the cultural centre were ridiculously cheap and he had thought, on occasion, of paying for the entire evening bar bill himself. He'd thought better of this idea, but it still irked him that he was unable to treat his village friends. It was instead they who treated him, making an indecent show of hospitality by buying him glasses and glasses of the astringent red wine that was the centre's only available drink. The wine had tasted fantastic to him. He didn't kid himself so far as to think that it was a good wine – as if he'd found an as yet undiscovered regional variety of grape. It was rather in himself that he thought he might have discovered something. He had the interest in wine befitting any educated urbanite, but in the village – and in relation to its wine – that interest seemed to represent all that was over-civilised about his life. He had a sense that things that should have been done for their sheer enjoyment had in his life become duties carried out in order to maintain an identity. Not here. The wine was good, enjoyable in company. How irrelevant his thoughts about its high acidity, lack of fruit and metallic tinge.

He learned to drink it, finding ways of making the passage of liquid into his body almost pleasurable. The trick was not to pour too much in the glass, so that one could sip at it undaunted by swimming-pool proportions. Having little liquid in the glass also gave the advantage of not risking serious spillage when dominoes hit the tables at speed. Though he never took to playing, he did, to his thinking, become quite a connoisseur of the game. He would sit at the table where he sensed the most intense match to be happening and look knowingly at the events of the contest as they unfolded. He was of course always careful to place himself so that there could be no doubt that he was unable to see the dots that each of the players had lined up. On some occasions the players became drunkenly angry on losing, and had even looked aggressively towards the cartoonist. These occasions tended to be forgotten, and who could say whether they contributed to his increasing alienation.

He still delighted at his own presence in the village, but the sensation became more introspective and self-conscious; whereas he had previously enjoyed feeling a part of something, his desire now was for a greater protagonism. He was no longer concerned with being accepted; it was as if he had learnt, through the many evenings spent looking at the photograph of the footballers, that there was an element of tragedy involved in forming part of a team. He wanted to be the person about whom the players were thinking as they posed crouched and diminished; he wasn't interested in falling in with their ranks. This change in attitude corresponded with his first attempts to write accounts of things that had occurred to him and things that he had heard about in the village. These he wrote in the third person as an attempt to distance himself from an identity that was clearly his own. He also tried to conceal the location of the place, not out of secretiveness but out of a feeling that the things he was writing might be relevant beyond his location, and this gave away his ambition. Although he never made a secret of the fact he was writing, when questioned about what the reasons for his activity might be he would respond that it was purely a personal enterprise, undertaken because he enjoyed it and not because he felt that there was any value for anybody else in the words that he so diligently orchestrated.

The Sidney Myer Music Bowl is a multi-functional outdoor performance area in a natural amphitheatre. It's used for all manner of concerts in the summer months, and in winter it is turned into a skating rink.

As in all other Spanish towns and villages, an annual feast is celebrated in the village. It commemorates its patron saint's day and is marked with the usual drunken merrymaking, as well as some organised competitive events. Most of these events aren't specific to the village; they are versions of sports that have developed in what could be termed the summer village festival circuit.

Some of the events are quite formalised, and constitute real competition: the slippery pole climb involves participants trying to climb unaided a five-metre-tall pole that has been rubbed all over with pig fat; in the boulder-roll they have to make a huge rock travel as far as possible across a field. In none of these events is there a time limit, and the competition often continues well into the evening until exhaustion or boredom sets in. By then it is quite clear who the winner is – no-one bothers with second and third places. At the end of the day, when all the competitions are over, and the winners of all the events have been declared, long tables with paper tablecloths secured with clips to their edges are laid out on the grass in front of the cultural centre. Some large dishes that have been cooked collectively by the villagers are placed on the tables. They are interspersed with smaller dishes bearing specialities that they have made at home. One might think that this arrangement would lead to a high level of competition and culinary back-biting – Señora X's *tortilla* not being up to its usual standard; Señora Y's *ensaladilla* being so much more refreshing than Señora Z's *menestra*. That these comments aren't passed is testament to the immense goodwill and generosity of spirit that the village feast inspires in the people. Once all the food has been laid out and everyone has had a chance to admire it, a number of ten-litre containers of wine from the local co-operative are funnelled into more manageable bottles. The party commences.

If one's first experience of the village were to be at one of these banquets, one might be forgiven for thinking that it was a place that was thriving, with a healthy mix of people from all generations establishing a functional social group. What one would not know is that many of the people are only there to celebrate the feast day. These are families, families formed by the droves of young men and women who left the village and their parents many years previously in order to find work. Many of them headed north, to the then successful industrial economy of the Basque country. There they continued to live through harder times and there they had their families. It was rare for any of them to return to the village – there were more exciting things to be done with their leisure time. Consequently, it was the rising fashion for rural living and rural holidays that inspired in many of them a desire to get back in touch with their roots. The village feast was the ideal occasion at which to demonstrate to their families the attractive authenticity of their place of birth.

The bull-run is quite a recent event at the village feast. It was established some ten years ago by a man who, sensing the resurgent desire for village holidays, had the entrepreneurial spirit to buy three bulls and a small lorry in which to transport them. During the summer months he takes them from village to village and for a negotiated fee allows them to be used for bull-running. To this end an enclosure is formed with a continuous ring of tractors and trailers. On top of the trailers sit and stand all the villagers and their visiting families. Despite the fact that many of the villagers are dressed in their best clothes for the feasts, it is nevertheless quite easy to identify them. Also easy to spot are those who have no connection with the village but are here for their holidays, and those who, having grown weary of city life, have made a home for themselves in the village. There's an attempt at mingling, single trailers bearing people of all the types, but still the divisions are clear. It is the villagers who are most concerned not to get their clothes dirty, while those from outside demonstrate their country spirit by neglecting to check for oil or cow-shit before they sit down.

Despite the fact that the bull-run is only ten years old, many of the men tell their new city families about their memories of the event during their distant childhood and adolescence. They construct the reminiscences as the event unfolds: one of the trailers in the ring belongs to the bull owner – it is the only covered trailer. He opens the trailer gate into the ring and after a few long seconds of apprehension one, two and then three young bulls nimbly blunder in. He tries always to have black bulls, because they look the part more. But because of this they are the most popular, so often he has to settle for brown or mottled ones among his small group. Young bulls are considerably smaller than the full-grown *toros* that are bred wild for the *corrida*, but at four to five hundred kilograms and with wild breeding they are still very powerful beasts. And these are all the ingredients in place for the bull-run. The next stage is obvious, men and boys pluck up courage and jump into the ring. The bulls are not quick to respond to them. Unlike the *toros* in the *corrida* they have not been spiked, and so they are not naturally aggressive. Much taunting is required to make them respond, and those that do the taunting are so cocksure in the face of the animals' apparent tranquillity that they forget about the size and the strength of the beasts. Their memory is kick-started into a pallid expression of panic when the bulls react. The counter-reaction happens more quickly than their machismo should allow, but appearances have at this stage diminished in their importance.

As the afternoon progresses the bulls get more and more tired, and the men get accustomed to the manner of their pursuit so that they are able to perform fancy manoeuvres that show off their bravery. These involve getting the bulls to collide with each other, or making them run in a perfect circle around the ring. Some, having judged the animals' tolerance, touch their horns and even pat them condescendingly on the head. The bulls look beleaguered by now, their coats shining with sweat and mucus streaming down their nostrils––as if they would be unable to summon up any significant energy. But this is a dangerous assumption.

Towards the end of the bull-run's third visit to the village, when the young bulls seemed so tired that even children and quite old men were jumping into the ring, and the owner was thinking of calling it a day, one of the bulls – a black one – squared up on one side of the ring with a red trailer on the opposite side. It lowered its head, thrusting its horns and massive neck forward, and sprang into a sprint for the trailer. Such was the momentum that it gathered that those aboard the trailer feared harm, and jumped onto neighbouring tractors with shrieks of excitement: surely the bull would meet a dramatic death with this collision. But the animal's intent was not to entertain, and just before collision, at the moment of maximum speed, it threw itself to the ground and skidded under the trailer and out of the ring. Very quickly it disappeared up the hill.

COLONIAL STADIUM

New 52,000-seat stadium in the Docklands area – a sporting and entertainment venue.

The car's rear is raised up on blocks so that to its back axle may be tied a rope that will be wound in when the accelerator is depressed: it is a Simca – the Spanish division of the Talbot company that was itself later bought by Peugeot. Simcas were ugly but reliable cars, the kind you'd expect to have been produced had the country suffered a lengthy period of Communist rule. As it was, the politics had been quite different. The terrorist organisation ETA used the cars in their campaigns as the car part of car bombs; they also made their escapes from assassination attempts in these vehicles.

The car is, of course, beige in colour – coffee with milk, as it's referred to here. They do come in other colours: a kind of ruby red; a pine green, white and navy blue. But beige is the most common, and the hue towards which all the others tend to lean with age.

Tied to the end of the rope is a dead hare. Its stomach is cut open so that the greyhounds might be lured by something other than its scuttling mechanical movement across the uneven stubbly field.

A book is run by a man that all appear to trust. The exact system of racing is difficult to discern. It looks as if the dogs are raced in heats that progress to a final. But experience tells that it's almost certainly not so simple, that there must be other rules involved regarding late qualifiers, fastest losers and other, less logical, exceptions. Since there are different breeds of dogs racing a system of handicaps might also operate, although how this might work is hard to fathom since the dogs in any one race are of mixed breeds and there is no-one performing any kind of timing on them. This would indeed be a difficult task because the manner in which the dogs are raced is very inexact.

When a race is about to start the dog-owners form a line on the side of the field opposite the Simca. They walk their dogs into position and hold them behind a rope that has been stretched out on the ground to mark the starting-line. Some of the dogs have never raced before and it is important to ensure that they run to the other end of the field. Those dogs that have raced before know that there is no real reward in such an effort and so their desire to get there must also be rekindled. A man makes himself known to the dogs by shouting and waving his arms in the air while all others remain silent. He then walks over to the hare carcass on the end of the rope and lifts it by the rope – dangling the carcass and swinging it gently. This has the effect of a hypnotist swinging a gold watch in the direction of a gullible audience – it is as if the dogs actually want to surrender the estimations of intelligence which are often invested in them. The man then draws from his pocket a white cloth with which he demonstratively polishes the hare. Never letting his audience lose sight of the cloth he replaces the hare on the ground and walks to the first of the dogs on the left of the starting line. He does with it what he proceeds to do with all the dogs, which is to hold the cloth around its bound muzzle. Like a reversal of the chloroforming that makes people go to sleep in films, the cloth drives the dogs wild and they follow it aggressively as the knowing man takes it to the other dogs. Then, keeping the cloth in full view, the man returns it to the hare and tethers it around its neck. The dogs are now quite fixated and ready to chase the hare. Those that have done so before forget the futility of their efforts and those that haven't harbour in them an expectant delight.

And it's all over so fast: the car is revved up, someone acknowledges this and waves a red flag, into first gear, the dogs are released and so is the throttle and the hare is animated to look like a cartoon water-skier heading for an unavoidable encounter with the back of the car. The dogs, which were so neatly spaced along the start line, form a messy pyramid with their running, and so well does the handicapping system appear to work that they all collide at its apex. This race, then, is about strength as well as speed.

Always a winner is declared. Of course it seems obvious that a winner should always be declared. What, if not, would be the purpose of the race? No, a winner has to be declared. What is less obvious is the manner in which the decision about which dog should be the winner is arrived at. There are beautiful neat races where one dog crosses the line so far ahead of the field that there remain no questions in the ignorant spectator's head. But these are a rarity, and in most of the heats a kind of mayhem appears to descend. Very often the car controller stalls the engine, or just doesn't rev it fast enough. All the dogs then fight over the hare and are dragged along the ground with it when the controller manages to get it going again. In many of the heats such an event takes place very near the starting line. But even so a winner is declared – a panel of judges make the decision, which none of the dog-owners ever seem to question.

Of course there are no published rules to the sport, the participants just develop an understanding of the ethos of the races as they get older and more experienced. The eldest have an amazing ability to discern a kind of order that allows them to make judgements from a situation that to the untrained eye has absolutely no meaning other than the slightly barbaric one that is immediately apparent. Certainly it is a spectacle to see animals running against each other; it's a spectacle that has been enjoyed for a long time, and as a spectacle it requires little understanding. But the understanding enables other kinds of more succinct enjoyment of the event, and the powerful ability to make judgements about the quality of the participants.

SANDRIDGE RAILWAY BRIDGE

The bridge once carried trains between Flinders Street and Hobsons Bay. It was in use until 1986. There has been talk of converting it into a footbridge. Premier Kennett raised the issue of the bridge's future in January 1999, declaring to the citizens of Melbourne that they must 'use it or lose it'.

Formerly, when I've referred to these creatures in conversation, people have addressed them as crayfish. But I insist that this is not their name. This is in part to do with that which I will tell at the end of this account; it also has something to do with wanting to keep the translation of something that I consider special as direct as possible, whatever linguistic clumsiness that might cause. The river crabs have now disappeared and all that I have left is their name. Their name was really all I ever had, for the culture of which I pretend to be a part exists in me only as a set of memories. So names are important for they prove that I know something about the memories that is direct, something that I have received not through translation or any other kind of mediation but something that I know – I can name it. I don't have to say that it looks like this or that, or speak of it in the terms of something else – I can name it. And I'll name it in such a way that I maintain the integrity of my knowledge of the name. I'll accede to changing the language, perhaps, but that is as far as I'll go. Linguistic equivalents might be acceptable but not equivalents of the object.

Even in their own right they were precious, protected by a very limited fishing season, to be enjoyed only by those with sufficient funds to afford the exorbitantly priced licences. Needless to say, many people netted the crabs without a licence, an act that was not seen strictly as poaching but more as the exercising of a right that was granted by a geographic privilege of birth. The rivers were quite strictly policed in an attempt to dissuade the illegal crabbers.

In an attempt to curb the poaching that resulted from the rarity and high price of the river crabs, the authorities decided to grant some licences for the creatures to be farmed in the rivers. This would be done by establishing large netted areas where the river crabs would be encouraged to breed and then be harvested according to relatively strict but market-led quotas. Within the first year of the scheme the entire population, wild and farmed, of river crabs was extinguished. Subsequent research showed that the species was very prone to disease. It had learned to combat this affliction by remaining constantly on the move and thereby allowing the long river to flush out its system. (This, incidentally, had been what made the best fishing sites so difficult to predict.)

The pens constructed to herd the crabs had concentrated disease to such an extent that even those animals that had escaped the farming were not able to survive the outflows of the infected tracts of river.

Some years later, after many recriminations and legal battles, the rivers were restocked with a Californian variety of the river crab – crayfish. These are larger and more resilient animals that lend themselves quite easily to being farmed, with the result that they are much more regularly available and cheaper than the river-crabs were. And so it seemed that the problem was solved – even for the better. To ease the guilt of those who had stupidly, but unwittingly, caused the extinction of the river-crabs, a large bronze statue of a river crab was erected at the outskirts of the main village along the course of the river where the river crabs once roamed. To celebrate the unveiling a new feast day was declared for the village, one that would not take the name of the local saint or deity but which would be known as the feast of the crab. Somehow the fact that they had perished could be seen to constitute some kind of sacrifice or martyrdom, and this made it OK for the animals to usurp the role of the religious figure. Certainly it was easier for the villagers to market the feast as that of the river crab, for though few people had ever tasted these rare animals, they had extensive folkloric and gastronomic fame.

Both river crabs and the new crayfish are cooked in exactly the same way: fried whole and with substantial amounts of olive oil in a large shallow pan. The creatures start out black, but as they cook they take on a deep red colour; this colour is one thing that the river crabs and the crayfish do have in common. This is not the orangey-red that lobsters take when boiled, nor the pale pink of prawns, but more the kind of red which would have to be reproduced with enamel paint, or lipstick. The river crabs used to be served as a luxurious starter, and those lucky enough to eat them would do so with great care and gratitude, making sure to ingest all the precious juices. Good families in the region would be sure to have a set of crab-eating implements in their cutlery drawer – devices designed so that heads and limbs might be severed without fountains of red grease erupting to stain clothes or white tablecloths. To see a group of friends now eating a huge dishful of the crayfish that they call river crabs outside some little bar is a sight that could be painted in two ways. One might see in their red greasy hands and faces the joy of sharing and indulging, getting dirty together, talking, laughing, drinking... These one might consider to be the best things in life, and of course how wonderful that they should be able to be enjoyed by all. But if there is to remain any of the value that used to be attributed to the crabs, the value indeed for which they are now considered so special, one has to see the scene in a different light. This is a harsh light that disturbs the well-being occasioned by food and drink and defines such excess as a gross and barbaric spectacle. No longer enjoyed for the delicacy of their flavour – a delicacy which the crayfish are, by local consensus, deemed to be without – these new animals are devoured like amusing pet food, as an excuse for drinking and smoking and passing the time of day. And this is not a view that stems from a puritanical sense of the way in which people should spend their time but from an idea about where that excess originates – in huge nets full of deformed creatures. Indeed, their appearance now changes little from living to the point at which piles of their shells lie messily on the kerb.

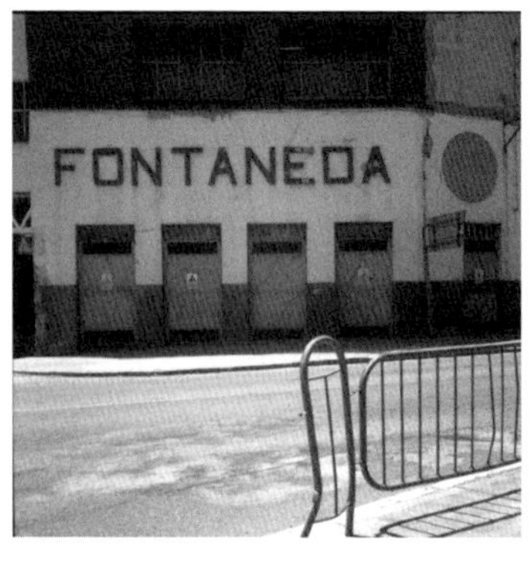

FONTANEDA

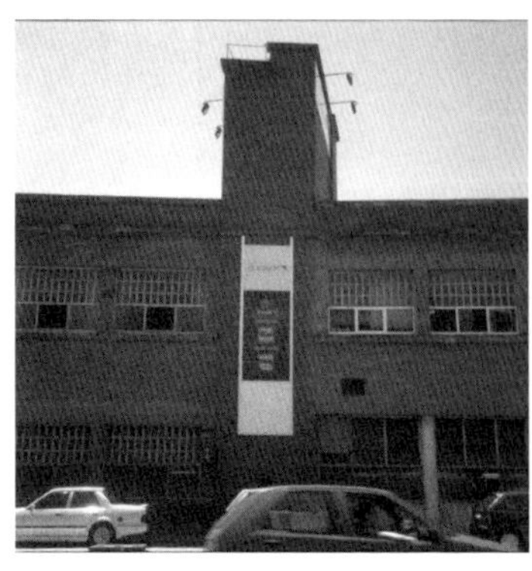

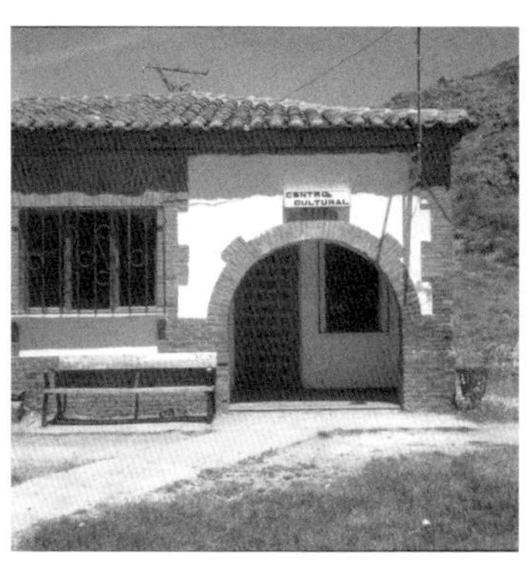

CENTRO
CULTURAL

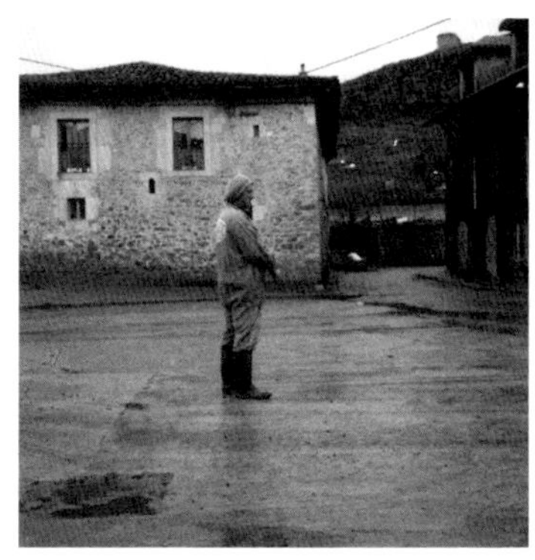

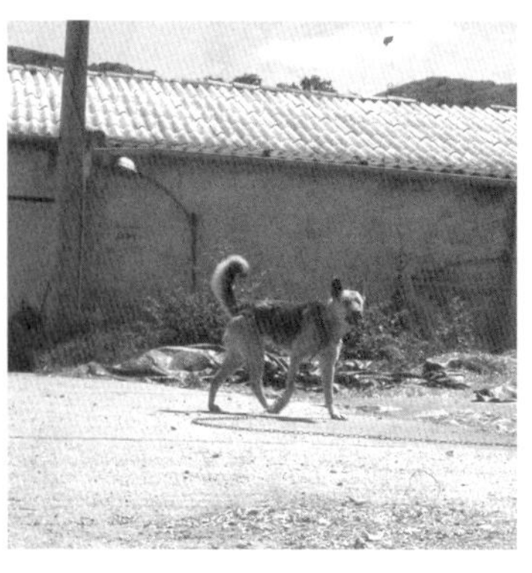

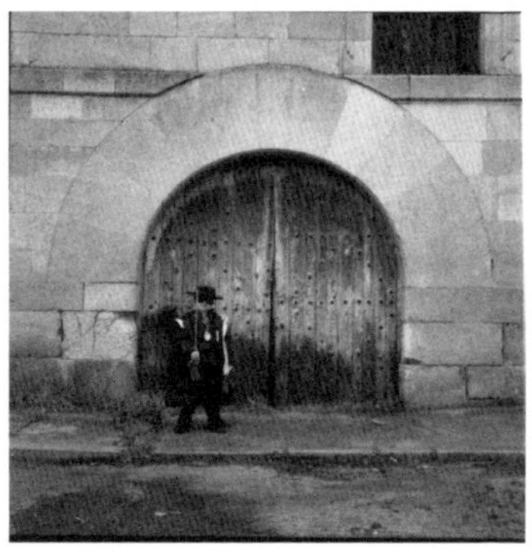

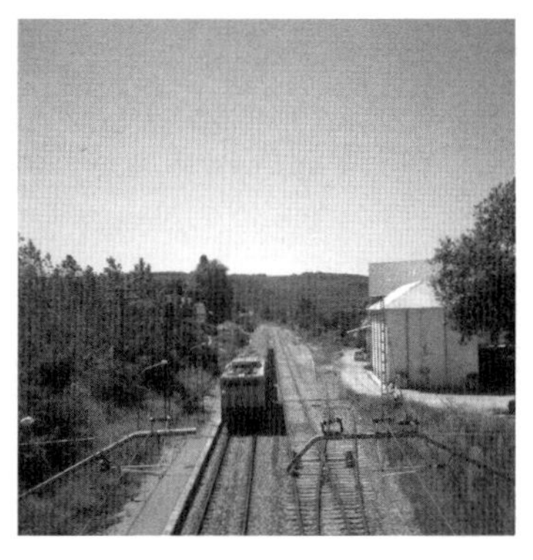
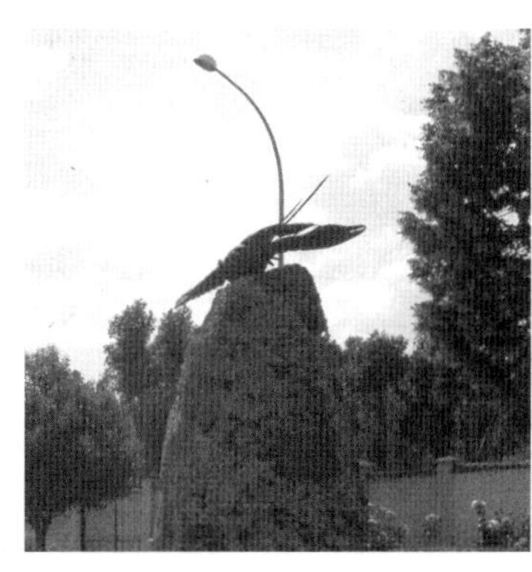

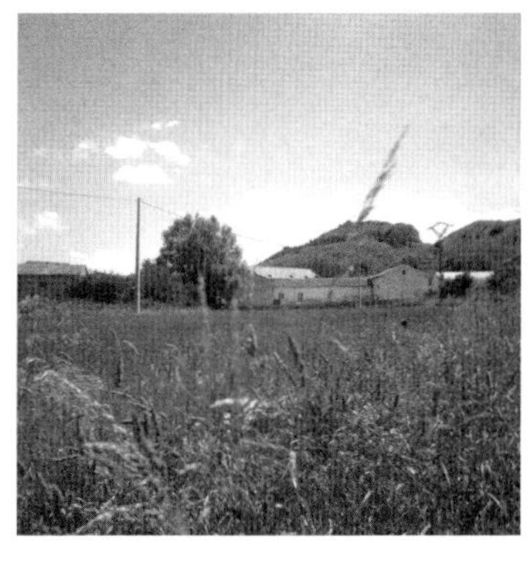
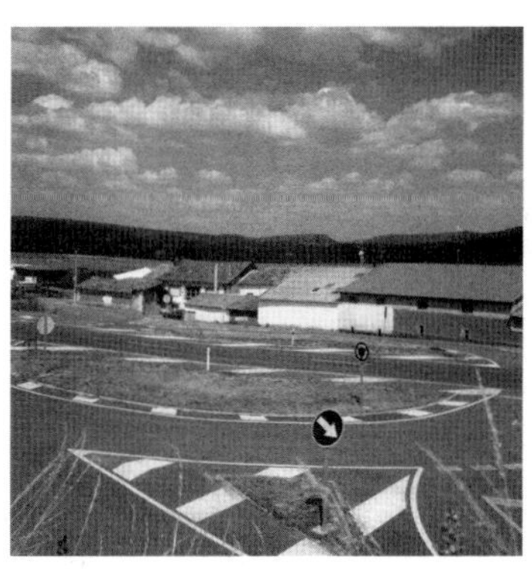

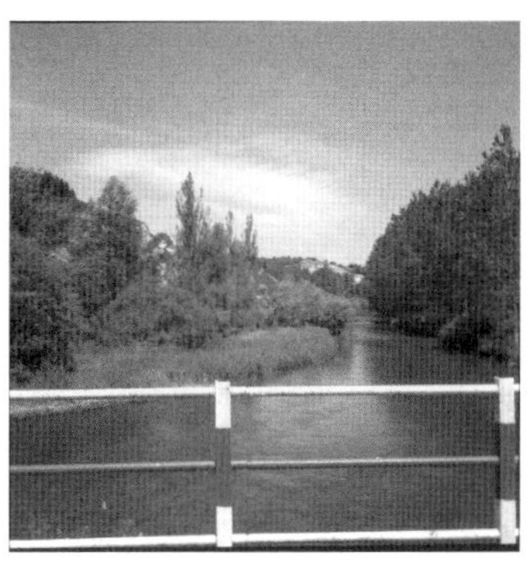
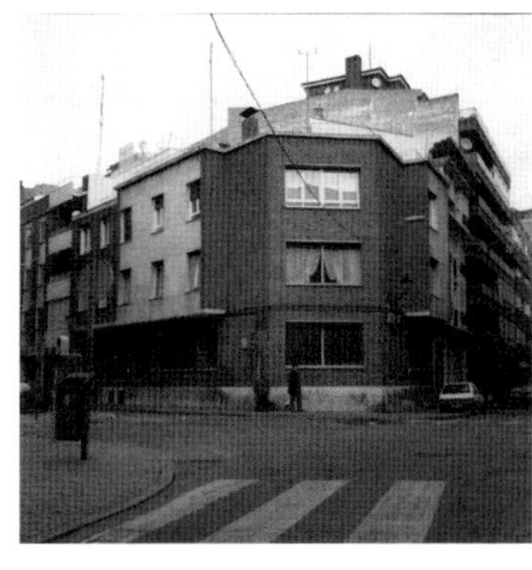

Two Cameras

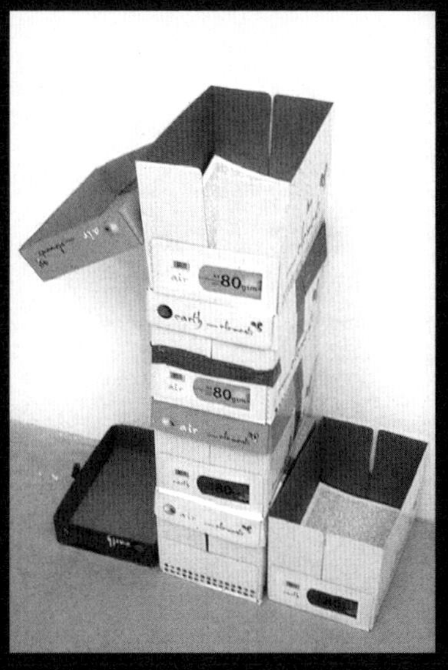

I've got two cameras. One is a Rolleiflex 3.5 F made by the
Franke & Heidedecke Company of Braunschweig, Germany.
I've looked all over the camera and through the instruction
manual that it still has but I haven't been able to find the date
when it was made. Neither do I know when my grandfather
bought it. This is something I could find out if I wanted,
but I still haven't decided whether I'm going to tell him that
I'm writing this. I would have imagined that he'd bought the
camera in Switzerland: a country he loves and to which he has
travelled often. But the instruction manual is in Spanish and
so I have to presume that he bought it in Fernando's camera
shop, which has been round the corner from his house for
about fifty years. I do think though that he must have bought
it after a trip to Switzerland. His visits there were partly for
pleasure but mainly for business – these two categories have
always been quite mutable for my grandfather, anyway. Not
that he didn't take holidays – he always had houses by the
sea and boats on which he would go on touring and fishing
excursions – but he managed his holidays with a kind of benign
severity. Switzerland was for him the land of precise machinery,
and whether it was to buy plant for his factory or to admire
clocks and chairlifts, his visits there would always involve some
enquiry in this direction. He must have seen someone using
a Rolleiflex on one of these trips, and he probably even spoke
to them and asked about the camera. On his return he would
have studied price, availability and reliability and twisted facts
and figures to make the purchase inevitable. Fernando would
probably not have had the camera in stock, but my grandfather
would have been able to give him precise directions on how he
might order it.

I'm sure my grandfather studied the instruction manual
very carefully. As I look through it now, I can imagine how the
rigorous sycophancy of its language would have pleased him,
with all its absolute claims about the reliability of the camera
and the precise calibration of its components. Instruction
manuals for cameras often have this quality. It is as if they
were written for a consumer with an intuitive knowledge of the
qualities of a good picture. The instructions aim to assure said
consumer that the camera shares his intuition and will help him

achieve his good picture. They also go on to suggest a few other options that the consumer might like to consider.

I was delighted that my grandfather should still have the instruction manual, together with another booklet detailing additional practical complements that one could buy: lens hood; external light-meter; filters for colour photography, filters for black-and-white photography; macro lenses; soft-focus filters, polarising filters; flash light; focusing disc; prism viewing device; pistol grip; supplementary hood with binocular lenses; 5 formats; panoramic head; tripod head; adaptor for flat film and plates; glass plate; telephoto system; wide angle system; long distance shutter release; case for underwater photography; device for microscopic photography; projection supplement; universal projector. The camera itself was in excellent condition, protected by a very lovely brown leather case. But it had no lens caps: my grandfather told me they were lost when he left them on the roof of his car after taking a photograph of a particularly beautiful valley.

My grandfather didn't give me the camera, I didn't even know he had the camera until the day he gave it to my father. We were staying at their house, a house he'd designed and in which they'd lived since before I was born. The design has changed while they've been there, according to their needs. Initially they lived on all four floors, then when some of their children left on three, when more left on two and when they got too old to negotiate stairs all the time, on one. It was not simply a question of closing floors when these changes in use happened; builders were always involved in pulling down walls and building new kitchens and bathrooms. Inside now it feels as if almost nothing of the house that was originally built remains. Only one room is untouched by the modifications, and that's my grandfather's study. It's clear that some important architectural compromises have had to be made in order to maintain his study intact, but it's also unthinkable that this shouldn't have been the case. He would have found it unbearable to be without his desk and his chair, his books and his papers, and without the pictures and ornaments that crowd the walls so completely. Photographs of all the family, original paintings of his factories, copies of masterworks by Goya and

Velázquez (and Renoir), my grandmother's embroideries and felt-tip pen drawings. In the far corner, on the wall above a leather sofa that is next to an oversized photocopier, is a vitrine housing a Chinese – at least we always called it Chinese – chess set with red and white pieces; the red ones are made of coral and the white of ivory. Each of the figures sits atop an ornately carved sphere. The carving goes right through the surface and reveals the sphere to be not hollow, but not solid either. Within it is another smaller but just as intricately carved sphere and within that another and another, and so on. The higher the value of the chess piece, the higher the number of spheres that fill its base. My grandfather always said that the set was made by very skilled carvers who in order to carve the bases would start with what I always imagined to look like a snooker ball and then carve into it to dislodge the centre from the shell. This exercise they would continue, having to carve through the ever-smaller holes that they had just completed. The vitrine was always kept locked, and even to this day I don't think I've touched one of those pieces. But I have spent a lot of time in the study looking at them. My grandfather and I are the only two members of really quite a large family who like to get up early. So when I was a child and we were staying with them I would always wake at my usual time of six thirty and find my parents sleeping. I knew though that at seven o'clock my grandfather would leave his room in pyjamas – cotton jersey – dressing gown and slippers – both tartan – and head for his study. I always gave him some moments to settle down before disturbing him. He was always generous with his time. If he was particularly busy he would give me a book to look at, and I would pretend to do that while I watched him work. More often than not though we would sit opposite each other on leather sofas and he would tell me about something. Most of these tales would be related to science, astrology or engineering, and often they would be accompanied by props: his sextant, charts, tables. I rarely understood, but the sound of his voice and the smell of his breath, and the fact that I was there alone with him made me stay and return again and again. When I'm there now I try to re-live these mornings, but it's much harder now. He gets up later, and has less energy, and the times when I'm there tend to be times when other people are also there: Christmas, summer – so it's hard to get him on my own. He's also, in the last few years, got more involved with using computers on which he writes and from which he handles his accounts. There's something very absorbing about this technology, and it does make him less responsive. The last time I spent any time of value in his study with him was the day he gave my father his old Rolleiflex.

We'd been looking through some old photographs in a box, black-and-white photographs with white serrated borders. These were family photographs and amongst them were images of his boats and his cars. In the box we also found some 8mm film that he hadn't expected to be there. I suggested that he could transfer these films to video and he shrugged, obviously thinking of something else. He left the room and asked me to wait there for him. I sat in the leather armchair and eased into memories that both celebrated and lamented times past. He returned after a few minutes. I stood up as if to attention when I heard his footsteps in the corridor and he walked in smiling and carrying an old projector that was black and rough-textured, like a cast-iron pan. He put it down and immediately tried to remember how to thread the film. I made moves to help him, but he insisted that this was his demonstration so I looked on in the attitude of awe and expectation that I was so used to assuming in this room. He asked me to plug the thing in and when I'd done this he flicked the projector's switch. Instantly there was bang and a small flash from the machine and then all the lights went out. He laughed as I hurried to unplug it. It was a naughty laugh, here we were, boys up to no good. He began to explain that it was the voltage that he hadn't considered. It had changed from 120V to 240V since the last time he had used the projector. I wondered out loud whether it could be fixed but he didn't seem to mind. My father, who had just got dressed, rushed in, concerned at the bang. His father sent him off to the fuse box to flick back the trip switch. When he returned, my grandfather and I were in conversation and he tried to join in. Despite our best efforts to accommodate him, it was clear that he had disturbed our reverie, and he was clearly hurt by this. My grandfather told us to wait while he went to fetch something and as we waited my father asked me what had happened. When I told him he expressed concern for his father. My grandfather returned carrying the Rolleiflex in its brown case. He told my father that it was for him, that he wanted him to have it. I tried to look pleased for him but I wasn't. Why should he have this camera? A camera that he'd never use nor truly appreciate for its sentimental value. Why should he be made to feel special, he'd only woken up at nine thirty, he didn't deserve it. I asked him if I could look at it, and he delighted in telling me to be very careful with it. I snapped that I knew about medium format cameras, that I used them all the time in my work, and went on knowledgeably to handle the camera. I wanted it so badly. I thought that if I had this camera I would be able to take inherently meaningful photographs. I was sure that he would give it to me, that I'd made my desire for the camera so clear that he couldn't possibly not give it to me. He had a new camera already. He'd remarried the previous year and his wife's parents had given him a fully automated top-of-the-range Nikon. I wished I hadn't asked him to give me his old Canon when this happened. That was the Christmas before this one, just after he'd received his new camera. He asked me what I wanted for my present. I thought he'd like it if I asked him for his old camera, but instead he looked distressed. Unfortunately for him – and now for me – I'd asked him in front of his new wife, who was quite keen that he should shed some of the appendages of his previous life. So he gave me the Canon which, because it had been his, I had idolised for many years. It didn't turn out to be such a good camera, though. The film counter went first and then the whole thing started to jam. So now I didn't have a camera of my own and I wasn't sure that I would ever have the Rolleiflex which I had so quickly come to covet. His wife was pregnant, and it would follow that since I'd had the Canon, the Rolleiflex would go to my half-brother. I sat all morning in my grandparents' living room with the camera and the instruction manual, trying to figure out everything about it, and desperately overstating my love and admiration for it. When other family members walked in my father would enjoy expressing how embarrassed and touched he was that my grandfather should have given him the camera. He squirmed

in that way that people do when they feel they have been paid
a compliment. I wanted to scream to him that it was only so he
wouldn't feel left out, that it was I he loved and not him.

★

When the Canon broke, and indeed before it had broken, I started
using my wife's 35 mm SLR automatic Pentax. I was extremely
snooty when she bought this camera. The money for it was a
present from her grandmother. My wife already had a camera:
a basic 35 mm Nikon, the same model that I'd had before it got
stolen from my studio at art school during a student sit-in. It was
a perfectly good camera, but she felt that it needed upgrading,
and the Pentax was the model she chose. When she came home
with it I was quick to point out its flaws. The automated shutter
speed and exposure were not a problem because they could be
overridden manually. The lens – a 28-75 zoom – was OK, but
I didn't really like the facility of being able to change the focal
length. Surely a fixed lens, devoted to one focal length, would give
better images than a flexible one. Though you could manually
override the auto-focus, the ring was very loosely calibrated and
didn't allow you to focus with any degree of sensitivity. I asked her
why she was annoyed at my observations, she'd bought the camera
for herself and I was sure it suited her requirements. I went on to
tell her that I found the viewfinder presented an image that was
rather small and dark, and I went to fetch my inherited Canon to
demonstrate the difference. Many of my prejudices were based
on my father's rhetoric about the Canon when the camera had
been his. He would often tell the story of coming across an old
acquaintance of his who was a photographer at a golf tournament.
He was there in official capacity, equipped with a huge grey
telephoto lens supported on a stick. My father went to say hello
and when the photographer saw his camera – the Canon – he
remarked how great those cameras were, because they were solid
and nothing could go wrong with them. So, largely because of this
story, I grew to an alarmingly advanced age believing my father
to have the best camera in the world. Even now, when I'd realised
it wasn't, I couldn't resist describing its virtues to my wife, at the
expense of her newly acquired Pentax.

I first started using her camera because I said it was lighter, and that the pictures I would be taking with it were not very important – just documentation, not work as such. I started to find the variable focal length quite useful, and also to enjoy the fact that her light meter provided consistently accurate readings, unlike the temperamental Canon. The focus was still a problem, but not so great as to stand in the way of me abandoning the use of the Canon altogether. This was aided by the fact that the thing just jammed one day, but by then I wasn't using it unless she needed her Pentax and I was forced to make do with it. I felt, and do still feel, inclined to fix it. I feel guilty when I think about the Canon and remember my father's panicked face when I asked him for it. I probably will take it to be fixed, but I don't know where. The camera's of an age that renders it neither modern nor antique; I can't take it to the vintage photographic shops on Museum Street nor to the more modern camera shops on New Oxford Street. I used to go into these shops quite a lot before I had the Rolleiflex, trying to ascertain the value of this camera that I so wanted and weighing it up against modern equivalents: a bit like buying a bottle of wine and looking it up in the wine book to see whether it appears, as if some degree of consensus were necessary in order to proceed with its estimation. I saw plenty of Rolleiflex cameras but my memory wasn't good enough to compare them to my (grand)father's. None of the ones I saw looked to be in such good condition. I asked a few attendants in the shops whether that model of camera was still worth using, and enough told me that they were fantastic and that they were all some photographers would use to make my craving for – my father's – Rolleiflex grow desperate. I thought that I would try to buy a lens cap for the Rolleiflex, to show how much I cared for it. I asked the assistant whether lens caps for Rolleiflex cameras were still available. He told me they were rare but that they did appear, but I would have to bring the camera in because there were many models with varied lenses and the distance between the lenses was not consistent. I asked him what difference this made and he told me that the Rolleiflex lens cap was a double unit – two caps hinged together like an ∞, or an 8 – so it was crucial that the distance between the two Os matched that of the camera's double lenses.

While at some of the shops that sold modern cameras, I started in earnest what had up until then been a fairly casual search for a video camera. I'd used camcorders before to document pieces of work that involved some kind of performance, also to make small bedsit works, familiar performative acts to no audience: tearing up a polystyrene cup into small pieces, filling up a red washing-up bowl with water. But these cameras belonged to friends or relatives. I'd also borrowed a camera more officially from CUMIS – Cambridge University Moving Image Studio – in order to make a video work for a final show to mark the end of a fellowship I'd done at Kettle's Yard. For quite a long time people had told me that I should work with video, that since I wrote and made images I would be perfectly suited to making film, or the art world's pretend version of film, which is video. So I'd been glancing sidelong at cameras for some time. And it wasn't even that they were that expensive. With digital technology arriving, those cameras that were slightly older fell in price dramatically. But I wondered whether it was worth investing in a camera that would be redundant so soon. My grandfather had lent me – which was his way of tactfully giving me – his old video camera: a monster old Sony. I'm sure it was state of the art when it was bought, and also that the quality of it would still take some beating, but the thing was huge, you had to support it on your shoulder, and the batteries didn't work, so you were rather limited to indoor shots. I'm sure that having this camera on loan also contributed to my lethargy about buying my own. It seemed to resolve a problem for me, a problem that is maybe about a fear of pragmatism. If I bought a video camera my intent would be to make a video, and I'd be determining everything right from the start. If, as was the case, the camera had been given to me, then my process was more speculative – if someone asked me why I was using such a camera I could just tell them that it was a gift and that there was really no option about using it, that it was just the camera I had. I could also elaborate on this and tell them about this huge and impractical camera being my grandfather's; I could tell them about his love of innovations, about the way in which he always had to have the newest and the best and how he had collected an inventory of possessions that I, above all his other grandchildren, craved. I could, effectively, tell a story that would divert attention away from what I had done and focus it not so much on why I was doing it but on how inevitable it was that I should be doing what I was doing in the way I was doing it. And this was also why I wanted that Rolleiflex so badly, because if I needed an external story to be able to make a video, a medium that is by its very nature already narrative, I also certainly needed it to take a photograph.

But the story pertaining to my grandfather's video camera was too boring and limiting, and I was really forced into making some kind of decision. I also had, for the first time in my life, some money. I started asking questions and found the answers as frustrating as the answers I would have given to questions on subjects about which I knew something:

– What's the best?
– Depends what you want it for.
– Yes but what's a standard good quality?
– There is no standard good quality; it depends what you want it for.
– Yes obviously, I don't want to make Hollywood, and I don't even know if I want broadcast quality – I guess that would be a good idea – but I don't know, I guess I just want a standard good quality camera.
– But there's no such thing not really, it's like with anything, you use what you need and you might also come to the conclusion that what you have becomes what you need – that it doesn't really matter what you have, that what is interesting happens in you adapting to whatever it is you have.
– Yes I know, I know, only too well, you don't have to tell me about these ethics of making, don't you think I've been through these dilemmas before, Christ!

There were four video cameras I was considering. Three were Sonya and one was a Canon. At the top of the range were the Canon and one of the Sonys. Both of these cameras were designed to look like miniature film cameras. The Canon evoked the form of a 16mm cine camera while the Sony had the shape of a miniature television camera. I think that this was probably intended to allude to both cameras' semi-professional status. I thought that if I was to take myself seriously as an artist I really should go for one of these two cameras, that their expense was actually an investment and that the quality would be important to me. I looked them up in catalogues and ascertained that they were able to do similar things and that they cost similar prices. So I moved from New Oxford Street and its apertures and shutter speeds and started looking around the more technological route of Tottenham Court Road. I walked into shops and asked whether they had both cameras; then, which one was best. Both very good, they'd usually say, top of the range, or they'd rank one above the other – but their judgement wasn't consistent as I continued along the road. I grew fed up of hearing that it was my preference, whatever I liked best. And then when some shop assistant would firmly endorse one over the other I'd feel suspicious of their motives – maybe they just had lots to sell, or they were working on commission. I determined that when I'd made up my mind to buy one or the other this would be the place to come. I would then be able to respond to the proactive haggling encouraged by the shopkeepers. Every time I asked one of them about the cameras they would ask me what price I'd been quoted already and then state a lower one, or show me things that they could throw into the deal – a strap, tapes, carry-case. I didn't call their bluff, because I'm a very bad liar, so I didn't have a very clear picture of how reduced the price of the camera could be. I think I probably didn't want to know what the price of the camera would be because I was so uncertain about investing in a piece of equipment – it wasn't like inheriting something. I had a hunch that I would use the camera; more than a hunch really, I even had ideas about what I might do with it, but I certainly had no sense that I would be committing myself to it as my only medium. I'd made such mistakes before, and bought expensive power tools thinking that they would be my work tools forever, only to decide to stop using them almost before getting them home. I had the desire to do what I did seriously, to be a professional with all the right equipment, but my temperament tends to be, or has been, more flighty than that: inclined to make do with what is available rather than determining the best recourse. And so I was aware that my idea that I needed a semi-professional camera probably had more to do with wanting to state some kind of seriousness of intent: with wanting what I did to be taken seriously even before it was done.

I was in the park one day, in the playground with my little daughter. She was playing with other children in a sandpit that has in it a slide and a series of pulleys and buckets that allow for construction site games to be played. It was one of the first times that I'd taken her to the playground and I did feel a bit uneasy. I didn't know the protocol about whether I was allowed into the sandpit to help her or not – she had just started to walk – and nor did I even know how I should speak to her. When you're on your own with a child you have no trouble speaking to them normally, even though they clearly don't understand. In public though, parents' voices modulate themselves towards a sound full of ridiculously long vowels and words that rise a few pitches on their last syllable. I hated the idea of speaking in this voice, but I also thought it was necessary, as if it would embarrass my daughter if I spoke in any other way. So I tried to say little, and helped her with her walking only when she got into real trouble. I was one of the only men who was there alone with a child, and I did feel as if I should be working, doing something more proper and manly. What if not that were the partners of all these women doing? I thought about the compromises of being an artist and making no money from it and having to teach for half the week, and the way in which that made the days on which one wasn't teaching feel like days off. It was about three o'clock in November, and the dim light that accompanies that time and month was making my thoughts spiral lower and lower. I looked at the men who were there with their children, unshaven men with faded clothes. The difference in appearance between men who are working and those who are not is much greater than that displayed by women. Most of the few men who were here were with women, and of course with their children. One of these couples was making a video of their child playing near my daughter in the sandpit. They insisted that the child should look like he was enjoying himself, regardless of his mood, because it would be silly to look so grumpy in the video. His grandparents would be very sad were they to receive a tape of their grandson like that. This was bad enough, it's depressing to see people documenting their lives – and even more depressing to see them construct what they want to document. What made it worse was their camera – the semi-professional Sony, the one that looks like a mini TV camera. The two parents took turns to use it, delighting in their own handling of the machine and tutting at each other's lack of care with it. They crouched at the edge of the sandpit, alternating between manual and automatic focus, and employing the powerful zoom to animate their pictures. They must have been quite rich to have such a camera, especially as they were not putting it to professional use.

★

The only one of the cameras on my possible list that I'd used before was the bottom-of-the-range Sony. I say bottom-of-the-range, but it was still an expensive camera. This was the camera that I was lent by the Cambridge University Moving Image Studio to make my work for Kettle's Yard. When I'd arranged this loan with them they had assured me that I would be able to borrow a higher range camera from them – the precursor to the TV camera lookalike. I was pleased about this, the work that I wanted to make with it was in Spain, and I would be staying with my father while I was there. I thought that this camera would express to him something about my professional status; about the fact that for me to take a picture or a video was not the same as it was for him. He had a video camera, a perfectly decent but pre-digital camcorder. He often tried to show me videos of his new family on holiday, or of my little half-brother dressed up at school functions. I always refused or found ways of not having to look at them. I hate such films for lots of reasons, but what I really couldn't stand in these particular instances with my father was the idea that there was nothing particular about what I was doing; I couldn't bear his reticence to recognise that what I'd chosen to do with my life was quite different to what he'd done. I was therefore quite disappointed when the technician at Cambridge gave me the smaller video camera. I asked about it – told him in fact – said that there was a mistake, that it was another bigger camera that I'd been promised. He told me it was broken and that this was all they had available. I was quite displeased, and I sought reassurance as to the quality of the smaller camera. I tried to see through his pragmatism as he told me how good it was and about the fact that I wouldn't be able to tell the difference. Of course he was right to patronise me, I'd revealed to him already with my questions how little I knew about video cameras. I also realised that those questions may have led him to believe that I was quite stupid anyway – I really hoped that this merely betrayed my insecurity and my panic to get it right. I was flying over to Spain specially to make this work and I needed my preparations to be perfect.

When I got there I asked my father whether I could borrow his camera, in fact I probably asked him whether I could borrow the Rolleiflex, unable as I would have been to employ any pronoun which might indicate his possession of the camera. I wanted to make still images of the scenes that I was shooting with the video, in a way just to get the feel of the Rolleiflex, and to think of the difference between taking a photograph and shooting video. I've always been quite keen on the work of photoconceptualists from the seventies. I like the scientific rigour with which they approach what they do. I also hate it, because in its logical kind of examination of the material things that are involved in taking a photograph it forgets that really fundamental desire just to make a picture. Actually, as time has passed around work of this type, elements within it have begun to look dated and therefore more incidental. I think this improves them, because it makes details which were once syntactically central to the work seem like peripheral eccentricities. My father said that of course I could borrow the camera whenever I wanted to, and so I spent that evening reading the instruction manual to make sure I knew how to load film and take pictures.

The Rolleiflex is able to use a variety of film formats, but I was only really interested in using the basic 120 format, which gave me negatives or transparencies of six by six centimetres.

The camera has two lenses, one above the other. The bottom one lets the image into the film chamber while the one on top serves the viewfinder. I remember thinking that this being the case the image I would produce would be a little bit different from that which I would compose. This difference would also be caused by the fact that in the viewfinder you saw the image in reverse: right as left and left as right. I tried to figure out how to work with this. Sitting on my father's sofa, way after he'd gone to bed, I pointed the camera at the knick-knacks on his shelves and then moved it round to the television and his plants. When I panned left the image moved to the right and vice versa. Neither was I used to the low viewpoint of the camera. Since the viewfinder is a hood that clicks open on the top you look down into it to fix the view. This means that the camera is always at the height of your chest or lower, and this makes quite some difference. What I most liked about looking at images through this camera was the size and organisation of the viewing screen. It is six by six, the same size as the film, and gridded up into small squares that I hoped would allow me to line up my images properly (This, incidentally, was one of the problems I'd expressed to my wife about her camera: that since it had a variable focal length, you could never be sure that your verticals and horizontals would be true.) Another thing I really liked about the camera was that it had a built-in light meter: all you had to do was make the needle and the circle line up. I turned all the lights on and tested the light meter readings of the Rolleiflex against those of my wife's camera, which I knew to be quite accurate. They were pretty much the same and I couldn't resist taking a picture, of the room, of anything. I had taken a picture of this room before, and I'd shown it – framed in dark oak – in one of my first exhibitions. It was a pretty oblique image, but a large palm plant, a glass coffee table and venetian blinds closed over a wall-sized window gave the image the air of a Robbe-Grillet story; I wasn't the only person to remark on this welcome allusion. I thought about trying to repeat this image with the Rolleiflex; I wanted to repeat every picture I'd ever taken, but with the Rolleiflex. That would give them meaning, rescue them from that fear I always have that to make and show a photograph is no different from showing people those pictures you take on holiday of a sunset or a building or a geological formation – those pictures that have no people in them and to which you're able therefore to attribute a different sort of value. I loaded the film quite easily and wound the handle till it was ready for the first exposure. I expected and wanted a satisfying clunk when I depressed the button to release the shutter, but the thing just made the slightest hissing click, and I was sure that something must be wrong, that my father hadn't looked after the thing properly for the short time during which it had been in his care. I tried again, taking the chance to line the same picture up a little more carefully, but I got the same noise. So I took the first film in a pathetic sort of hesitant yet hurried manner, with the attitude that I'd probably have to repeat all the shots anyway. They came out fine. Anyway, they were just trial shots. I had them processed while I was still in Spain to make sure that it was worth proceeding with the images I really wanted to take. The contact sheet was beautiful, there's a kind of goodness to an image that's square in format, a decency. The video camera I'd borrowed had the facility to make stretched wide-screen images, 16:9 ratio as opposed to the more usual 4:3 TV ratio. It was a facility that I had thought I might use, but seeing the square images on the contact sheet just made me want to go the opposite way – the squares seemed so honest and the wide screen an attempt to disguise the tools of a tourist as cinema.

My intention with that work, no, I don't need to tell you the intention, it's the mechanics you need to know: I needed to shoot a number of images of a short (about 3 km) stretch of road. I planned to stand at the beginning of the road and, facing in the direction I wanted to go, centre the image on the point at which the road disappeared from view. Then I'd walk to that location and make my next image from there, centring the image again on the point where the road disappeared. And so on until I got to the end. I wanted these to be video images because I wanted to have ambient sound and to build in some sense of a slowly evolving narrative. But the video camera was a very blunt tool to use to get these centred images, because it had no indication of where the middle of the image was on the viewfinder. I hadn't expected it to have the Rolleiflex's fantastic gridded-up viewfinder, but even the Pentax had a little circle to mark the middle of the image. I did determine that in future I would have to use a more professional video camera, but then I just persevered with the one I had.

★

I made the work and showed it at the end of my fellowship at Kettle's Yard. When I'd been thinking about what to do for this show I had considered making a work that was set or had some relation to the city and the university. But I decided not to, and I think some saw this as a kind of failure – the institution's and mine. I was very nervous to reflect publicly in a place about a place, particularly a place that was so sure about itself anyway. I spent much of my time there driving around the countryside just north of Cambridge. It was here that I found the disused railway track, about which I wanted to make a work for the show that I was about to discuss in Rotterdam. I thought I knew that I'd need a video camera for this work, and I think I'd decided that I would like to have my own, so that I could return often to the railway tracks without having to rely on loans. I thought I might try to get the institution to buy me a camera for the work. For a previous exhibition in Rotterdam I got the venue to buy me a MiniDisc recorder and microphone in order to make a work. But the video camera would be that much more expensive, and I knew it was unlikely that I would have the cheek to ask the institution to make such a capital layout.

My preferred way of getting to Rotterdam is to fly there directly from London City Airport. KLM run a Cityhopper service that employs small propeller-driven Fokkers. There's a practical dimension to my preference in that City Airport is very easy to get to. But at the heart of it lies a less prosaic reason, and this is the perspective on London and then the Thames broadening out into the Thames Estuary that these low-flying planes afford. You have to sit on the right of the plane as you face forward on the way to Rotterdam. From the window you see the river widening, gradually fanning away from the city, the buildings populating its banks changing in scale as their function suggests itself to be more industrial. And then you get to the sea and very quickly you've arrived. It's the kind of flight where you really feel you're flying; where the act isn't abstracted into something else. At City Airport you walk onto the plane, up a little ladder, and then you come down it again when you get to Rotterdam. I don't think it's nostalgic to prefer this, more to do simply with being able to grasp what you're doing. So when I was invited to Rotterdam I asked whether I could be booked on this flight. Unfortunately, though, this is a flight that is used primarily by businessmen and the tickets are quite expensive unless you are able to be very flexible. My schedule was too tight to juggle dates, so I had to take a regular flight from Heathrow to Schiphol and then go on the short train ride to Rotterdam from there.

The Heathrow Express was more efficient than I had imagined and I got to the airport far too early for my flight. I checked in and went through to look at what used to be the duty-free shops but which were now just airport shops, keen nonetheless to have offers that might convince travellers that it was worth buying things here. This was the first time that I really looked at a Bally shop. I thought I knew what those expensive Swiss leatherwear items were about and had consigned them to the naff rubbish opinion. But I was surprised at how stylish some of their stuff was when I looked at it. I also considered the merits of buying a jumper at the Scotch House. I thought about the fact that I would never dream of shopping there when I was in London, but that their wool was probably of very high quality and that their prices – in relation to that quality – might be quite reasonable. Then a sandwich – pleased to see that Pret A Manger had got a footing in the airport lounge. I've always thought that it would be a good idea to have hairdressers in airports; it always seems such a waste of time to have a haircut and this dead time could provide the perfect moment in which to do it… Really, I was just desperate not to go into Dixons and look at the video cameras. It was so predictable, almost every time I flew I'd end up looking at the cameras, and I'm just not the kind of person who would ever buy something that expensive from an airport shop, whatever the deal on offer. But the shop was there, and I could see that they sold Fuji film, which I needed to buy, and that was the excuse to enter. They didn't have Provia – the particular type of film I needed – and so I pretended to engage in conversation about film types with the woman behind the counter while eyeing up the video cameras in the glass display cases. It was gratifying to see such variety in an airport shop; often they don't stock the top end of ranges, but here they had all the cameras that I'd been considering. I went to the counter and looked more closely. It was the three Sonys that now appealed more, because the more I thought about it the more mannered the shape of the Canon seemed. I'd also had advice from CUMIS that it was probably better to stick with Sony since they marked the industry standard. A friend had also told me that he'd used one of these Canons at his gallery recently and that he hadn't been too impressed with it. Blunt, unsubstantiated advice was what I needed, and I was happy to take it where I could. I found myself standing at the counter and inevitably the assistant asked if he could help me with anything. Probably because I was travelling for work, about to visit quite a prestigious venue in which I was to show my work later in the year, I felt self important enough to let him think that I was interested in buying a digital video camera. I told him I knew all the models but that I did have some questions. For instance, did they all have fire-wire in/out connections to be able to edit in and out of a computer? Yes, they all had that. Even the small one? Even the small one. And to what extent was it possible to override the automatic settings manually, did the larger ones have any advantages in this respect? No, you could manually override on all of them. And the 3 CCD? The larger ones both had 3 CCD and the smaller one didn't. This just meant that a separate chip took each colour, so for broadcasts the colour would be truer. Would I be using it for television broadcasts, though, he asked me knowingly. I was desperate to express to him that no I wouldn't but that I was a professional, that I didn't want the camera to record my children's lives but to make work with it – it was video, artists made work with video! I translated for him that I wasn't interested in all the features, effects and labelling options that the camera would give me, I just wanted something that would make decent quality images and which would have some facility to be overridden manually.

He told me that there was a special offer on the small camera: 15 % off the selling price and a guarantee that if I didn't like it I could return it to any Dixons branch within three months and get my money back. Of course it entered my mind immediately to buy the camera, do what I needed to do with it and then return it. But I knew that in acceding to this offer I was blowing my cover. I'd attempted to come across as this kind of affluent professional and here was I now feeling like an opportunist scally trying to get something for nothing. So I told him that his offer was all very well but that I wasn't sure that was the camera I wanted. There was a flash in his eye for a second, as if he thought he might be able to sell me something more expensive, but he changed his mind quickly. He told me I'd never be able to notice the difference in quality between this camera and the one that was one up from it in the range. Against my better nature I asked if I could see them both, and he made it clear to me that it was an effort for him to fetch them, as if to suggest that this had better be worth his while. He put them both on the counter and talked me through their functions, indicating what you could and couldn't plug into them. He did this excited at the bored tone that he was able to muster about his subject; as if saying that he liked his subject so much and was so knowledgeable about it that it bored him. I've met academics like that who, understandably perhaps, react with some contempt to questions around their subject that are designed to surprise them maybe or to rekindle their interest. It would take more than the sale of a glorified camcorder to kindle my shop assistant's enthusiasm for electronic items, this was the mainstream, and the expert likes the peripheries. He had quite chubby fingers that handled the cameras' small buttons and switches with surprising agility. He could barely be bothered to speak, the cheeks wobbled and there came out a continuous murmur full of 'basically's and 'to be honest's; his head seemed disengaged from what it was saying. The brunt of it was that I'd be better off going for the smaller camera because it was smaller, he repeated, and more convenient; it was a newer model than the larger one, and it had incorporated many of its features – and there was the offer to take into account, apparently I had nothing to lose. I tried to pretend that I might also be interested in the top-of-the-range camera, but he saw instantly that true as my professed interest might be I would never buy that model. So, kindly I think, he skirted over my question. I asked him if I'd understood right, that it was the small one he was recommending, the 3 CCD was the only real difference and that I wouldn't notice that unless I was playing my footage back under very strict quality conditions. He nodded, bored and waiting for my decision. I looked at my watch, nervous that I might be missing my plane, but unfortunately I had plenty of time left – that wasn't going to make my decision for me. So I can take it back within three months if I don't want it? – I conceded that I was interested in the offer and his face opened slightly. He started to close. To any Dixons he told me, within three months, and they would take it back, no questions asked. He asked his colleague whether they had any of the special offer cameras left. They let me think that they weren't sure, that they might have one but… the colleague went to the back to look and returned carrying a box – the camera ready to go. He said that it was the last one and my assistant looked at me with a suggestive twist of the head. I asked if he could give me a couple of minutes with the cameras to decide. He agreed. I tried to think through every good and bad reason for each of the cameras, questions that involved my whole life, self-esteem and future. I looked over towards him and asked what it meant that each of the cameras had Carl Zeiss lenses. He told me that basically, Sony had an exclusive contract with Carl Zeiss and that they were the best lenses you could have. I asked him what was so good about them, what characteristics they had that other lenses didn't. He told me it was the quality that was so good and I realised how petty it would be to press him on this. I did anyway, what were the qualities that made them better. Amazing clarity, he said, and excused himself to attend to another customer. Small victory won, but none the wiser about the cameras. He returned to me, and I asked for clarification about the offer. So I would be able to return this at any branch of Dixons and get my money back – even if I'd used it? He reassured me of this and added that I wouldn't even need to return the packaging, as long as all the contents were there and not broken I would get my money back, no questions asked. And what if when I went to the shop they declined? I could hardly return to the airport just to return a camera, and I had no access to this branch unless I was flying. I tried to imply that I flew a lot but that it wasn't certain that I would go through that terminal again within three months. He assured me that he understood my concern and gave me his card and circled his number saying that I should call him if I had any problems returning it. And then I crumbled in front of him and asked him whether he thought I was doing the right thing in buying this camera; please would he reassure me that what I was doing was right, that I wasn't selling myself short. He said just the right thing, that it was an amazing piece of kit. I gave him my credit card and asked him whether he'd throw some mini DV tapes into the bargain. He told me he couldn't, not with the reduction I was already getting, but he suggested an economy pack of three on which there was also an offer. I accepted.

In Rotterdam I checked into my hotel straight away. I wanted to play with my new camera immediately, but I was distracted by the ornate and arabesque nature of the room, and anyway, I needed to charge the battery. Later, after I'd had my meeting and dinner and drinks, I lay in bed looking around my room through my new camera. The Moroccan brothel aesthetic reminded me of my grandfather's chess set, and I also remembered the photograph I took in my father's living room.

It's a Sony DCR-PC100E, the new version of the camera I'd borrowed in Cambridge to make my video in Spain. It retains an upright book-like shape, and functions in much the same way as its precursor. An innovation is the DV in/out socket which allows one to digitally transfer sequences to a computer from it and then get them back to make master tapes. Another difference is that the new version has a 'Night Shot' facility which allows you to make green grainy unintelligible images in low light. The new version also has a memory stick port and in the packaging a memory stick and a thing to be able to attach it to a PC. I'm a Mac user and this function is of no use to me. Other than that it's the usual range of effects – Negative, Sepia, B&W, Solarized, Slim, Stretch, Pastel, Mosaic – and different kinds of exposure settings – Auto, Spotlight, portrait, Sports,

Beach & Sky, Sunset/Moon, Landscape, Low Lux. I looked at my room through all these digital filters and on all the different exposure settings. The auto focus seemed to do quite a good job, and it was possible to override it manually. But it wasn't like focusing a camera, I don't know how it worked but I didn't get that satisfying sense that a camera gives when you're focusing and you feel as if the lenses are moving into correct relation to each other at your command. But it did focus quite accurately, if incomprehensibly, so loose was the ring. I was particularly impressed with the zoom, though this also seemed to confuse the digital and the optical, the illusory and the mechanic. The lens is labelled: Carl Zeiss, Vario-Sonnar 1,8/4,2-42. This probably has little to do with the zoom, not sure – I'm sure my grandfather could tell me. Never mind, when you press the zoom button, something seems to move physically in the camera – probably the distance between the lenses. But there is a point beyond which the lenses stop moving and yet the image continues enlarging, as if the zoom function were continuing. This is an effect that is called digital zoom. As far as I can gather all it means is that there is a physical magnification of the image – like cropping the edges off something and then blowing it up to the same size again. So it is a type of zoom that results in quite severe loss of picture quality because the pixels become so large. It is also the kind of zoom that makes you think that zoom is like a kind of concentration. I remember thinking that if one were able to concentrate hard enough one might not need a zoom at all, or certainly not a digital zoom. But I couldn't deny how effective and amusing I found it. I lay on my bed and zoomed in on fingernail-sized areas of the light switch.

★

On each of my visits to Spain I would now use, or at least examine, the – my father's – Rolleiflex. I started to incorporate the camera into my work, using it in conjunction with my new video camera to make different kinds of images. In my father's house it was an ornament on a shelf, amongst many ornaments and trinkets that I'd photographed before. I was quite happy for this to be the case because it meant that no one else was using the camera. It was with some arrogance that I took it from its place and made as if I was breathing life into the thing. It was after buying my video camera that I noticed that the Rolleiflex also had a Carl Zeiss lens. It was a detail, but it felt like the coincidence that one experiences when reading something that appears to be just too relevant, or thinking that you have just the anecdote to tell for an occasion; a feeling that you're blessed with the ability to tie all of your life's ends up. And this made me want the camera even more, it was another reason why I should have it. But when my father offered it to me I refused. He said I should have it because I used it and he never did; that if it was left with him his son would break it one day accidentally while playing. I couldn't give him the pleasure of letting me have it, I'd have to rearrange my whole picture of things if this were to happen. I've also been brought up always to refuse things twice before accepting them, brought up by my father to do this, and this is indeed what I did with regard to the camera. On the third offer I accepted, making it clear that I would love to borrow it but that the camera was his whenever he should want it. I promised to look after it, and I did find myself eager to inform him of the important use to which I was putting it, or of the money I was spending on complementary components for the camera.

Even before the camera was mine, the initial use to which I put it was quite austere. I believed that this camera would help me to achieve straight and parallel lines in my photographs, and that this made it specially useful for architectural images, the kind of images I might want to take for documenting my work. I thought this because of the ample grid on the viewing screen, because of the way that this might help to line things up. But the camera isn't actually very good for this kind of work. Maybe it's to do with the double lenses, with the fact that you don't see exactly the view to which you're exposing the film, maybe it's this that causes the slight inaccuracies in alignment. What is really impressive about the photographs the camera takes – and this is something I never expected – is the colour and the contrast of the images. I always thought that the quality of colour was purely to do with the film that you chose to use, or with the kinds of filters that you might put on the camera. But when I took my pictures to be developed the people at the lab, people who know a lot more than me about these things, remarked on the quality of the colour and said that what determined this quality was the lens, the Carl Zeiss lens. This was surprising for me because my small knowledge about the function of lenses is based on those black-and-white diagrams where you see lenses in profile with lines representing light changing direction and then converging as they travel through them. These diagrams seem to suggest that it is the lenses' function just to change the direction of the light – the alignment of the image – and not the quality of the light. There is such a diagram in the Rolleiflex instruction manual that shows the convergence – and the differences – in the way light travels into both the camera chamber and the viewfinder. I know that Carl Zeiss was a German optician who was born in Weimar in 1816 and lived until 1888. In 1846 he established a factory at Jena which became noted for the production of lenses, microscopes and other optical instruments. His partner, Ernst Abbe (1840–1905), was a German professor of optics born at Eisenach. He deduced the mathematics of the optics of the microscope, and this enabled him to design microscopic objectives scientifically, working with Otto Schott (1851–1935) to perfect optical glass and in 1886 producing lenses of the highest possible quality for scientific research. That is to say that whereas the production of lenses had previously been a craft, an artisan trade, new advances made it possible to determine optimum function though numerical values – through measurement.

In what might have been a similar spirit, I thought it would be a good idea to buy a small spirit level attachment for my cameras. I'd seen one that a friend of mine was using some years before and I considered that it would be wise to have one. The purpose of it was to ensure that one's camera was level with the tangent to the sphere of the earth that is what one thinks of as the plane. It's a pretty thing, like a hollow ice cube with green oily liquid inside and some lines etched onto the surface. It is grooved at the base to allow it to fit onto the small brackets at the top of cameras that usually house the flash. My video camera had these brackets for a lighting unit or an external microphone, but my Rolleiflex didn't. At the moment of considering the camera spirit level the principal thing for which I needed it was to take some static video shots of the disused railway tracks outside Cambridge and then one 180° pan at the end of the track. The attachment would keep my camera level for the static shots, but when it came to the pan I needed the tripod on which it swivelled to be level as well, or the circumference which the pan described would be at angle to the level of the aforementioned ground. I was looking at tripod heads with integrated spirit levels when I experienced a crisis in confidence that led to me walking out of the shop and leaving an assistant in mid-sentence about the advantages of Manfrotto tripod heads. I bought a packet of cigarettes – ten Camel Lights, because I liked the light blue packet – and went into the Museum Arms on Museum Street where I ordered a pint of lager. I used to love doing this, having a drink and a cigarette on my own in the afternoon, and I tried regularly to relive my pleasure, but by the time I sat at my table that afternoon it was clear to me that my life was no longer so straightforward. The mix of lager and smoke just seemed to produce unpleasant mucus in my gullet. I thought about why I'd come here and remembered that it was to reflect on the spirit level, to think about what it was that had made me doubt its usefulness. I soon realised that this was not merely a mechanical question, and that to raise it would suppose some fundamental changes in my attitude and approach. This was alarming because I wasn't sure what it meant for the work that I'd done previously, nor the projects which I was currently completing. I'd lost my faith in something that had been a part of my work for some time. Not that it was central to my work, but it was certainly present in the background, like an unspoken structure of belief. It wasn't just a question of my pictures being level, it involved all sorts of other things like why I should block out background noise on my videos, or why it was important to make sure that the right white balance was selected. Editing, too: the way in which the process of editing made work seem proper and professional. All these rules, borrowed indicators of the value of things, now seemed phoney, worse than phoney; they were like a conspiracy that I'd maintained against myself.

My grandfather's visit to Switzerland was probably because he liked to go there. He liked to go there so much, in fact, that he chose to do so at a moment in his life when he needed the greatest consolation. At the outbreak of the Spanish Civil War my grandfather was in Edinburgh undertaking medical studies. He returned to Spain to be with his family and his fiancée. When the war finished he saw himself unable to complete his studies and yet needing to make a living for himself and the beginnings of what he must have known would be a large family. If anybody were really interested I could give them the detail of it, but for the purposes of this story it's enough to say that he began to produce vitamin A from the livers of bluefin tuna that were caught in the south of Spain. He developed a relationship with the tuna fishery in Sancti Petri in the province of Cadiz and established a factory in Palencia to extract the vitamin from the livers. He came from a long line of pharmacists and so he knew the commercial side of vitamins and pharmaceuticals well. Furthermore, he benefited from the drive towards self-sufficiency that so informed post-war policy-making in Franco's Spain. This opened up Spanish markets to him, and so profitable did these prove that he was able also to invest in an international export strategy. By the time World War Two broke out he was exporting vitamins to France, Germany and the UK. Evidently this was not sustainable. Though remaining strictly neutral through the war, Spain's sympathies were clearly on the German side. Even if he had wanted to, my grandfather would have been unable to stop trading with Germany, and this made it impossible for his UK clients to continue trading with him. He was blacklisted, and was unable resume his trading contacts, even after the war. It was not sufficient to break him, for there still remained a substantial national market for which he could cater. This kept him afloat and at times thriving into the early fifties when a chemist at the Kodak laboratories in the USA discovered a procedure by which vitamin A could be synthesised and therefore produced at a fraction of the cost of extracting it from tuna livers. My grandfather was terribly excited by the discovery: his first thoughts were not of the ruin that this discovery could suppose for him, but of the great scientific advancement that had been achieved. He went to visit the Kodak company at George Eastman House in Connecticut and familiarised himself with the synthesising technology. He figured a way that he could do the same thing in Spain, and began to make arrangements to purchase and transport the appropriate machines from the Kodak company. Since it was not their main activity, Kodak were quite lenient about the patent rights for their procedure in Spain, and anyway many of the people with whom my grandfather spoke were intrigued by this enthusiastic Spaniard with a passion for science and photography. He returned to Spain with crates carrying the equipment to synthesise the vitamin, but these were held at customs and refused an import licence. It appeared that the Spanish government had just negotiated a contract to import various products at low prices from the USA – including vitamin A – in exchange for allowing them to have air bases in the country. My grandfather was ruined and began the process of shutting down his factory.

By this time my grandfather already had six children, and there was seventh on the way. He didn't know what he would do. He thought and thought about his possibilities but was unable to arrive at any conclusions because always the fear of financial ruin clouded his more lucid moments. He decided that he must go away on what he was unable to term a holiday. His wife and two of their younger children would accompany him on a caravan trip to Switzerland – a land where he thought he might find some inspiration. It was to him a therapeutic place, at a time where everything seemed to be falling apart around him he wanted to be somewhere that was as ordered and regulated as possible, somewhere where he could think straight. From previous visits he knew that the Swiss could be quite prejudiced against Spaniards. They were seen as the paupers of Western Europe; he had once come across a sign outside a restaurant that declared: NO DOGS OR SPANIARDS. And he didn't hold this against them (he is a man who also suffers from quite marked misanthropic tendencies). Switzerland was also quite an expensive place to visit. The peseta was worth very little, and my grandfather's supplies of pesetas were anyway quite limited now. So he decided that they would take as much as they could from home in order to avoid unnecessary expense on the journey. He had a good supply of tinned tuna from the fishery in Sancti Petri, and his godfather had a fig plantation near Badajoz in the south, so there were always boxes of dried figs in the cellar. During his stay in America visiting the Kodak company he'd seen instant coffee, which was not available in Spain, and thought it such a good idea that he tried to produce his own version of it using the now redundant equipment for extracting vitamin A. He made coffee through a filter, added milk to it and then evaporated and dried the liquid in his ovens so that he was left with a powder which he hoped he could rehydrate with boiling water in his caravan. During the trip my grandfather was unable to rid himself of the financial worries which he knew he would have to resolve on his return. He did consider various possibilities such as the industrial processing of cereals and the production of chocolate, and he did research these ideas, but without much inspiration.

On his return he met with many of the men who had invested in the vitamin company. The purpose of the meetings was to inform them face to face that their investment would longer make profits for them and to discuss the fate of the plant. These were not difficult meetings, for such had been the success of the factory during its brief life that these men had already seen their initial investment returned with profit. By way of revealing to them a novelty, and in order to lighten the atmosphere of what were for him quite depressing meetings, he served these men the version of instant coffee that he had considered to be quite successful on his trip. He made it in front of them, dropping a spoonful of the powder into a white cup, pouring boiling water over it and stirring. This familiar procedure would have seemed then like alchemy. A few of these men asked if they might have a jar of this magic powder, and then some of their friends asked for the same, and soon my grandfather found himself with so many requests that he was forced to charge some money for the instant coffee. There was probably a moment when he realised that the coffee was becoming a potential livelihood. I don't know how he made the

decision to pursue it, but he did, and he pursued the business
with the same exactitude with which he had pursued all his
other ventures. Paintings and photographs in his study attest
to the changes and expansions of the plant, which began as
a pharmaceutical enterprise and continues life as an instant
coffee factory. The first fleet of vans, the decaffeinating plant,
all the landmarks in the history of the business amongst
the reproductions of Goya and Velázquez (and Renoir) and
photographs of his family. A space left for the prized Chinese
chess set but resting above it a hand-drawn diploma by the
management of the tuna fishery in Sancti Petri, thanking Don
Antonio Cruz for his loyal custom.

★

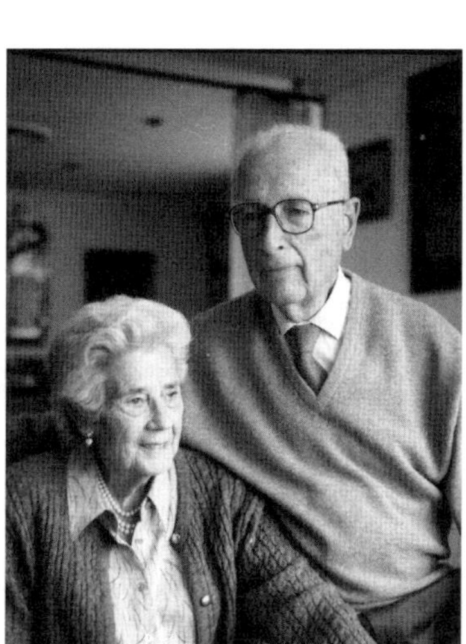

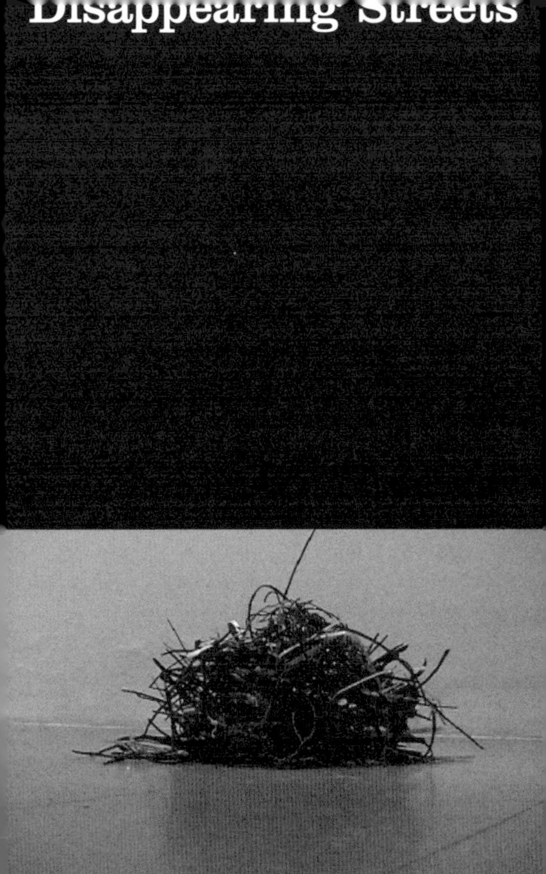

Disappearing Streets

I've been taking photographs of disappearing streets. I'd
wanted to do this for a while, but couldn't figure out a rationale
to guide me. I suppose I mean that I had no idea what these
photographs would be, and I felt that I had to determine this
before I set about taking them.

There was one photograph I took, not exactly accidentally,
but without the sense that I would want to take any more.

And neither can I really say when I decided that I wanted
to take more of these photographs, or indeed why. What I
can say is that when I realised that I did want to take more, I
surrounded myself with problems:

1. What film to use

2. What camera to use

3. How far a field could the streets be

4. If they were to express a typology, was there a place – a
   generic place that might pertain to all my sites – from which
   the photographs could be taken so that the typology would
   be clear.

5. Should I go out specially to take the photographs, or should
   I always have a camera on me so that I could take the
   photograph whenever I came across a street (this relates back
   to 1, 2 and 3)

Also on my mind, though less pressing because I thought I
could delay the decision, was the question of how I'd show the
photographs once I'd taken them. But inevitably this question
also related back to 1, 2 and 3 because I knew from experience
that it's much wiser to select the appropriate film-stock for the
job than making do and then transforming the thing later. It's
not such a problem for single images, because you can just pay
more attention to the quality of the images, but if it's a case of
a work comprising a set of images, and if the inter-relation of
the images is important, then to maintain this inter-relation
through the processes of transforming one type of film to
another creates a horrendous problem. I encountered it when
making a work that comprised twenty-four photographic prints
in one form and a video projection in another. I'd taken the
original images on 35mm transparency film, and so in order
to make the prints the lab first had to make what they called
an inter-neg, from which they could then print. The printing
process then allowed for a certain amount of variation and

change in the prints, but this was not limitless, and the
possibilities seemed lacking when trying to match the print
to a transparency. The people in the lab explained to me that
it was a different medium, that the mistake I was making in
assuming that what you'd get on a print would be the same
as that which you'd get in a negative was one that a lot of the
customers made. And they were fed up of telling them that
it was a different medium, that it couldn't be the same.
How could anyone expect to achieve the same luminosity in
a print as one could perceive in a transparency when it was
luminosity – the desired quality – that was essential even
to the seeing of the transparency: one saw it because light
travelled through it, unlike a print which reflected light in
order to make itself visible. I couldn't argue against this,
but I was also suspicious that maybe they were abusing my
ignorance, that they could perhaps try harder. So I pointed
out the differences again, trying to let them know that I did
have some tolerance but expressing the limits of it. I also tried
to look downhearted, as if this dissatisfaction with the prints
was something that really might break me. This expression
wasn't entirely manipulative, either; it wasn't so much that
I was angry with them but potentially angry with myself for
not making my case strongly enough, for being too polite to
conduct myself in a manner that might seem unreasonable.
And it is a problem, to think that one's demands might be
seen as unreasonable. I've been in a number of exhibitions
where the stroppiest and most unreasonable artists ended
up getting the best spaces, or the greatest attention from the
curators. That would be OK if one were sure that one had
negotiated accurately that line between getting what one
thought one ought to get and seeming unreasonable. Because
there is nothing worse than feeling that you haven't stood
up for yourself enough. You find yourself skimping, cutting
corners so that you don't waste resources or take up people's
time. Then the curator, who sees in you some reason, talks to
you and you act as their kind of counsellor. They criticise all
the other artists, and you agree but feel slightly uncomfortable
because they're your friends – although there's nothing
nicer than hearing your friends, particularly professional

friends, criticised. They tell you how nice and easy you are
to work with and you take the compliment like a long, slow
shafting that reaches its climax after the show has ended, when
in the curator's mind all those unreasonable artists become
interesting... temperamental, and desirable to work with. It's
not always like that, and neither is it anybody else's problem to
make sure that you get that to which you think you're entitled.
I think I must have been about eleven when I let the girl next
door borrow my bicycle, only for her to let her boyfriend scratch
it and damage the brakes. Next time she asked for it I let her
borrow it again, and it returned damaged again – and she didn't
even dare to ask again. More recently, though, I've learnt to be
more assertive, even to the extent of asking the young man who
was cutting my hair last time I went to have it cut to stop half
way – or, luckily, before he'd got to the half-way, and probably
irreversible, stage.

It was at the barbers to which I've been going for the past
two years, a barber that was recommended by a friend who
had been living for a longer time in the area. He told me how
good they were, what a decent job they did, and I went along
pleased at the recommendation. In the past I've enjoyed getting
my hair cut when I've been away in different places. It's one of
those mundane kind of tasks or services that can make you feel
as if you're bypassing a kind of tourist existence when you're
away, because you're doing something that everyone needs to
do, or that most choose to do anyway. That level of normality
often enables the extraordinary to happen: in Newlyn a barber
insinuated that I might like to have sado-masochistic sex with
him in his back room; in Cadiz the barber handled sardines
that his friend had brought him and then without washing his
hands returned to cutting my hair; in Madrid – a hairdresser
this – tried to sell me products to restore my thinning scalp.
It's not the events themselves that are appealing, but putting
yourself in a position – a vulnerable position – in which they
might happen. The most I'd ever before told a barber not to
do was to cut my neckline straight: I like it to follow its natural
shape, but often I've even let them get away with this; I've had
old men with hands far too shaky to handle a cut-throat razor
scuttling just this implement – a blunt and rusty version – on

the back of my neck and around my ears; when they ask if I use product on my hair I say no, but don't complain when they don't ask and smear it on regardless; when I look in the rear-view mirror tray I always say it's great, just right, really what I wanted, and wait until I'm a good distance away before fluffing away the blow-dried, gel-set quiff.

Though I had sought these types of experiences I was nevertheless relieved to find a local barber whom, on the strength of two cuts, I had come to trust. At £10 his cuts were a little more expensive than many others in the area, but he did a good job. The first time I went in he knew exactly what I wanted when I said that I wanted it short all over: really quite short, but scissor-short, not done with clippers. I've had clipper cuts before; there was a time when this seemed to be the only haircut that it was possible to have – variation existing in the grade of the clippers and in the variety of grades that were used on any one cut. But I never quite got rid of the idea that this cut was a skinhead cut and that I felt more comfortable with a clearer indication of choice and preference on my head. A clipper cut suggested that choice and nuance could play no part in a haircut, like someone suggesting that a certain simplicity constituted neutrality, as if things could exist without being designed. If you had a clipper cut you'd gone beyond choice – you'd achieved the destiny of all haircuts and could not be criticised for your style in this area since you were not really demonstrating a style but a fundamental state. I came to mistrust the clipper cut but still needed to have my hair cut quite short or else it began to look like frizzy '70s performance-artist hair. Thinning scalp with remaining strands all too keen to respond to the slightest static and fly up at strange angles. This is how I came to the scissor cut – short, but only as short as scissors would allow. I felt that with this cut I gained some dignity – an old fashioned kind of virtue elicited through my visible relation with choice and taste. I also felt that the cut ennobled the barber, made him more than a barber – a hairdresser, a man with skills and aesthetic judgement. And this barber I'd found lived up to those expectations.

The shop is much like all the barbers' shops in the area, a bit grimy and with floor unswept. Quite unlike those hairdressers I remember being taken to by my mother, where all the instruments would be in blue-lit sterilising cabinets and a girl would come to sweep the floor every five minutes. Here there are coloured Formica chairs, that have now achieved some degree of interest in their appearance, and magazines: *FHM, Maxim, Loaded.* Customers come in, and without asking know that they are to sit and wait their turn. It is the kind of ritual which now seems quite rare when there is a requirement for greater precision in knowing when one will be served or when things will happen. An old-style air then about this barber's shop. Everyone there must support the same football team, and most seem to know what the others do: not necessarily their jobs, but certainly their attitudes and general areas of work.

Though there are three chairs in the barber's shop, only one of them is usually manned. The barber looks resigned to what he does. I don't know whether this is because he is embarrassed about his profession or because he really doesn't like doing it – as if he were aware of this as his fate. More than in a job, he looks as if he is indulging a habit when he cuts hair. He seems to realise something about it being a bad thing for him to be doing, but he can't stop, and the pleasure of it brings pain to his face. He knows that pleasure and he greets it with a downturned face, as if it were a priest to whom one had just confessed. As soon as your turn comes and you sit at his chair he seems intuitively to know what you want, and I always take pleasure in his tacit suggestion that my desire is a fine choice, something of a challenge.

The customer who preceded me on my first visit was a child: a young boy, about seven. The barber took as much care about his cut as about anybody else's and talked to him all the way through, seeking his, and not his father's, opinion. When he finished he asked the child what he thought and they had a laugh and a tease about something. He helped him off the chair and then before he left insisted that he gave him a kiss. The child was embarrassed, but his father insisted and so the barber got a quick kiss and a bit of a hug as the boy said goodbye.

I was still smiling at the scene as the barber called me. I thought he was annoyed with me, but if he was he behaved entirely professionally in asking me what I wanted done. He began spraying my head with water as he stroked my hair and rubbed the water in with his other hand, all the time looking carefully at the shape of my head and the consistency of my hair. I made to tell him things, areas to look out for, past experiences, but his hands and face did something to indicate that he wasn't interested in my history, only in the moment. He began to cut, and there was a calm about us as it became clear that he was working while I received a service, as if only within this silent and clearly defined professional relationship could either he or I allow for the intimacy of the way in which he looked at me and caressed my head. I broke my silence when he put down the scissors to take up the razor, told him that I wanted the line at the back left natural. He took in breath and nodded with his eyes closed, as if suffering that I shouldn't have appreciated that he would have known this even without being told. He continued and I hoped he wouldn't notice the goose-pimples running down my back as he scraped my neck.

When he finished we performed an evasive glance ballet as I tried to catch his eye to express how pleased I was with the cut. He humbly refused to meet my eyes directly, preferring instead to use the buffer of the mirror's reflection, but he nodded at my appreciation. I'm used to people becoming arrogant when they feel that they've done something well, but he instead seemed overcome with humility, as if embarrassed about his own talent.

My next visit was just before Christmas, and the barber's shop was quite full. Unusually there were three barbers working, with customers occupying all three chairs. My barber was working at his usual chair at the back of the shop. There were several people ahead of me but I waited nevertheless, judging that my turn would not be long in coming. When one of the other barbers had finished he requested the next in line but this person stated that he was waiting for my barber; the next did the same, and it was only the third in line that acceded to the request. The next request came from my barber and the first in line accepted. Following this the middle barber called and was again refused by number one. He turned to me and unfocused thoughts rushed through my head as I said yes, of course, and stepped towards him. I didn't feel I could be so fussy about my hair as to refuse his offer. If he worked in the same establishment he must perform a function of similar quality. He was a young man and his English was poor. I sat on his chair and he robed me with the cotton gown and asked me what I wanted. Short, but scissor-short, I said, I didn't want him to use clippers. He told me not to worry, that he would use clippers but that it would be the same, that I wouldn't notice any difference. He would use a high grade and this would do the same thing as scissors. I told him that I didn't want to argue with him, he was a hairdresser and I wasn't going to question his professionalism, but I wanted my hair cut with scissors and not clippers. He insisted again that it would make no difference and I repeated my assertion. Our disagreement drew the attention of an elderly man who acted as if he was the owner of the shop. He tried to reassure me that there would be no difference and I again repeated my case, adding that if I had to I wouldn't mind waiting for the man who usually cut my hair. I looked over towards him trying to seek support, but he wouldn't enter the discussion; he made it clear that he was concentrating on another customer. I made to get up from the chair, saying that I would wait, pleased that I had made the decision. But it was too late; the young man picked up the scissors and obliged me to resume my place. He looked at my head from all sides. Then he pinched a tuft of hair and sheared it off with the scissors. I was reminded in the clumsiness of his actions of the dexterity with which my customary barber performed: that dexterity whereby his hands would work in synchronicity with the scissors so to make it feel as if he were not cutting the hair at all but teasing it into shape. After a few more hacks of hair I told the boy to stop. I asked him if he'd ever done this before and he looked aggrieved and guilty. There was also anger in his eyes and I feared the scissors. I turned towards my barber half imploringly, half-asking him to explain, but again he wouldn't be drawn into the discussion. I asked the boy to show me what he'd done with the aid of the tray mirror. Bald uneven patches were beginning to develop. I pointed them out to him and his nervousness stretched as he told me that he hadn't tidied it up yet. But I want it like he does it: please tell him, I implored my barber, who could no longer refuse to answer me and softly told me to wait until he was free and he would continue the cut. This I did with great clumsiness, apologising to the boy who was

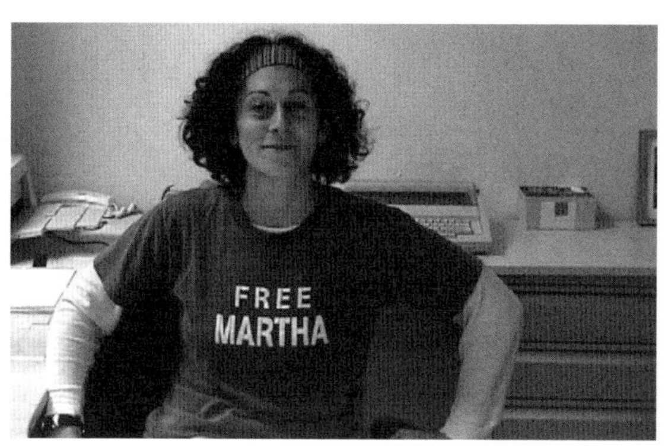
FREE
MARTHA

himself, I think, relieved not to have to continue the deceit. He was quickly patronised by another customer who was happy to demonstrate his manliness in being less concerned about the appearance of his hair. I did get the cut I wanted eventually: my barber performed with customary grace to mend the mess made by his colleague. I judged this boy to be a relative who was here for holidays. It may have been that he had never cut hair before and was forced to do so in order to earn his keep. Not that I would hold this against him: everybody has to start doing what they do somewhere, and the beginning of that trajectory is the best place to fuck up. It's worse later when you get so confident about what you do and so fed up of the long hours that it requires that you decide to ease off a bit. Why not? All your colleagues work much less hard than you, and their work is not so bad, in fact in many ways it's quite good. Perhaps it's your fastidiousness that's holding you back; perhaps if you weren't so critical of yourself and let yourself get away with those things that those around you let themselves get away with your work and your enjoyment of it might increase. This is very dangerous ground, for to stand on it supposes an admission that you know how to do what you do; to stand on it means that you can't move. Much better to fuck up at the start, when you're at least trying: people will tend to forgive you this. The boy was learning how to do something that might become his trade, he fucked up and I told him so and he may have learnt from that. Another Italian barber I met learnt his trade before he left Italy, though how good he was prior to his departure I don't know. I met him thirty years after this, and by then he owned his own shop in Melbourne. It wasn't the only barber's shop I tried there; I'd been around the corner first and walked into a much fancier-looking place. All around were posters of a man in leathers on a motorbike. In some – mainly the action shots – he wore a helmet, so you couldn't tell who it was. But since it was one man who was pictured in all the helmetless shots I presumed that it was the same person all round doing wheelies, being draped on by girls in bikinis, drinking beer from a bottle and I can't remember what else. The shop was empty when I walked in and I had some time to look and develop and internalise smug criticisms of the place. When the man walked in through the back I wasn't sure whether my critique was validated or rendered so obvious that it just lost all relevance. It was he of course, the man in the pictures. I didn't want to tease him, but neither did I want to flatter him, so I kept the conversation to hair and asked whether I could have a cut. He told me that I could make a reservation for the following day. No good to me, this, and I asked whether the afternoon would be at all possible. He told me he was all booked up. His own hair was long and dark and extremely well kempt. He ran his hand through it as he told me of his bookings as if to let me know how good he was, let me understand that I couldn't just walk in and expect service. I mistrust hairdressers with overly indulged hair, like I do artists whose lifestyle is too nice – it's too obvious.

I left and walked round the corner to a grubbier-looking barbers I'd spotted whilst riding on a tram a couple of days before. I hadn't then thought I'd risk it, but I was here now, and I'd put an hour aside for this. It was called Felice's and the hairdresser had very dark black grey hair cut in a short angular quiff and a carefully shaped tiny little goatee beard. Yes, he could cut my hair right away, and I explained that I wanted it short but scissor-short, not done with clippers. He was unfazed by my directions and began immediately with a fast and efficient clipping action. He identified that I wasn't local and used this to start conversation by asking me whether I was on holiday. I told him I wasn't, that I was working there on a project for the Melbourne Festival. I told him I was a photographer and a writer, and that I was doing some work about some places in the city. He said I could take a picture of him and write about how he ruined my hair – we laughed. I asked him where he was from because I recognised his accent as foreign. I knew it was Italian and he confirmed this, said that he'd come here thirty years ago. He had been a hairdresser there, but had left for work and a better life. I asked him whether he returned often and he said yes, but it had been twelve years since his last visit. By way of a kind of consolation I told him that it was a big journey. He asked me where I came from and I told him that I lived in London. Had I heard the Tottenham/Man U. result? I hadn't, and he told me that having

had a 3-0 lead at half-time Tottenham went on to lose 3-5.
We talked about what a fantastic team Manchester United
were, but also about the nature of the English game; about the
unwillingness of English teams to hold on to a lead; about the
kind of heroic dignity that suggested that attack was the best
form of defence and the morality that would see it as just plain
wrong to insist on a defensive strategy. He asked me why the
English were so stupid about that, and I told him I didn't know.
I added that I'd been talking about something similar during
a radio interview I'd been asked to give to a radio station the
previous day. The man had asked me whether London was the
capital of art still, following its acclaim through the YBAs. I
had no idea, but I made an argument about English pride and
nationalism, suggesting that there was a jingoistic attitude at
play in English culture that manifested itself by having to assert
its own as the best or the worst. This had been a very humble
interview. The interviewer – a Colombian who had been, and
still aspired to be, a playwright – had Miles Davis' *Sketches of
Spain* playing in the background, and was determined to lead
me to talk about my work as some kind of enterprise involving
an exploration of human loves and passions. This was a
Spanish-language slot in the programming of the multilingual
SBS station, and the themes covered were naturally broad.
But nevertheless I felt effectively deflated by the fact that my
interview was followed by a piece about the dangers of anti-
inflammatories. It was probably because of the evident lack of
importance of the interview that I chose to aggrandise it for my
hairdresser, believing that he would be proud and impressed
to be dressing the head of someone so prominent. The effect
was predictably counter to my intent: the hairdresser saw
through my bluster and was irritated by it. His clipping action
got curter, the manipulation of my head less gentle. He told me
about the architect clients that he had, about their fame, and
the way in which they travelled round the world. I'd probably
seen their work, the modern architecture that was all around
the city, the monument that I would have spotted on the way
in from the airport. I said that of course I had, one couldn't
help but notice the preponderance of sharp jagged architecture
that there was all around the city. I added that the building

where I had done my interview was of this type, and went on to say what a peculiar thing SBS was, a channel that broadcast on television and radio in such a range of languages. I wanted to regain some ground by admitting how unimportant my interview had been. This was motivated by an unreasonable fear that he would cut my hair in the style of the architecture of his architect clients – a style that he seemed to have adopted for his own head. So when he came to cutting the back I asked him not to do it as a straight edge but to follow the natural hairline. 'Natural' was in fact the way I wanted the cut to be, not too sharp and angular. He repeated the word and I reiterated it: yes, natural. I told him I'd been on the Spanish slot, and countered his surprise by telling him that I was originally from Spain, and that Spanish was my first language. He seemed delighted and said that he often watched the late-night Spanish films because they were hot. What did he mean, hot? Hot, you know, dirty, he told me.

When he finished he showed me the back and I attempted to show my appreciation. I asked whether he'd mind if I took his photograph, and he was clearly delighted for me to do so. I wanted to picture him in the shop, and I wanted the two images that hung on opposite walls to appear in the photograph. One was a naked calendar girl and the other a large fake silver pencil nude on a black background – hot, dirty pictures. I had to use the mirrors to achieve my shot. He asked me to send him a copy and he gave me his card, told me also to tell my friends about him, so that when they came here he might cut their hair.

It was during my time in Melbourne that I started again to think about the disappearing streets. This city is mainly on a grid, and so the streets don't disappear at all. This suited me, because my main concern was to keep moving, and I could see that there was always somewhere to go. I had that anxiety that comes with being in a distant foreign place for a limited time and feeling that I might miss something. The work I was doing there forced me to visit a number of places in the city on various occasions. The route around these places soon formed a circuit for me that I was able to follow and complete with increasing ease. So I began to explore those places to which I had no obligation to go.

Being alone in a city allows you to choose what you might present yourself as being – to yourself and to others – and then the opportunity to try to act out the possible actions of this determined self. I found it hard to think beyond two types: one of these was the studious, rigorous type who would stay in his hotel room despite the novel attractions outside, and read and study. Being in a new place would not for this type signal excitement and novelty, but rather indicate a time outside of the normal distractions that he would encounter in the place where he usually lived. The other type is the one that would indulge in all of these distractions. Either way, you find yourself acting or performing whatever it is that you do. But it's a type of acting that is quite close to behaving naturally, whatever that may mean. Maybe it's to do with the fact that when you are in these situations you're very aware of how you construct your identity, aware of this in a real affecting way and not as a theoretical concern. I always find it very tempting to smoke when I'm abroad, because it feels like something you can do that does declare something about you, a private but public performance; one that you do for yourself but through the eyes of others.

Back home I'd given up thinking about the disappearing streets. Partly this was to with formal problems that I had around the presentation of photographs; about how I printed them and then presented them, about what I might want them to be. I think these problems prevented me from considering the photographs more attentively. But I did come to realise that what I needed was to look at the photographs less attentively. I mean by that that I was so keen to identify what these places were, and what the images I was making of them did, that I never thought about what they didn't do. It took travelling to a city that is based on a grid to realise this, or to get a hint towards it. In such a city almost any image you make of a street will have it disappearing away in perspective. But this kind of disappearance will suggest that there is more going on beyond the image, will suggest that the image is inadequate in relation to the real that it attempts to portray. And there may be a kind of sublimation in relation to this, a sense of the real escaping representation. These straight streets are made impossible by their image. I'm more interested in those streets that have their representative potential enabled by the image that might be made of them. Put simply, I'm interested in streets that disappear because they curve away and visually close themselves; I'm interested in taking pictures of these streets because it is only in still images that this enclosure is possible, and I'm interested in this enclosure because it seems to me potentially to constitute a space for thought and reflection – a space that can only exist in an image and which therefore has allied to it implicitly a sense of fiction.

This is a very structured and contained space, a bit like a stage, of course, but hopefully not alluding to that cliché too rabidly. I'm not interested in the performance that might occur within that stage, what you might call the human element; all the lives that one might imagine in the houses and in the characters who sometimes find themselves in the images. Not interested in them at all, only in the space that the street defines as it stops the view from continuing indefinitely.

The burglars came in through the ceiling. We live on the top floor and they gained access to the communal loft space and then kicked their way through the plasterboard. Fortunately, the front door was deadlocked, so they couldn't take anything large, but this did concentrate their attention on smaller items such as our cameras.

We contacted the insurance company and they told us to make a list of everything that had been stolen and to provide, where possible, receipts or other proofs of purchase or ownership. For most of our cameras this was impossible, since they were items we'd bought some time ago, or that we had inherited. In the case of my Rolleiflex I at least had the instruction manual which my grandfather had kept so carefully for many years.

I was determined that the insurance company should not replace the Rolleiflex for an equivalent second-hand camera. I'd never considered it to be second-hand, it had been handed down to me and this was an altogether different story because I knew who had used the camera before me and I also knew the manner in which it had been used – sparingly and carefully, like a piece of machinery, the performance of which had always been scrutinised not just in terms of its output but also in terms of the sound it made, of the ease with which the dials turned. Neither did I think I wanted the camera replaced for a contemporary medium-format camera that would be of an equivalent price to a second-hand replacement. Such a camera would certainly be of sufficient quality for my purposes, but within that certainty there was a doubt, the doubt that I might be selling myself short and that someone might be able to notice that.

Some months before, when I'd been taking a coffee break I'd noticed a Rolleiflex on the table of a man who was alone drinking coffee. I sat near him and spied on the camera which I could see was the same as mine in size and structure, but which had certain details and features that made it look more modern. His looked chunkier, the edges had been rounded slightly to give the thing the appearance that it was more of a coherent unit, a bit like the transformation suffered by cars as time has progressed, where the aesthetics of a moulded bubble seem to have dominated design thinking. His Rolleiflex also had a small green LED light on the side, which indicated something about light metering, I guessed, but also that, unlike mine, his camera had a battery. He got up and I let him go for a couple of seconds but then surrendered to something between curiosity and the desire to declare something to him. I apologised for bothering him – needless, as soon as he realised the enquiry was about his camera. Your camera, is it a Rolleiflex? I didn't realise they still made them. He told me that they did, or that they had when he bought his which was five years ago. I told him that I had one of the early ones and he assured me and himself that the ones now were essentially the same, that all that had altered were a few design features and the light metering system. I wanted to ask him what he used it for, or why he used it, but I didn't want to express surprise. So I asked him in which department he worked, premising my question with the information that I worked in visual arts – this explained why I had such a camera. He was in sociology, where they were conducting much research around photographic documentation. We bemoaned the fact that departments didn't collaborate more, and fantasised for a bit about how wonderful it would be to cross disciplines a little more easily and with some more support. I told him I'd love to see what they were up to, and when he told me where they were based I pretended to know exactly where he meant. It's not that I wasn't interested. I was also interested in a talk that an anthropologist gave where he discussed the way in which film was used by his colleagues: Their use of film, he maintained, was not just another way of recording the same stuff, but a way of creating new knowledge; knowledge that could only emerge through this medium.

I've been stopped myself when using my Rolleiflex. It's a camera that must have a friendly look, the look of a scientific instrument that is too cumbersome to be used. It's also the kind of device that triggers memories in people, memories of their grandparents – real memories and imagined memories. People say that it will last you forever, or that it's got such a fantastic back-plate. And I nod and smile, often touched by their enthusiasm. Almost always I tell them that it was my grandfather's camera, thinking, rightly, that they will like this, think what a nice young man I am. Because usually it's older people who comment. Not I think because it's they who remember it, but because it's they who are able to ask without fear of other implication. When it's happened I've felt lucky to have the camera, felt that even if I had the chance I wouldn't swap it for any other model. I remembered this feeling when I thought about replacing my stolen camera, and I also remembered my encounter with the sociologist, and the hope this gave me that I may be able to replace like with like.

I called the company that distributes Rollei in the UK and was put through to a man who could help me with questions concerning Rolleiflex cameras. He sounded as if he was close to retirement age, and I imagined him alone in a small office which was concerned to maintain the availability of this aged product with the real business of the firm being conducted at a faster pace around him. I explained about the burglary, and about my concerns regarding the replacement of the camera, that I didn't want it replaced with another second-hand model but with a new one that was as close as possible to that which I had lost. He was delighted to talk about the Rolleiflex and the features that were the same and those which had been modified. I took pleasure in his assertions about the quality of the product, but my questions were not as innocent or desperate as they may have appeared, or as they may have been in the past. Thy were motivated by a scenario that I had imagined in my head where the insurance company, through the loss adjusters, would contact this man and consult him about an accurate replacement. I was priming him to voice my concerns, but also trying to reassure myself that I was making the right decision.

★

In the months preceding the theft of the cameras I had been considering changing our car for a bigger model. Our own was still at the stage where it would be worth something in part-exchange and I thought it wise to capitalise on this before it became worth little and we would have to run it until it stopped. We also thought that we might have another child, and that we might need more space than that which we currently had. Although our price range was limited, we did have some savings that would allow us to get something relatively new and large, and I began to do some research into what might be the most appropriate model. I asked friends and family about their experiences with their own cars, and looked carefully at cars that I saw in the street. I'd never chosen a car before – those we had had we had inherited or bought advantageously from my wife's family when they upgraded theirs; so the idea of deciding upon something gave me the sense that I had reached an important age. I called the garage where we serviced our current car for some more objective and practical advice. I asked them if there was a dealer that they could recommend and they didn't hesitate to give me the number of a man who I discovered didn't operate from premises but instead acted as a kind of broker between those that wanted to sell their vehicles and those who wanted to buy them. Almost immediately he told me that he worked mainly for the pharmaceutical industry, healthcare professionals he called them. I didn't ask him why he didn't just refer to them as sales reps, but instead tried to express the confidence that his statement was intended to elicit. I told him that I didn't know much about cars, that I had a Peugeot 306 and I wanted something larger. Cars I had seen

and quite liked were the Peugeot 406 and the Volkswagen
Passat – both as estate models – but I would be happy to listen
to other suggestions he might have. He told me I had made
wise choices, but asked me, when I told him my price range,
whether I had considered the Ford Mondeo or the Nissan. I
don't know why exactly, or I'm reluctant to admit why, but I
said that I'd rather not consider these models. He asked me if I
had any preferences regarding the colour and I said, trying to
suggest that such superficial considerations were beneath me,
that I wasn't concerned about the colour, though I knew that
I would never drive a green car – because my mother was
superstitious about them – and that I'd rather not have red or
burgundy – because I fancied a change from the colour of our
two previous cars. He said that he would call me when he had
found any appropriate cars and he asked me if was in a hurry.
I said I wasn't, pleased that this might ease the pressure of
making a decision.

I've always found it quite difficult to spend what I consider
to be large amounts of money. By large I mean those that
might be involved in the purchase of something like a car or
a computer. This is mainly to do with the fact that I've never
had much money, but even when I have spending it has been
difficult. I don't think I'm tight, but I have never had the kind
of security that assured me of my ability to generate more,
and, as any economist knows, lack of security slows down
spending and leads to stagnation. Buying a car was a kind of
therapy for this. Recent experiences in my work had begun to
show me the value of security and confidence over fear; that
only by being secure could one invest in the risks associated
with working hard.

I bought magazines and looked at websites about cars,
trying to augment my knowledge about the subject. Other
men with whom I'd often found it difficult to talk suddenly
became my buddies and I would call them to discuss models
and prices. I realised that this is what people did, that this
was what all that excitement was about. As I drove around
or walked the street I would stop often and look though car
windows; I would measure the length of cars out in paces and
compare them to that of other cars. My magazines became

my only reading, and I came close to tearing out the pages
and sticking them all up on my wall so that I could more easily
make comparisons and come to some objective decision about
what would be the best car to buy. From the initial pair that I
had suggested to the dealer my list grew. Every time I became
enthused by a new model I would call him and tell him that
he too could add it to his list. I apologised for my enthusiasm,
said that I wasn't trying to hurry him but just attempting to
give him as many options as possible so that his job might be
made easier. I went through Volvo, Saab, Skoda – only the
new ones, though, which after long research, consultation and
successful publicity reception I judged did not have the old
stigma attached to them any more. I cleared up the kind of
engine range that I would be prepared to accept in any of these
ranges – preferably diesel, but only so long as it was turbo diesel
and could give the car some power. I was intensely excited, and
I began to extend my enquiries when I realised the possibility of
buying an older but better quality car.

It was a Mercedes I was thinking about. A big, proper,
quality car that was designed to last. I could afford to get an
older one, and I imagined myself driving it around casually,
as if I'd forgotten, or not even ever thought about, the vehicle.
There's an appealing identity associated with easy wealth, one
that allows for dirt, even, and creases. The sense that fabrics
may be draped everywhere and precious things allowed to
tarnish. An old shirt, but the right shirt, and likewise the
jumper that also displays the good sense of investing in quality.
This is to know norms, and then to be able to stray from them
but still to demonstrate that knowledge, to express the value of
that knowledge. A question of how many buttons are done up,
or the extent to which a shirt collar might toy with flicking over
the neck of a jumper, V or O neck, depending on season and/or
occasion. You have to know about these things if you aspire to
wear loafers and make it seem as if you're not dressing up. It's
impossible to buy them with that easy off-brown reddish colour
in place; the colour is achieved in the admirer by the certainty
of the wearer.

All the Mercedes were either too old or too new. Too old and
they betrayed my budget, betrayed the fact that I didn't have so

much money to spend and that it was as an economy measure that I was buying a car of such an age. Too new and the car suggested that I had more money than I would want people to think I had and that I was trying to show off about it. What I wanted was a car that would be understood as being the car that I would inevitably own. Then there were the running costs, which many people told me were exorbitant. The man from the garage did say to me, when I asked him about the relative merits of buying a newer but not so good car like a Peugeot or a Ford compared to those of buying an older Mercedes, that the Mercedes would always have the edge for him, because of the greater mileage that they were capable of delivering. He also cited their reliability and stated that if they were serviced in independent garages there was no reason why repairs should be more expensive. But the fact that he was in the trade didn't give me the confidence that it should. It made me think that there were things he might appreciate that I didn't.

It would have been much better if the insurance company had arranged credit at Jessops like they did for the smaller cameras. Then it would simply have been a question of going in, choosing goods up to the amount available and leaving with them. But because there was some uncertainty as to whether it would be possible to obtain a Rolleiflex replacement the insurers consented to send me a cheque for the full replacement value that I had stated. This was quite a large sum of money, more than I would usually spend on anything. It was more than I would have needed to buy the scooter that I had coveted so much. That started as a style choice, a desire for an old Vespa because I liked the speed at which it could carry me around. I also liked that it wasn't necessary to wear particularly special gear in order to ride a Vespa. Not like a motorcycle, for which leather and waterproofs seemed obligatory. Vespas didn't stop it raining but they did allow you to stop when it was raining and wait in a café until the sun came out again. They were things you could ride with loafers, or classic trainers, and with jeans and a polo shirt with a crocodile logo. Done properly it could exude the most powerful ease.

It was the old model I wanted, with the manual gear change and the flat front. Vespa had introduced a new version of this with automatic twist-and-go gears and a contemporary bubble inspired update to the design, but I wasn't interested in this, because it seemed too practical, like an alternative to a second car. I wanted the Vespa for capricious reasons, and much as I tried to explain to myself the practical benefits of owning one I wasn't prepared to allow practical considerations to influence my choice.

There were those who said to me that Vespas were unstable, that their small wheels were a danger round corners, in the rain and going over bumps and pot-holes. But there were also those who stated the virtue of being protected from splashes, and of being able to store one's helmet in the under-seat compartment. It was suggested to me that if I wanted to develop my riding I should consider a small motorbike instead of a scooter because it would give me the opportunity to progress. I wasn't interested in developing my riding, I just wanted a Vespa, but I heeded the warning, nonetheless, and when I came to take my two-wheel motorised riding test I did it on a small motorbike. I passed.

Of course passing on a motorbike brought up all the problems with choice again. The instructor, who must have judged me to be quite talented, allowed me to ride his big black Yamaha at the end of the test, and I was delighted to realise that it was much the same as riding the little 125 on which I had done my test and on which, or a variety thereof, I would have to ride until I passed the next test and the next. I started envisaging this progression through bigger and bigger bikes, and remembered having seen people – admittedly in good weather – riding big bikes while wearing fairly casual clothing. I was also told that a motorbike was far less likely to get stolen; the kids on the estate were mad about scooters, and since we had no yard or garden whatever I got would have to live on the street and be very prone to being taken and toured triumphantly around the estate. The kids preferred the more modern scooters, had little time for the older design that I was interested in, but a scooter, whatever its age, is much simpler to ride than a motorbike – I think that's the point of them – and so any scooter would have been more appealing to them.

★

The burglary made me feel uneasy about the place where we lived. People talk about feeling violated after a burglary, about feeling that their space is no longer their own. I had no such feelings, but I did have a more structural sense of unease. This was to do with the fact that we lived in a flat and that the ceiling was made of plasterboard. This was all that separated us from the communal loft area through which the burglars had entered.

Owning property is an abstraction at best; that idea that a piece of land and some structure belongs to you is difficult enough to understand. It is made more difficult when the structure is attached to other structures, so that you actually share the walls but own the space that they define. When it comes to a flat the thinking is even more complicated because the space that you own, unless you are on the ground floor, is not attached to the ground and does then really define itself as a chunk of air. And it's particularly difficult in a big city such as London, where so many people inhabit different chunks of air. It seems illogical that you should have to travel often long distances to return to your own chunk when there are so many adequate ones all around you all the time.

I wanted to simplify my thinking, feel more connected to the place where I lived, and thought that the way I might achieve this was if we were to sell our flat and buy a house. We considered leaving London, because we could get so much more for our money elsewhere. If we left London we could buy a bigger place, with some land, perhaps. That would really give a sense of ownership. If we were to stay in London the most obvious option was a Victorian terraced house, the kind that so ubiquitously makes up the landscape of the residential part of the city. The flat we lived in was a modern flat, ex-local authority in estate agents' language. Its status was the reason why we had been able to afford relatively spacious accommodation in a decent location. People are prepared to pay more for property the older it is, because they are probably susceptible to the same kind of fears about the abstractions of property that I have just described being susceptible to myself. A Victorian terrace gives a sense of the ownership of real space: a patch of ground, some of it edified and some of left as a garden or a yard

I'd love to have a yard, with large garage doors onto the street that I could secure and so turn the yard into my small piece of private street, a transitional area between the domestic and the public. I'd like part of the yard to be covered, so that I could store things there securely. I don't just mean the scooter, but other things as well, things with no purpose or function. There's a kind of smell that these places develop that I find extremely appealing, and though I doubt my ability to create such a space it seems almost like a bastard destiny that I should have such a space. Often these spaces function in relation to both a kitchen and a bathroom. So one might find in them empty bottles and jars, a washing machine and a clothes line, shovels and forks, bicycles, baskets of apples, gloves. All these things contribute to the smell, the dusty dampness that occurs immediately prior to decay. This is the quality that my aunt always looked for in her fruit. She would seek the softest piece that was on the verge of wrinkling and even growing mould. I always took the harder pieces, because one's involvement in eating them was less intense. A crispness, a sharpness, acidic cleansing. Where she would peel her fruit and prepare it into pieces before eating it I would eat mine whole, leaving only the stalk of an apple. It's people like her who can develop the kinds of spaces that I love, because they have a sense of the validity of waste, of the fact that time is able to nurture things beyond their actions. And so they have no urgency to rationalise things towards function; they know that to get the best out of something there needs to be something that is left over, and that there needs to be a space for that which is left over.

The man in Newington Studios told me that I wasn't winding the film tight enough. He asked me what camera I had and I told him, told him it was a new one that I'd got thanks to the insurance company. All right for some, he said to me and went to get his to show me how to wind the film properly. His camera was battered in the way that only a professional's camera could be battered, in the way that only someone who really knew what they wanted from a machine could tolerate, because someone who didn't know might well panic at the cosmetic damage and assume that such a sign indicated deeper wounds.

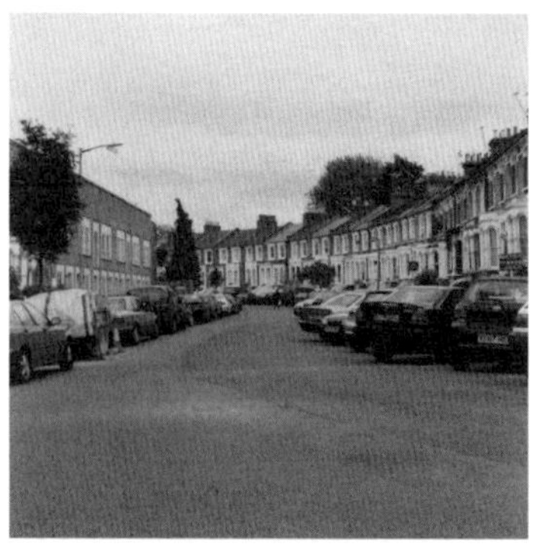
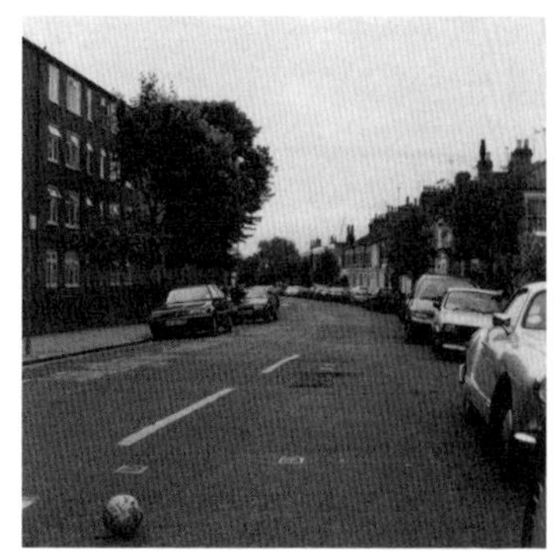

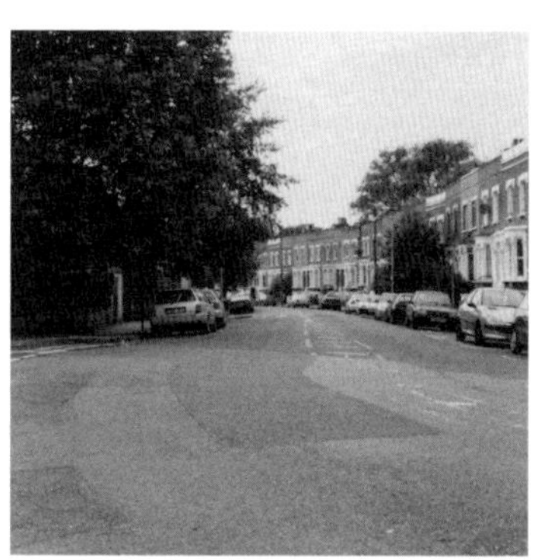
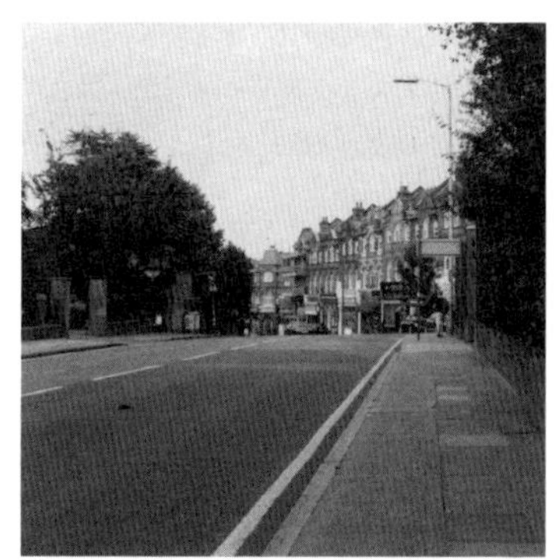

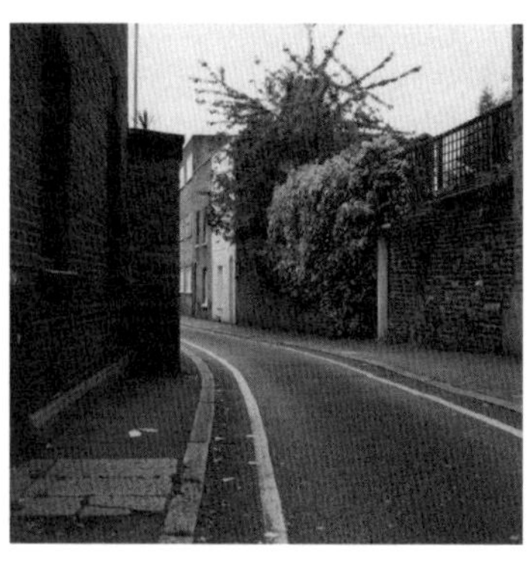
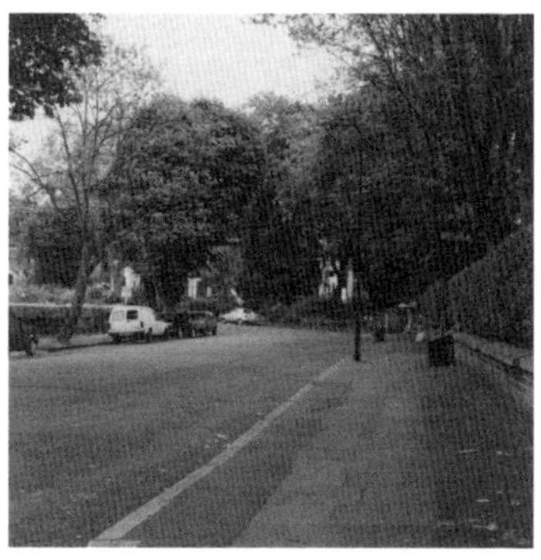

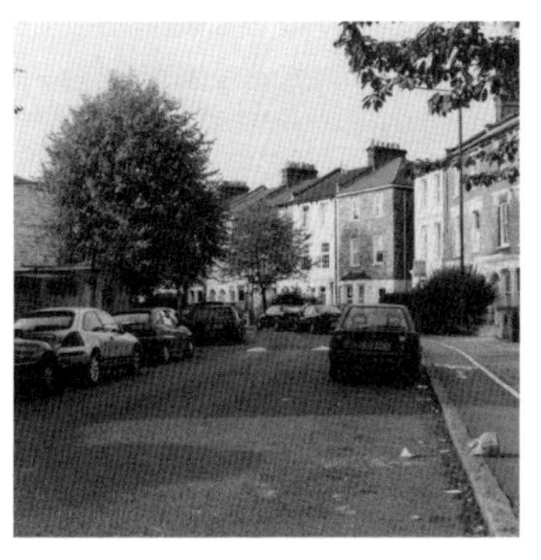
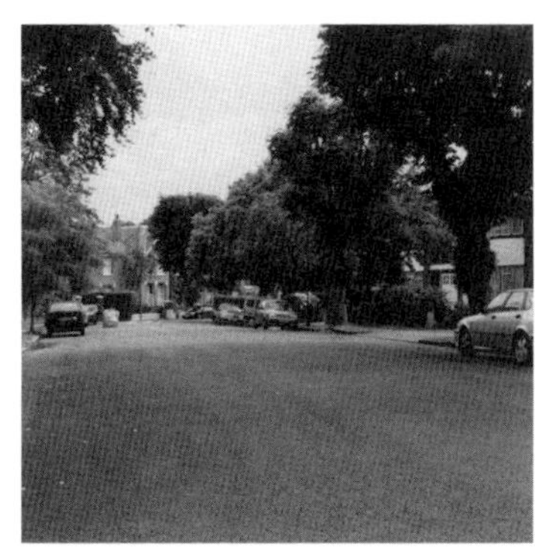

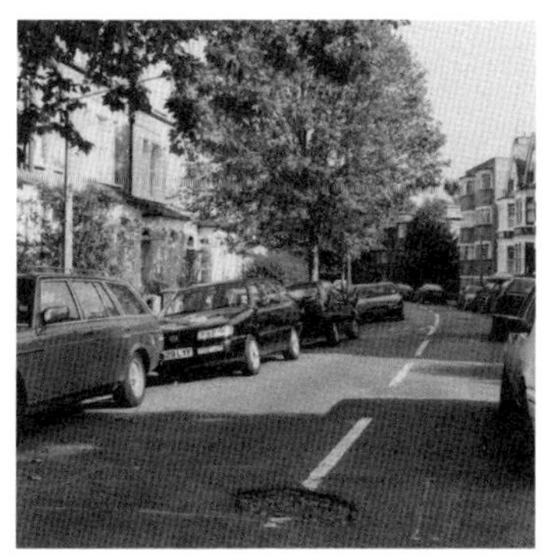
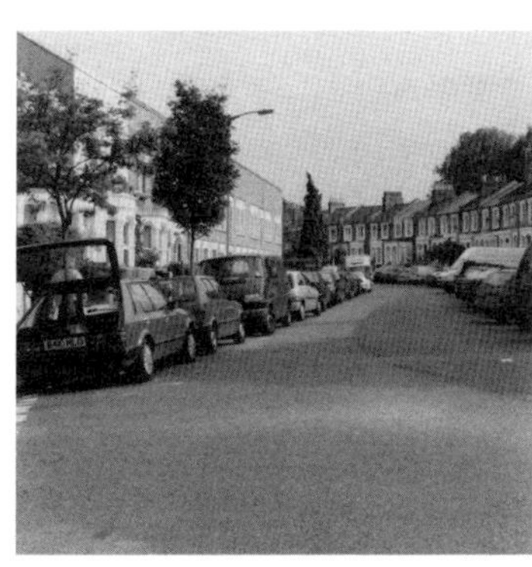

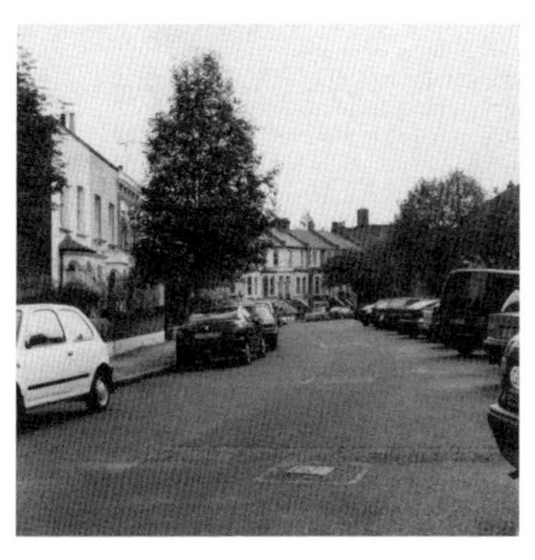
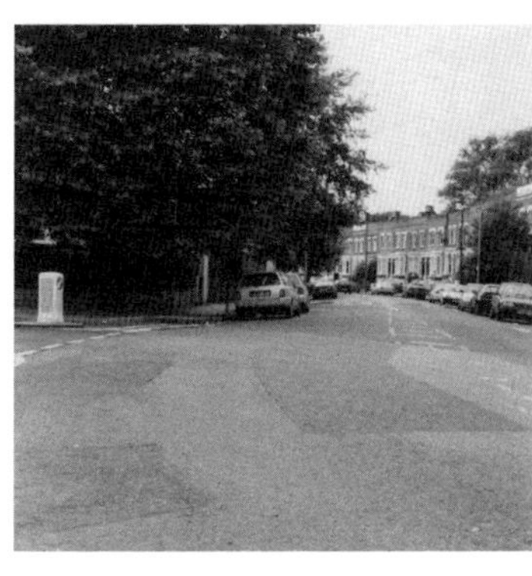

I had asked him for a contact sheet but he had told me that he couldn't do that, that he could only make individual prints. I'd always assumed that from a contact sheet I would choose the shots I wanted and then get them printed by people of quality whose standards I was familiar with. I had also thought that I might just stop at the contact sheets, but this seemed so keenly to labour the process that it quickly, slowly actually, subsided as an idea. The idea that someone could just print the images that I would use straight off and have immediately in my possession was very attractive. It meant that there would be more proximity between what I was working on and what I was showing, that there wouldn't be this moment where I sent the things off to get printed and then see them for the first time in the exhibition. I enjoyed the idea that the prints might gather fingerprints and dust while I looked at them and that those might form part of my trust in them when I came to show them. Again I was determined to show them on their own, convinced that I had achieved something of a material approach to this project that made it OK for me to show things without explanation or without a kind of narrative surrounding them. This was exhilarating, to think of the open poetic of these things, these small conventional things. The idea of he conventional was very present in my mind. I thought that I might have achieved something to do with a practice that is motivated by one's own questions and not by the space that is opened up for one by the culture. I'd been working for some time on other people's projects, situations where there might be established already a space or a context that already held value and meaning and it was my job to direct the nature of that. This was useful because it lessened the focus on my own concerns, and spread it around things with which I would have to be concerned just to entertain the notion of working in this space. This put me in the position of a concerned agent, one who would be managing inevitabilities and trying to encourage reflection upon them. It seemed then that what one offered as an artist was one's presence and thought in relation to an event or a place, and that this place gained some cultural validity by supporting within itself an activity that was potentially critical. Essentially it bought the critique, and thereby redeemed itself.

This has something about it of art as penicillin: administer
a small dose wilfully and internally and you secure a kind
of resistance to the cultural and aesthetic problems that
cannot be contained. It is a system which allows for art to be
manufactured quickly and emblematically. The artist soon
realises that it doesn't matter what his work is just so long as it's
there and so fashions something that is emblematic of the kind
of concerns with which he needs to be associated if he is to be of
any use as the mild and contained irritation that is required.

It's easy to speak of resistance, but if it's to be real enacting
it is really very difficult. I talk about the photographs that I
get back from the wedding photographer being the work itself
and not just a sample. This suggests that I accept a certain
arbitrariness or contingency with regard to the quality of the
images. That they look the way they look, and that I accept that
as a part and even a whole of the way that they are. In a sense
this is a question and refutes the possibilities of the printing
process; with a negative I could make or have made by others
as many prints as I want, and there is some scope to change
the quality of the image through this process. Clearly I don't
want to accept the contingencies of the prints I'm getting just
because I have the negatives and am able therefore to consider
that I can at any later stage make new prints, for this attitude
would compromise the very contingencies in which I'm so
eager to profess an interest. So I think that I should destroy
the negatives and have only the prints left as a record of the
work. Prints from which I will nevertheless have to make a
selection, thereby again compromising my intention. There is a
sensible way forward, which is not to dwell on the absoluteness
of any decision, not to see these decisions as absolutes but as
points of thinking which are strong enough to survive, despite
maintaining escape routes. The thing is that it seems much
harder to manage this flexibility and what might be called
common sense than it might be to impose a more identifiable
structure upon the decision. Artists often quote their structures
like a credo, as if the structure gave value to decisions that
might otherwise seem unimportant because they are subject
to the same kind of rubbish that everyday decisions are. They
say things like: I always destroy the negative; I only take one

shot; I only work with my shoes on; I only use found materials; I never take the pictures myself; I only ever use one brush – and there's an implication that it is the limitation that makes the work interesting. Maybe this is to do with a confusion between limitations such as those listed above and what might be a more useful kind of essentialising process in one's work. I think of essentialising work as involving oneself almost unconsciously (and by that I mean that it becomes part of the work and not something that is imposed upon it) in the kind of criticality that does not impose rules but that affects the practice continuously and is the practice; where the questioning and doubting is not imposed after the activity, or indeed before, through rules, but in the moment of making or doing always; so that the critical is cause, action and effect. I hope this isn't a rule in itself, just an indication or a reflection on something: that's what I'd like it to be. Not a position – you learn that from people who've seen enough of what positions can inflict that they disallow in themselves the arrogance that might enable them. We met a man from Northern Ireland on holiday and his character had just this kind of conciliatory nature. That's the kind of nature that isn't surprised by things and that doesn't declare them wrong just because they might be unusual. He would let his children have two ice creams after lunch, and didn't worry about it if they didn't socialise or weren't as charming as many people like their children to be. It was impossible to get him to moan about anything, because his attitude was simply to receive experiences and information and not to find a way of thinking that he was in control of them. This man's tolerance made you feel very aware of your own prejudices, and of your eagerness to criticise things. I'm using him as a model for something that is not actually able to accommodate the irritating smugness that he had about himself. When some islanders told us that there were snakes as well as lizards on the island we recounted the story to him. He said that he hoped he was lucky enough to see one, in an attempt I understood to undermine the mild critical panic that was growing in us, and the fear that he feared in his children. But I imagine that there was a time when his attitude hadn't yet solidified into this kind of smugness, when there was about it still the kind of suppleness that would enable him to perceive situations as if he could presume no prior knowledge of them and therefore in this way abate the prejudice that he might otherwise treat them with.

We were staying in a villa next door to the one the Irish man shared with his wife and children. It took us a couple of days to get on name terms and then we let the relationship peak at that. It seemed important to allow for this reticence on such a small island as this. From our balconies we could see each other's evening preparations spilling out into the sun, almost smell each other's desire always to live with that level of ease. We would always wave on first sighting and make nice faces at each other's children, but there it stopped, and we were able easily to get on with our own non-activities. We tried for a day or so to do just what we felt like doing at any one moment, but after that day inevitably we began to consider what our programme of activity might be. There was a walk that must have taken about 15 minutes to get to the beach, and it was over a hill, which in the heat took some effort to climb. On the way we passed what efforts at vegetation the island could manage and small lizards, which seemed ideally suited to the hot dust of the terrain. At the top of the hill there was a small military base, and across the track from it a helicopter pad was drawn onto the ground with white painted stones. I thought it looked quaint and wanted to take a photograph of it but remembered then that some months previously a group of British plane spotters had been arrested for spying. The quaintness of the base belied the strategic importance of the position of the island. It wouldn't really have made any difference, because we lost all the films that we took some time during packing for our return. This was a blow: it's sad to lose those images that you've never seen. Most of these images would have been sentimental reminders of happy times on the beach, aboard a boat, swimming in the sea, etc. And these were the ones I missed most of all. This was despite the fact that there were a couple of images that I had taken as work, not as images in themselves but as research towards another possibility. On the island the street lighting, and it's grand to refer to it as such because there were no streets really, just lanes connecting the houses, was attached to the posts that I guessed would have been erected in order to carry electricity.

They were dark wooden posts, which retained a very clear sense
that they had once been trees. That is to say that they were not
the result of thick trees being scraped down until they became
posts of uniform size and shape, but that within a fairly limited
range these were actual trunks that had been turned into posts
by being de-barked and de-branched. So there were small
variations in their appearance – this may have accounted for the
attention that I gave them. There was one of these posts a few
steps from our front door. It was at night, because it had to be
at night that I noticed the phenomenon that inclined me to take
a photograph of the post. At about three metres, or maybe even
a bit less, from the ground a lamp was attached to the post a bit
like this:

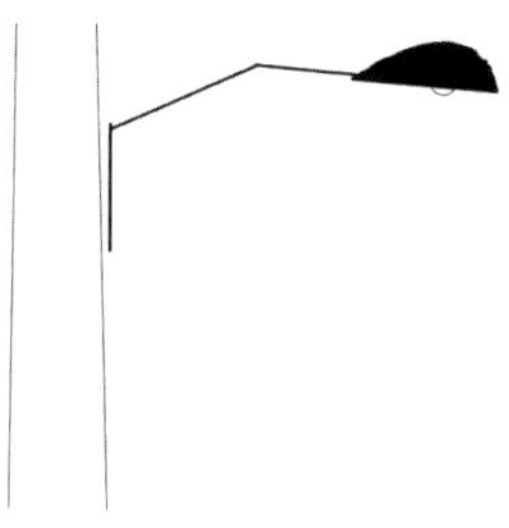

Because these posts were quite sparsely situated, the effect
at night was that the ground and the bottom of the post was
illuminated while the top of the post disappeared into the dark
sky. I liked this invisible image of the post going on forever,
and I sensed all the posts on the island together forming a kind
of inverse scaffolding that held our place in the universe. I
thought of Manzoni's plinth, and considered that I too might
be able to make a sculpture detailing this phenomenon. It
would be easy enough to rig up a similar apparatus and to put
it in a dark space so to light up the bottom and the ground
but not the top and the sky. This was the reason for the
photograph, and for a small drawing that I made of the lamp. I
made two photographs – during the day, so that the mechanics
of the illusion would be revealed. One image was of the whole
post and the other a close-up of the lamp fitting which quite a
fragile old tubular tin look to it: I think it was painted white, or

green perhaps; either would do so long as the particular colour gave some sense of age.

Manzoni's plinth is a plinth that is upside down so to suggest that the world is on it. It works both in a literal and in a figural way. Literally the world is actually as much atop it as it is underneath it. One thinks about gravity, and about the fact that everyone, wherever on the planet they may be, thinks that they are the right way up. But as the literal is further explored it starts to collapse. The work tends to be seen indoors – it has at least always been indoors when I have seen it, and so if it is really to be thought of as a plinth one must think of the building upside down and dug into whatever space it is on which the world is displayed. Even if the work were outside, the plinth is not so tall; surrounding buildings, trees and even people would beat it for height and it would therefore be these things on which the world would rest, and not the plinth itself. This challenge to the literal is important to the work, for it stops it having to perform and allows it to signify something in a more figural way. This is not a way that disavows all the playful literal intentions to which the work points; on the contrary, it rescues these intentions from having to be tested in relation to mechanical function. Maybe it's this urge towards mechanising ideas that the work is testing.

I don't think that I could achieve such a balance with my posts and lights, largely because the interest lies in something perceptual that would need to be recreated artificially if I were to make something that acted accordingly. I have no problem with the work having to be indoors in order to establish this kind of control over the light conditions. You might have thought I had a problem with that, because being indoors the illusion that the posts might go on forever would be counteracted, but I wouldn't mind this: in fact I would like it, because this would not be a reality that I could expect anybody to countenance. The problem I have is in the setting up of a perceptual illusion, because it seems to me that this confuses the relationship of the figural and the literal, confuses it by admitting the illusory, a kind of space which for some reason I consider wasteful.

I remember being seventeen and seeing a full moon that looked shaded on one side so that it appeared as the sphere that I knew it to be. This reflected back and turned the stable surface on which I was standing back into the sphere which I also knew it was. An elated kind of vertigo followed as I thought in disbelief about the fact that I was standing on the surface of a planet. I think that something of this feeling motivated my interest in the disappearing streets: when it came to selecting – though this seems an overly controlled and determining way of describing the act – places to photograph I thought that it might be this sensation of being on a planet that I was looking for; this extraordinary sense that was only interesting and affecting to me if it was grounded in something that I could, by employing my everyday pragmatics, think of as real. I considered how I could cast these spaces that I was turning into flat images by flooding them with some kind of moulding material. But I'd have to fill everything, and the filling would then become a casing out of which I'd have to cut the planet.

I wasn't, and am not, interested in things flooding over. What I like about the images is their limitations, that – as I have already said – the space which they represent is limited pictorially. I don't think they give the illusion that there is nothing beyond them, perhaps because the kinds of places they picture are so familiar. If they were to do this they would certainly fail.

The woman asked me who I belonged to, and I told her that I didn't belong to anybody. I must have said it suspiciously, for she gave me a look of contempt the nature of which I've only felt when I've known it to be merited, when I've felt guilty enough to internalise the implied criticism. The woman probably thought that I belonged to the council, or to a developer. People often think such things when they see you out in the street with a camera. They ask what the plans are for the area or for a building, or whether you're part of an action group campaigning against the building of something. Her first question was a little less intrusive, but she did not speak literally: can I help you, meaning: what the fuck do you think you are doing taking photographs on my street; or on our street, even.

My first art teacher told me about the power of looking, about the power of the gaze, if you like. He said how strange it seemed that when looking was about receiving light it should so often be understood as something that emanated from the body, as if by one's looking one were actually and even physically affecting what one looked at. Certainly a camera is a more obtrusive looking tool that the eye alone, and yet the camera can often serve as an excuse to look, can provide a kind of alibi for looking. On the day when I was asked to whom I belonged another woman approached me as I was preparing to take a photograph by reading the light off my subject with my light meter. My subject was an application for planning permit that had been displayed in order to fulfil the requirement to inform people of proposed developments to a site. I don't remember what the site was, nor of what the proposed development consisted – even though I photographed many of these permits I rarely read what they actually stated. She thought that the light meter was a scanner and she asked me if I was scanning the permit: I said no, that I was photographing it. Then she asked me what it was and I explained to her about planning permits and their purpose. And you're interested in this one? No, I told her, just in the general idea. Then she asked me if what I did was lucrative, and I told her that it wasn't. Well, I hope you haven't taken my picture, she said, and left with a kind of disapproving flirtatiousness.

Her chin, or rather the bit that connected her chin to her neck, was covered in hairs just longer than stubble.

The question about to whom I belonged remained with me. It seemed preposterous that I, an artist, an independent free thinker who valued the subjective above all else, should be asked such a thing. And yet I also knew that I wasn't just doing this for myself, that part of my motivation was dependent on the fact that I was doing some kind of job for others. I don't mean this in an altruistic way, that way in which one might consider one's motivation to be about the benefits that one's work has for society. I mean it in a much more direct way: I was essentially being paid to gear my subjectivity towards a context created by someone else, where I was in a sense performing the labour that was required by someone else's idea. I had tried to resist this way of working by establishing patterns of work for myself that were not linked to anybody else's requirements. But I doubted the authenticity of this approach because of the joy with which I greeted others' appreciation of my efforts.

You may or may not have noticed the plastic cable clips that are fastened around lamp-posts, traffic lights and railings around the city. They are remnants of notices and adverts – among them the planning permits – that people and organisations have wanted to make public in a cheap and effective way. When one of these announcements is torn down to make way for another the plastic clips that held it remain attached to the support. I had used these fastenings myself for a project, the funding of which depended on the work inhabiting the public realm. In that capacity the fastenings were merely functional, but I became interested in their appearance and perhaps in their significance, and considered the possibility of collecting them. I thought about this as something I could do independently; something that did not require any kind of funding and which I could pursue with my own time and lack of resources. It was not until I was offered a suitable opportunity to exhibit these things that I actually started collecting them, but my memory about the independence of the idea remained intact somehow, despite my having needed this spur to get going.

It sounds simple enough, a pair of scissors and a plastic bag the only equipment needed. I left the house with this equipment and walked to places where I'd noticed there to be a preponderance of the cable clips. These were junctions, usually, places where many people passed and would be sure to receive the various intended communications. On the walk to these places I considered the way in which I'd work. I knew that I would have to be somewhat opportunistic and this entailed finding a way of being able to have the scissors to hand but not visible, so it didn't look as if I was carrying an exposed blade. To this end I wore an old jacket, the pocket of which I didn't mind snagging with the black plastic-handled kitchen scissors, which for ease of access I had to carry blade down, like a gun in a holster. Previously I'd also had the foresight to choose quite a strong plastic bag in which to carry the cut cable clips because I knew their cut edges would be sharp enough to puncture a weaker bag. Most of the strong bags in our cupboard were from clothes shops and they had on them the logos of design labels.

I was equipped but I couldn't stop, or therefore start. I walked past a number of suitable and laden sites but at none of them could I bring myself to stop and start cutting the tags off. I told myself that I didn't want to panic people by taking out a large pair of scissors in broad daylight, and I thought that I would be better going out after dark – though I soon realised what a dumb idea this was. I reconsidered, and thought then my paralysis to be just like the one that accompanies the beginning of making any piece of work, that it was nothing to do with the public dimension of this act. I was also surprised at the narcissism that disinclined me from appearing to be a council cleaner or rubbish collector. I'm not even sure that this was a result of narcissism, but perhaps something that had more to do with my uncertainty regarding the way in which I might respond to people's approaches. I felt sure that these would happen; if taking photographs had elicited responses and comments from passers-by then the action that I was then postponing was bound to see me answering questions or responding to comments. I'm never quite sure as to the part that these incidents might play in my work. They do become useful things to talk about when people ask questions about the work, because they operate as charming asides, anecdotes, which if told properly can seem to shed light on what might be the motivation and meaning of the activity – as if carrying it out allowed one to gain certain insights.

Once I'd cut the first cable clip off the subsequent ones became easier. And it became easier still once there was a sufficient mass of them in my bag to keep it open, stable and receptive. Some of the clips must have been on the posts and railings for quite some time, for they were encrusted with dirt and painted over. Even those that looked to have been attached more recently had taken on the circular curvature of the post. This made them tangle around each other in the bag and form a kind of mass. I thought about the sculptural process to which this alluded. The individual clips, having been cast into a shape by the post, were re-cast collectively by the shape of the bag in which I was collecting them.

In the Tyrol, one is only allowed to pick mushrooms and other fungi on alternate weekends. This policy ensures the necessary replenishment of various species and formalises the self-imposed restrictions that any serious fungal forager would follow. It's not enough to know where the fungi grow, for they do often inexplicably favour some locations above others: one must also understand the cycles that will lead to the greatest crops. It's important never to pick all the fungi that one finds in one site, but to leave enough there to encourage subsequent growth.

Some people choose to eat the fungi when they are as fresh as possible. Their flavour then is delicate, so they are better eaten alone, for most other flavours will overwhelm them – light scrambled eggs are a good vehicle for them, but even with these it is crucial to maintain a low ration of scrambled egg to fungi. Those who allow the fungi to dry out for three, four, five days, and even weeks and months, enjoy the mustier and more powerful taste that they develop. This enables them to be used to flavour a number of dishes, and sometimes in combination with the most powerful ingredients such as game and red wine sauces.

Palms

Wanting the pictures to stand in for all these other things

Relationship of words and images – narratives and pictures

He might be talking to another person, and that other person
might just listen

**You're here now, and I don't care what you think about
what I'm going to tell you. So stop trying to get your face
to respond – forget the empathy, just listen. And I'm not
expecting you to interact either – no need for appreciative
comments. You said you wanted to see these, so here
they are, and you'll just have to listen to what I say.**

**Walk on to the stage and over to the table at which
there is a projector, a desk lamp and an A4 typescript.
Examine them both in a not too careful manner. Realise
that there is no chair there and go and fetch the one that
is at the piano. Place the chair at the table and sit on it.
Put down this sheet of directions on the table, pick up
the A4 typescript and follow its directions.**

Switch on the projector.

**Raise the light level on the projector to maximum light
setting – as you do this the lights in the room should
dim.**

**Switch on the desk lamp and angle it so that it allows
you to read this typescript.**

**Press the green button on the cable control to advance
the image – if it doesn't advance try pressing it again
until it does: it will jam relatively often. When you see
the image look at it for a few seconds and then read the
following aloud.**

Man walks on stage carrying a cue card and finds a table
on which is a projector, a desk lamp and an A4 typescript.

He examines this set-up and realises there's no chair so he goes to fetch the one that is at the piano. Seated now, he puts down his cue card and picks up the typescript which he begins to read. He switches on the projector and raises the light level on it to maximum. As he does this the lights in the room dim. He switches on the desk lamp and angles it to allow him to read the typescript. By pressing the green button on the cable control he advances to the first image. If the image jams he tries again to advance it using the green button until it is visible. He looks at the image for a few seconds and then begins to read out loud.

Press the green button again to advance to the next image. If it jams try again until the image is visible – when it is look at it for as long as you need and then read the following aloud.

36. THIRTY-SIX

You probably don't need to know about the previous stuff. Enough to say that it was more programmatic, designed to counter any engagement with things of unexplainable interest.

You can set yourself rules in order not to have deal with the randomness of your interest, and you may even be able to follow them.

Press the green button again to advance to the next image. If it jams try again until the image is visible – when it is look at it for as long as you need and then read the following aloud.

I've been looking for something to remind me of the possibility of things being special. I look for it in various instances, not because I want a typology of this subject, but because I want to see it appear easily – I want to persuade myself that it is available, that I don't have to grab it at the first instance.

EGG YOLK

BLUE CONTACT LENSES

See, these are things you can't take a picture of, some because they're private, and others because they don't keep still, because they're about something happening.

Press the green button again to advance to the next image. If it jams try again until the image is visible – when it is look at it for as long as you need and then read the following aloud.

It didn't happen suddenly, no more suddenly than anything else. When used in writing narratives the word 'suddenly' tends to refer to the writer's state of mind rather than the circumstances of the event he is writing. In this event what I am about to describe happened as suddenly or predictably as any event might happen. It just happenned; to say it was sudden would be to confuse the unexpected with the immediate.

This is it: the first man reached over and with one of his chips broke the yolk of the second man's fried egg so that he could dunk said chip in it and then eat it whilst continuing the conversation. The second man tried to hide his surprise and what might indeed have been his indignation. Instead he chose not to comment on what the first man had done, pretending that he considered it normal. He could not remember what they had been talking about, and since it was he that had been driving the conversation felt responsible for resuming it as quickly as possible so that the first man should not suffer his surprise. There was something quite noble about his actions in this respect, something that demonstrated his will to learn and not to remain entrenched in the way he was accustomed to doing things or thinking about them. His strain showed though in the nature of the dialogue which he attempted to launch.

– when I'm abroad I sometimes don't feel that they know how
to do proper meals there. For an Englishman a proper meal
is like this, with lots of things on the plate. The most typical
would be roast meat with potatoes and lots of different
vegetables, all on your plate together. Abroad they give
you your meat and then, after that, salad, and often with
no vegetables at all. It's like, I don't know how to eat it.
Not that it's the only way to eat, I suppose it's just habit.

The second man nodded in an interested way and continued
eating his chips, never again dunking them in the first
man's egg.

**Press the green button again to advance to the next
image. If it jams try again until the image is visible –
when it is look at it for as long as you need and then
read the following aloud.**

When asked to explain abstraction, the painter referred to
eggs and bacon.

**Press the green button again to advance to the next
image. If it jams try again until the image is visible –
when it is look at it for as long as you need and then
read the following aloud.**

The two men in this story will be refered to as the older
man and the younger man, for this was the most salient
differentiation between them. And the difference was quite
extreme: the older man in his mid-fifties and the younger
in his late teens.

**The are sitting opposite each other on the tube and
conversing in a language which is the younger man's
native tongue. Despite the fact that it is a language that
the older man speaks quite fluently, he is nevertheless at
a slight disadvantage. But he is experienced enough to
turn this disadvantage to his favour by drawing from the
younger man a caring and considerate sympathetic tone.**

They were talking about bread. Their words are translated here
from the younger man's language. The younger man spoke first:

– Is there still anything you need to buy?
– Only bread, but I'll get that at the last minute
– Bread?
– Yes, for toasting, I can't get decent sliced bread there
  for my toast in the morning
– Doesn't it go bad?
– No, I take a whole suitcase full and freeze it as soon as I
  get there. I can put it in the toaster from frozen, it's fine
– But you can get sliced bread there, my mother has it
– You can, but it's crap
– You're not set in your ways at all, are you!

**The older man chuckles, pleased that his little
eccentricity has been noticed. The two smile at each
other. Almost immediately the train arrives at their
stop and they get off together.**

**Press the green button again to advance to the next
image. If it jams try again until the image is visible –
when it is look at it for as long as you need and then
read the following aloud.**

They spoke little to each other, and their silence granted some
dignity to the act. The younger of the two men held a rope to
the end of which was tethered the top half of a pig's snout; the
lasoo secured behind the animal's teeth. As he pulled on his
rope the pig backed down and away in the opposite direction
and thereby made his body taught.

  The older man had been standing by the wall of the sty,
sharpening his knife. It was an old knife, sharpened so many
times that the act had long ago began to wear away the blade.
It was now a thin and delicate instrument that the man rubbed
on his stone.

  When it was done, and the pig lay on its side at peace from
the convulsions that only seconds previously had jerked its
corpse into reflexive life, the elder massaged it tenderly, to let

the last of the blood out of the small incision he had made in its throat.

With care they picked it up from the hind and fore legs and carried it into the barn, where they laid it on the stone floor. Steam from the large water boiler had warmed the space up and made it comfortably damp. The younger poured some of the boiling water on the pig's skin, and the older vigorously scraped off the hairs that seemed to lose their attachment with the heat. They worked their way around the pig's body and once all the hairs were removed, the elder yanked off its hoofs with a spike at the back of his scraping implement. With this same spike he exposed the tendons at the extreme of the pig's hind legs and used these as eyelets through which to thread the hooks of his weighing scale. This he then lifted and secured to a beam. After shuffling the pig into position, he began to pull: this set pulleys in motion that in turn lifted the pig into the desired position, head down and with stomach facing outward. Before anything else he cut out the animal's rectum, making sure to cut out more than he needed, just to make certain. He threw this away and then cleaned his knife almost too carefully, almost as if wanting to delay things a bit. The younger meanwhile stroked the carcass up and down. He was trying to get a measure of its size, but was also finding some delight in what they had achieved thus far. The both strained to read the weight of the pig by the glow of the single exposed bulb that gave a minimal light in the barn. The younger then placed a large black plastic bucket under the head for the bowels. These fell into the bucket with a huge slop when the elder sliced the pig's stomach open. Beige and snot green bowels that the older had only to guide down and out of the cavity. He used his knife again to release the bowels from the last anchor that they retained on the pig's throat and then with his hack-saw cut open the rib-cage and removed the head. This he placed nose up in the bucket, atop the bowels like a garnish. With the same saw he sliced the carcass in half down the spine and then he and the younger each took one of the two pieces to the farmer for approval.

Neither the younger or the older were able to make any sense of the farmer's decision not to make black puddings with this pig. If these had been required they would have had to collect the blood in a bowl as it first spurted and then streamed from the animal's throat when they killed it. Whilst it collected one of them, probably the younger, would have had to stir the blood vigorously with sticks, to avoid coagulation. It would have been wrong for them to take the blood themselves, and so it was wasted as a stain on the yard.

Press the green button again to advance to the next image. If it jams try again until the image is visible – when it is look at it for as long as you need and then read the following aloud.

From her perspective it must have made sense to tell the story. When you feel embarrassed about something you can either abandon it or expose it to such an extent that your own publicised awareness of the thing renders it no longer embarrassing. She chose the second option because she wasn't prepared to give up the beauty that she felt the blue tinted contact lenses gave her.

She wasn't going to lie about it; every kid in her class knew that she didn't need glasses. It would have been nice to produce some practical reason for which she might have to wear them, and then to portray the blueness as a mere eccentricity. 'Well, if I have to wear them they might as well be blue', she could have said, as if considerations about her own appearance were secondary. But without recourse to such a justification she had to confront the pure narcissism of the act of wearing the lenses by exaggerating the practical difficulties that they caused her. She would excuse herself from class in order, she said, to reposition one of the lenses correctly; spend half an hour each morning and night on maintenance; attempt to get excused from games because of eye irritation; refuse to go swimming. Even on holiday she would refuse to swim, despite the desperation of her parents who were exasperated that her urban vanity should have travelled with her to the Caribbean beach. Her grandmother, though, in whose house they were staying, seemed to understand. Despite the fact that she objected to the lenses, she was proud to see in the girl's reluctance to remove them something of the vanity that she had expressed

in her youth. This was a vanity from a time when people took
more care in their appearance; when people would not let
practicalities stand in the way of looking smart.

At the end of the girl's first day back at school she waited
for the bus home with her friends. 'It was so hot and dry there',
she said, 'that my contacts stuck to my eyes'.

**Press the green button again to advance to the next
image. If it jams try again until the image is visible –
when it is look at it for as long as you need and then
read the following aloud.**

There was no reason why he should have minded the comment.
He knew himself that it was awful stuff to work with,
particularly in the cold. Cement dried his hands badly enough
in the summer, but in the winter they got so cold that they lost
all sensation and therefore also the wisdom to know when to
stop, the wisdom that would have allowed his body to define
its own limits through pain.

It was while he was taking a break from his work that he saw
the man, and he nodded out of politeness, to try to put the man
at ease. He'd often experienced the discomfort that people felt
around him manifested through reluctance to engage. Being
a builder made him something close to a criminal in the eyes
of many. He imagined this man thinking that the only reason
he had been acknowledged by a builder was that he had been
mistaken for a master criminal on the lookout for some muscle.
He wondered how the man, if he were a master criminal, would
manage to approach him without compromising his secret. He
imagined the man saying something like: you look like a man
who could break something. To which he would answer: and
what kind of breaking have you got in mind? Oh, the lucrative
kind. That would have been the conversation that would have
seen him involved, and who knows what excitement that might
have brought. Instead of this the man tried clumsily to suggest
that he knew something of the builder's work: don't envy you
working with cement in this cold. A simple extension of a
weather conversation, to which the builder replied: that's right,
feels like your hands are in ice, still, you've got to use it.

He wasn't sure why he allowed himself to be patronised so easily; he did have some sense that it was wise to avoid confrontation, that this would help him beat his stereotype. But he had bright red plastic gloves on for fuck's sake, of course it was horrible to work with cement in this cold, it was horrible in all weathers, but it was his job, what made him think he should say anything about it?

Press the green button again to advance to the next image. If it jams try again until the image is visible – when it is look at it for as long as you need and then read the following aloud.

He'd picked the kind of glasses you'd have expected him to choose following a trauma: thick-rimmed, big and rather square. His clothes still gave off that vegetal smell of hash, but there was something different about his levels of concentration and attentiveness. The visit was unexpected. In the past he would have to be almost bullied into coming to see his family. Now he was seeking his place here, demanding it quite gently, as if to acknowledge he needed it.

★

When he got to the railings at which he'd normally lock his bike, he realised that he'd left his lock behind. This meant that he had to cycle all the way to work instead of leaving his bike here as he usually did. It surprised him how quickly he got to work like this, but nevertheless he spent half the day devising a scheme that would make it impossible for him ever to forget his lock again.

Press the green button again to advance to the next image. If it jams try again until the image is visible – when it is look at it for as long as you need and then read the following aloud.

The man eating the 99p sandwich facing the pillar by the door, with another sandwich bulging out of his jacket pocket.

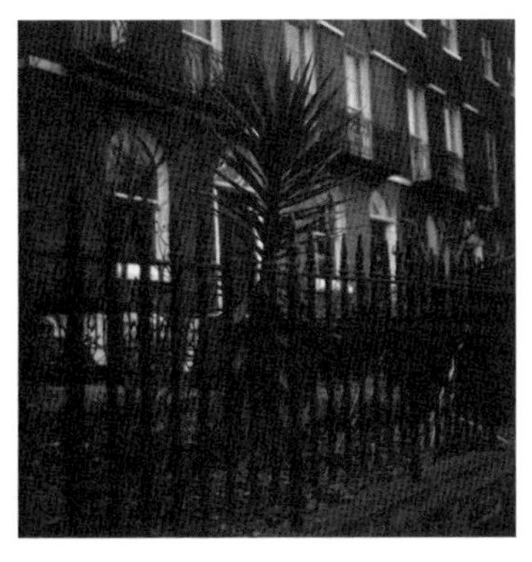
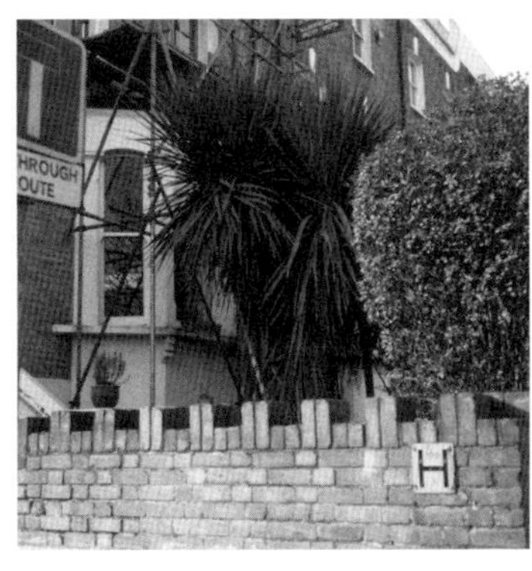
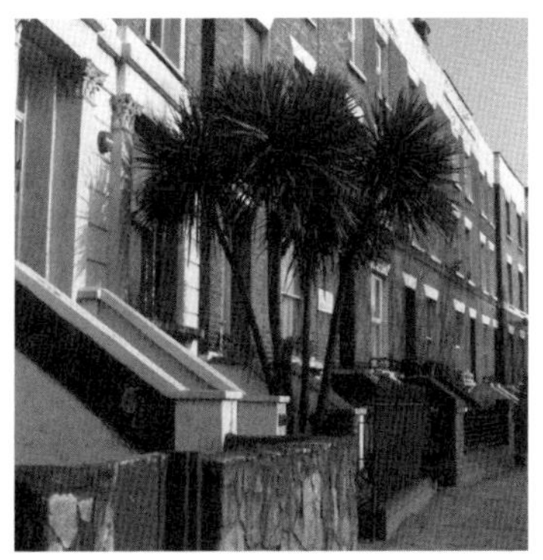
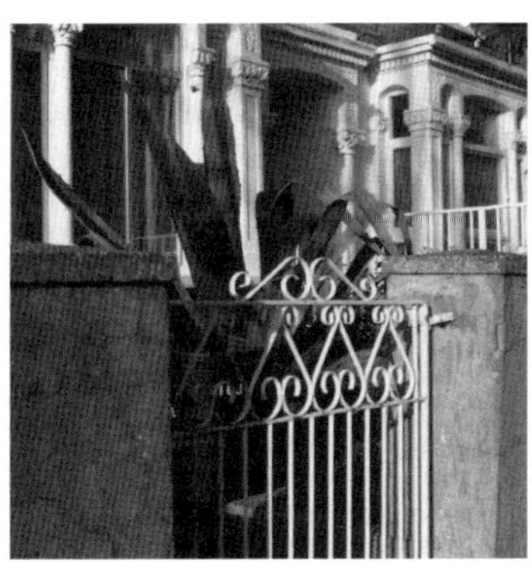
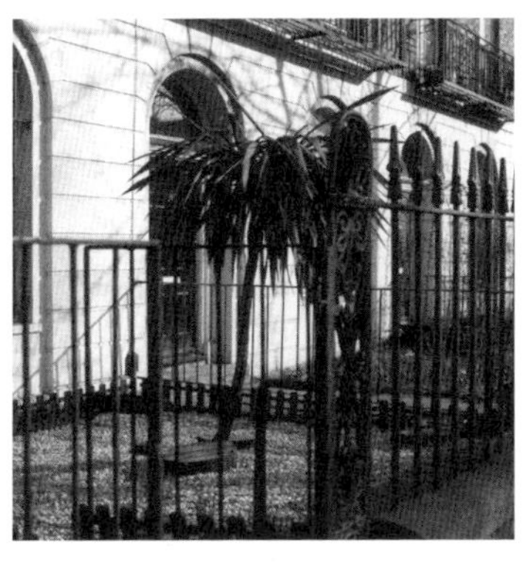
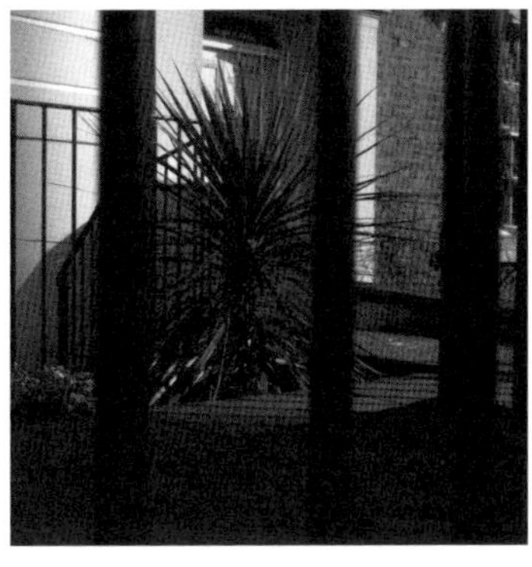

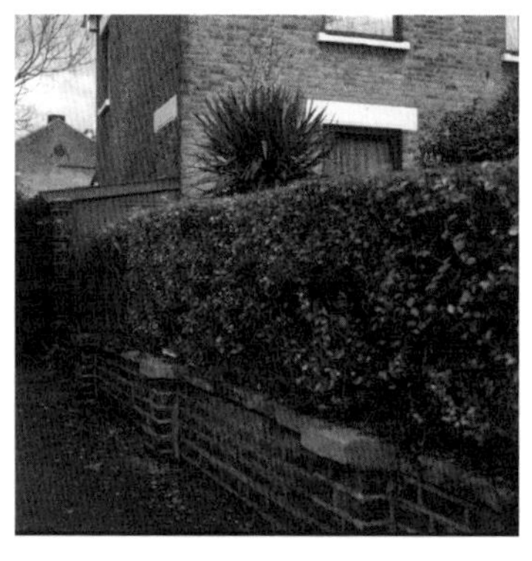
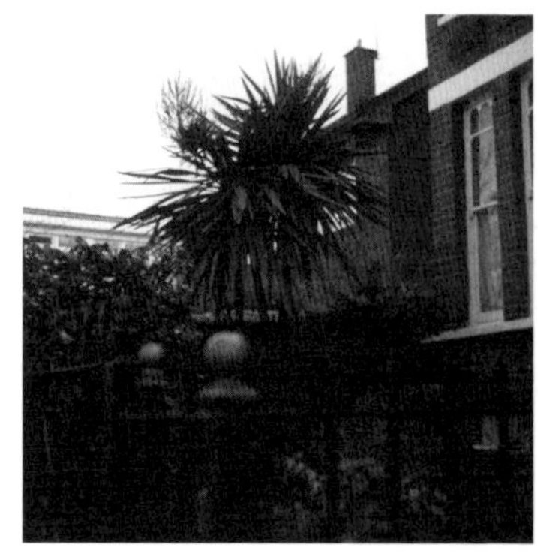
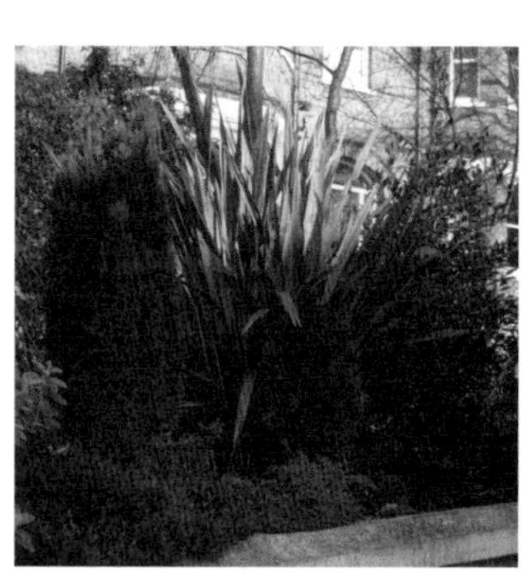
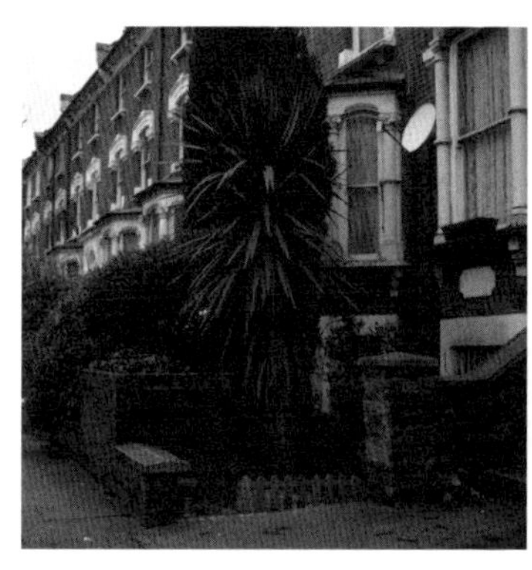
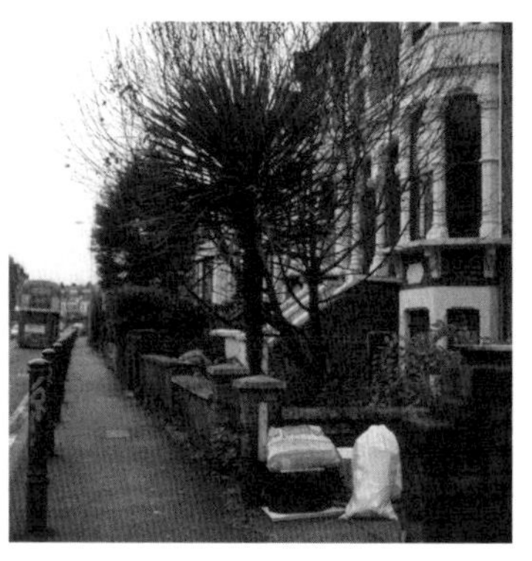
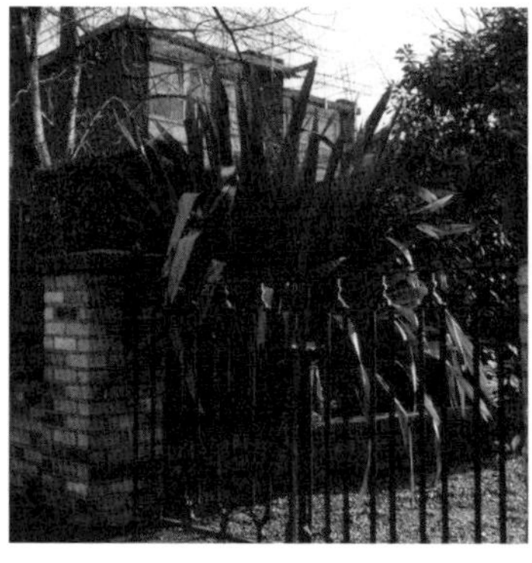

Three Shows

Part 1

Jason told me that he thought a lychee stone could help him to explain what he feels when he sees some people's brown eyes. He said they made him feel the sensation of swallowing them, not the whole eye, but just the iris.

I asked him if that was why he took the photograph, and he said that it was, but that it wasn't enough. He explained that he'd also tried to paint it, the object and the sensation, despite the fact that he'd found it very difficult to paint before.

When I asked him why he wanted to paint it, he said that he had this thing about all the materials: the paints, the brushes, the canvas, and setting up the space. The smell also, he loves the smell of the turpentine and the oil.

I told him how great I thought it was that he had the space and the imagination to do what he wanted, and in a way he agreed. But he also tried to tell me how he felt it was easy to enjoy the space, with all the materials and the smells, but that it was something else to have to live with all the things that he did.

Part 2

I told Jason how nice his place looked, with all that space, and the garden… He agreed, but said that he didn't really want a garden, but a yard, with large doors onto the street. He wanted to be able to keep things there that he would otherwise have to throw away. Some of the yard he wanted to be covered, but I think he must have meant that he also wanted something like a cellar or an old utility room when he talked about the kind of space in which you'd find things like shovels, broken bicycles, baskets of apples… He said part of it was about the dank smell that these places have. He told me that his aunt had a room like that, and he remembered how she liked her fruit to be really ripe, almost going off, and that she prepared it with a knife and fork before eating it. The thing was, that she was happy to keep stuff around, even though she had no immediate use for it. I said that she must have been very patient, he said that was what he lacked.

When I asked him whether he didn't need patience for his
garden, he said that some things just grew by themselves,
grew bigger than you could imagine. He told me that their size
wasn't actually a reflection of their favourable conditions, but
that they only bother to grow this tall when they can't get the
sun lower down.

And he explained that despite all his best efforts to control
everything, it was impossible to avoid what arrived from
elsewhere. A dahlia of pains and joys which my hot heart wept
for you. That was how he described it. Otherwise what, he said?
Pink and purple flowers against an old brick wall.

He didn't answer me when I asked if his aunt was still alive,
but he told me that she'd had a conservatory built at the top of
the house to show off her pot plants, glass tables, ornaments
and framed butterflies. When he stayed with her he'd get up
early in the morning and go to the conservatory to look at all
the stuff and to read the magazines in the rack, which she
was very proud of because it was hand painted. He said that
he thought the real reason he went there was so that his aunt
would find him there when she got up, so that she would think
he liked the same things as she did.

And he said that she spent so much time on her conservatory
that she stopped looking after the orchard. The house had been
her father's, but he had never lived there, he'd had it as a kind of
weekend place outside the city. He told me that her father knew
she wouldn't look after the orchard, and even though the trees
he had worked so hard to maintain were going to ruin, he was
content. I asked him to explain, and Jason said that it was as if
he didn't really care about the trees themselves, but more about
being remembered as the person who had been able to nurture
them. Jason seemed to understand this.

Part 3

Jason told me that when he started to look for his own space,
he didn't even know what a field looked like. He comes from
somewhere much flatter than this, where the fields aren't tipped
up for you to look at. He didn't know how they divided the land

there, only that they had no hedges. He said he didn't want to go back there, but he did want to find a place in which he had some reason to live. It wasn't enough for him just to like a place, or to find it convenient – he thought he needed a better reason.

I didn't know how you would go about finding a better reason, and he said that he didn't either, but that learning to say the names of the fields had helped him to feel a part of something.

I asked him if it had taken much time to establish something, and he said that it had, but that he'd enjoyed how the labour had made him feel. He told me that he'd promised himself that he'd remember this when he started doing his own work again. He tried to use the room which had been the base for all the labour, where all the tools and materials were kept, as his work-space. He said that he thought this would make it easier to start again.

I wondered whether that had worked, and he said that for a while it had, though he was also drawn to working outside, especially when the weather was still nice. He said he'd made this out of broken bricks and cement but that he'd had to break the bricks because he'd only kept those that were intact. He hadn't wanted to break the bricks into pieces that were too small because then, when he mixed them with cement, they would just have formed concrete. Neither though did he want the pieces to feel like blocks, because he would then have had to build it in a regular manner, and he didn't want to do that. He said he had wanted it to appear complete, rough but also complete, so it had to be made out of these small pieces; bricks would have made it look as if it could carry on growing. He'd decided that to make it appear complete the pile should be more or less spherical, and when he came to building it he realised that he couldn't do it unless it had a flat base. I didn't get the difference, and he said that he could of course have built something like it that had no base, something very similar but which would not have been built in the way he wanted to build it

It seemed to me that he must have been pleased about how he had achieved the transition, about how he had managed to use the materials of one kind of work for another. He asked me not to forget that he used to live in a flat, and that because he now owned the outside as well as the inside, it was more difficult for him to know where the edges were.

Part 4

He explained that it was one thing to own the inside of something, just a contract really, but that it was quite different to own the outside as well. He said that in a hotel you don't even own the inside and that, weirdly, that makes you look after yourself better. You pamper yourself more I guess, and take a bit longer to do things like getting dressed and brushing your teeth. He told me that the first time he'd stayed in a hotel was with his father, and that he'd found a camera that someone had left behind in a drawer.

He said that he hadn't wanted it to be in the middle of the picture, because he didn't want it to look symbolic. He wanted the feeling of the thing, and the feeling of the place, but he didn't want it to mean anything else.

I wondered how he decided what to photograph, and he told me that even he couldn't remember why he'd taken many of the pictures. With this one he said he thought it must have been quite a hot day, or else he wouldn't have stopped. He didn't think it was to do with it being a quarry, but maybe more about the blocks being piled up and looking like bricks.

With this, he thought it was about it casting a shadow, even when it was folded up, tied together and vertical. The colour too, the way the pink and the green were affected by being what they were. He said something about their colour only being possible because of what they were.

Part 5

I asked him what that stuff about swallowing eyes was all about and he tried to explain that when you blow onto a baby's face, it will try to suck in your breath. It's a technique that you can use when you take a baby swimming and you want it not to be scared of putting its head in the water. You blow on its face just before dunking it, and because it fills its lungs with air, it won't take in any water. He said that this was called the paradoxical reflex, and that it must be called that because most people would expect the baby to resist their breath rather than inhale it.

He asked me also to think about the way in which coloured contact lenses change people's eyes, the way they make their eyes look opaque. This had made him realise that people's eyes normally look transparent, so that you almost can't look at them, that it's as if you look through them. He said that the first time he'd realised this was at a bus stop where he saw a girl wearing purply-blue contacts. He noticed a wasp landing on her black leather coat. He could have ignored it, but then he would have felt terrible if it had stung her. He could have told her about it, but then she might have panicked and made the wasp sting her. Her bus arrived before he could decide.

I still didn't understand and I asked him to explain more. He said he didn't know himself what it was about, but that he'd try to tell me what it felt like. He asked me to imagine one brown eye, and actually only the iris. He said it was as if he swallowed it without having put it in his mouth, and he made that popping noise that I can't make when you put your finger in your mouth. Then he described it falling slowly down his throat, and constricting his breath. He said it never reached his stomach, but that it became something else instead. I think he said something about it transforming itself into the substance of the shape it had cast.

Two Clamped Books

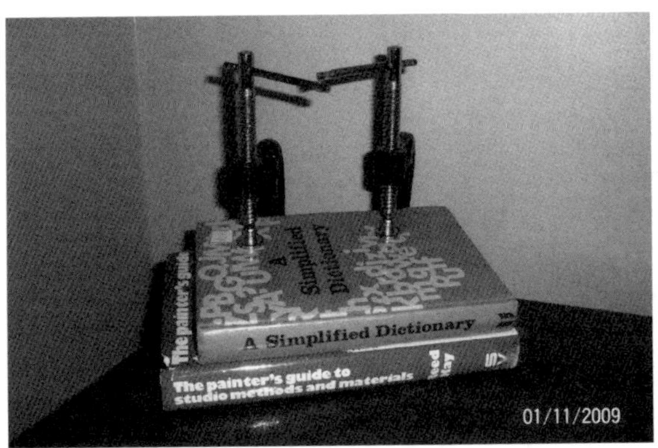

In the Shape of
What We Know

He called first thing that morning to tell me she'd died the night before. His voice quickly lost its initial serenity, and turned into a high-pitched whinny of fake-sounding emotion. Despite the hurt he must have felt I resented him succumbing like this. I think he may have taken my coldness badly, as an insult even, certainly a reproach, because later, when he called to tell about the funeral, it was my brother he chose to contact.

I started anyway. I'd been meaning to do it for ages, and today was the day I'd set aside. I think you have to flick it on bit by bit and then spread it later, leaving it meanwhile to adhere. I'm no good at it. I try to save time by spreading it before it's ready, and most of it falls off. So I scrape it up off the ground not to waste any, and then I'm using stuff that's full of grit and even harder to work with.

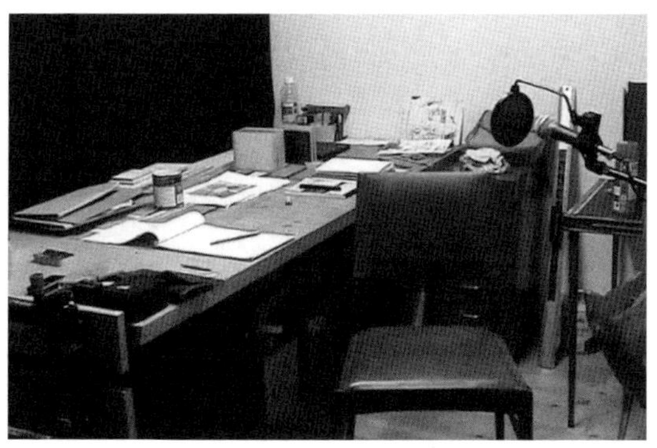

After the service she was driven to the cemetery and we all made our own way there. By the time I arrived she had already been put into the mausoleum, and the opening to her tomb was being bricked up. We stood around in rough order of seniority waiting to do something like pay our last respects, waiting to satisfy our curiosity by having one last look at the coffin.

When my turn came a man in blue overalls was rendering the brickwork that sealed the tomb. Sweat ran down his face, which, through its concerned expression, betrayed its proximity to death. He was using a much wetter mix than mine, softer and

more malleable, which he worked easily and at great speed –
even with all these emotional people unwittingly scrutinising
his performance, he did his job expertly.

I had wanted to build a shed in the garden where I could work,
so that I wouldn't have to spend money on a studio outside.
I was also uncertain about the aesthetic of a studio, and the
way it pretends to a division between one's life and one's work;
the way it pretends to shut out the aesthetic of one's life, those
sentiments that can overwhelm any interest one might have in
one's own work.

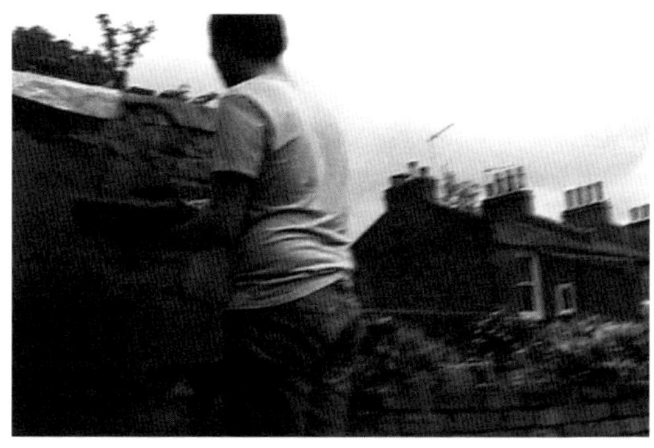

I invented the principle that it was important to build the shed
only with materials that I had already and, because I didn't have
enough, was then able to give myself the excuse to build a small
hut for the kids instead. That phrase: 'for the kids' sounds so
falsely naturalistic: as if I were quite at ease with having these
three dependent creatures in my life.

I put together a sub-structure made from a combination of
scaffolding planks and other bits of timber left behind when we
had had some work done a year before. ('Having work done'
was and sounds like another badge of responsibility.) I shutter-
boarded the walls with flooring material and mirrored the shape
of our house by giving the hut a single pitch roof.

Where I was short of materials I scavenged the Hackney streets, which are rich with the leftovers of home improvement. By the time I got to installing the fixtures on the doors, I had become tired of how long it was all taking and I skimped, and neither did I bother to glaze the windows.

I did not presume the design was original, but neither did I realise that the hut was so similar to the garage next to which I lock my bike at work. The work that saves me from doing that which I would do in the shed that I never built for myself. Blindly susceptible to the most immediate influences, I seemed to have absorbed this structure and reproduced it integrally.

After the funeral everyone was confused about what to do. She would usually have been the one to make sure that something was organised by booking a venue for a family lunch. No-one had thought to do anything like that, or at least those that may have done so had considered it too crude to show concern for such practicalities.

It was somehow decided that those who lived there would make their own plans, individual or collective, while those who had come from out of town would accompany my grandfather home for lunch. We were told that some dishes had been ordered from what had been for many years their favourite restaurant.

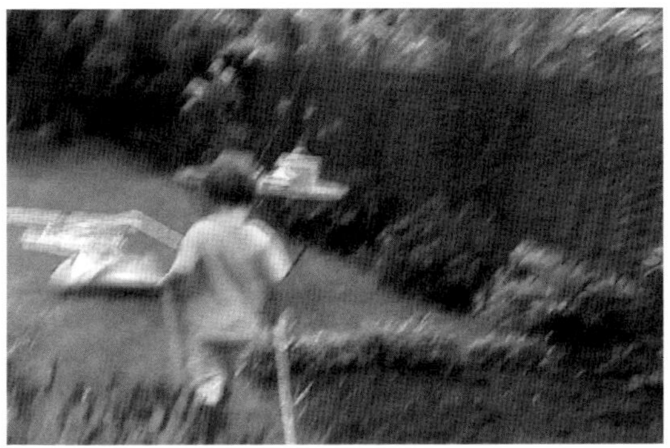

I went with my cousin to collect the prepared lunch from the restaurant and we were greeted with much commiseration. Passing the kitchen, in which large women prepared vegetables among the stoves, wood grills and dull red pans, we were shown to a back room where the waiters waited for their shift to begin, already dressed in their white jackets and black ties. Table waiting is still a profession there, and not a job young people do during holidays or while holding out for something better.

The back room had a bar in it and felt as if it might sometimes be used for functions for which the dining room was too small to cater. Extra chairs and tables were kept there, along with the table linen and coat racks. There was a dim light, a theatrical light, dramatically redundant now but nevertheless the light by which we saw. Drinks were served at the bar for the waiters to take to table.

I hoped they would offer us a drink while we waited. They didn't and I didn't ask because I know how quickly news travels in small towns like these. The lady owner of the restaurant pretended to try to console us in order to reveal to us her own anguish. She dressed in a young and glamorous manner, as if to stress the self-conscious effort it took to maintain a restaurant in such traditional style.

Back at the house we ate gloomily and talked about what we could. This included the food. 'How delicious,' we all said. 'As ever,' my grandfather said, 'it never changes, as good as it always is.' This was food to be judged in relation to how closely it met its paradigm, which was established through time in one's gustatory memory. It was not about what new sensations it introduced but about how well it reproduced something already known to us.

His understated assertion urged us to value what we knew, and always to use these occasions as small reminders of what was. Truth, he seemed to imply, lies in being able to perpetuate and continue to bridge time with an ongoing formulation of the known.

Any instrument has its own discipline, and the cello, because it has no keys or frets, teaches her to make judgements that are not predetermined; in order to confirm that the notes she is playing are correct, she cannot rely simply on having put her fingers in the right places. It teaches her to listen, and to make decisions based on an assessment of her own judgements. She also learns about musical principles, about which she already knows much more than I do.

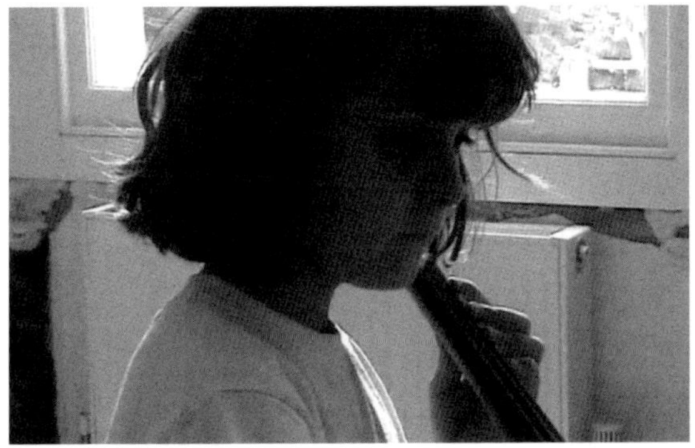

It can be hard to get her to practise, and it's difficult to know how hard to push. She's quick to notice me succumbing to the temptation of getting her to fulfil my own frustrated ambitions, of denying her the indolence that I so readily perform before her. One fights so hard against the inevitability of their mimicry.

They ask me what I teach them, and I have to say that I try to teach them anything they want to learn, as if it were all there in the landscape of the future, bound to no past and waiting to be collected. I'm not able or prepared to configure it for them, or indeed myself, in the shape of what we know.

Mensch

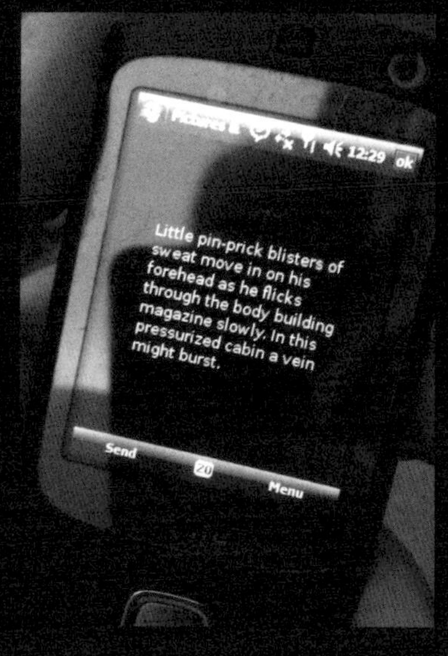

Throughout the service
he tries to insist on strict
adherence to the liturgy, and
in his sermon he confesses
himself to be a devoted fan
of Shirley Bassey.

He makes the communicants
who are shuffling slowly
towards the alter listen to a
recording of a sentimental
ballad from 'Mamma Mia.'

Many of the dads sway
from side to side as they
sing hymns accompanied
by guitar and flute.

*

Little pinprick blisters of
sweat appear on his fore-
head as he flicks through the
body-building magazine slowly. In this pressurised cabin a
vein might burst.

After some drinks his skin
turns red and the thin strands
of dyed yellow hair on his
head are cast into stark relief.
He says he used to be a straw-
berry blond.

His high-waisted trousers are
designed to flatter his bulging
stomach, and his long jacket to
make him look taller.

*

He uses art as an excuse to
disengage himself from the
pursuit of his ambitions.

He tends to write objective
texts that imply universality
and is resentful of those whose
work employs more particular
and evocative language.

He tends to try to establish
rules and simple patterns but
is aware that he operates best
in a more complex and less
regimented manner.

*

Seconds after the Falangist
song begins he puffs out his
chest and raises his right arm
aloft before him. With his left
arm he supports his new folding bicycle.

Every morning he winces at
his dishevelled image in the
shaving mirror and is thankful
for the fixed co-ordinate of his
small moustache.

Those who know him so-
cially can be offended by the
offhand manner in which he
treats them.

*

At the car boot sale he
was suspicious about his
motivation to buy the carved
wooden stool in the shape of
two cupped hands.

As items that evinced a
self-evident function, the two
small G clamps seemed an appropriate purchase. That they
were painted a deep brown
colour was an added benefit.

Because he couldn't choose
which he liked best, and
because they were so cheap,
he bought all seven walking
sticks.

*

He embraces men he knows
and has not seen for some
time firmly, and palpates the
fat around their back to know
their state of health. He deals
in percentages.

He leans out of the car window to point out the place
where some years previously
they had found a rock with
an ancient carved image of a
sheep's head.

He carries the debris close
to his body, supporting the
weight on his chest and
stomach.

*

They rest together on one-
piece wooden picnic tables
drinking tea and smoking roll-
ups. As others arrive they are
greeted warmly and quizzed
about their journey.

Young men who ride without
the appropriate safety gear are
subject to angry derision and
sharp criticism.

In order not to fail the MOT
he bombed home and changed
the rear tyre. He then raced
back to the garage with a loose
axle. The mechanic said he
was crazy.

*

When his wife asks him where
he is going he happily replies
that he is going wherever he
wants to go.

He is currently separated from
his wife because he went out
to buy a new tyre and came
back with another bike.

The lane discipline on a nearby roundabout is impossible
to fathom. On his approach
he has to slow down from
110mph virtually to zero in a
very short distance.

*

He refuses ever to plan ahead
and is outraged when others
do the same. This makes it
difficult for any of them to ask
for the help they so desperately need.

He has scant regard for line
management, and even takes
pleasure in undermining
those who have a lesser
responsibility than he.

He has achieved his position
without really knowing anything and now resents having
to rely on others to deliver
content.

*

He imagines that conditions
need to be absolutely perfect
in order for him to achieve
anything.

To move on he distances himself from what he perceives to
be the mistakes of his past.

Because of a long series of
aborted and unredeemed
projects he now finds herself
advanced in years and with
little to show.

*

Translating
Chapter 2

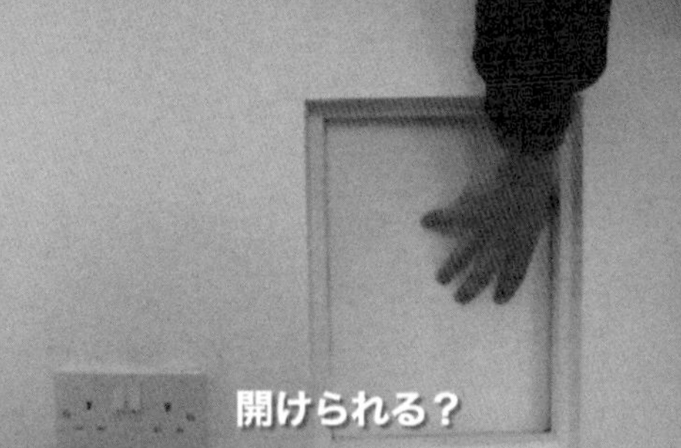

– Okay, this chair you mean?
– By the window is nice.
– By the window.

– Start again. Let me just get a pen.
– Rugatka
– Rugatka?
– That's the word in Hebrew
– Sling I think

– Do you want me to pull the curtain a bit?

– I'm not going to say the title, or do you want me to say
  the title? No. The Chasm. The landscape was severe.

★

– So I gucss we'll get there…
– We'll get there, we'll go to the space. It's just, because,
  because the original idea had been to go to the space and
  do a performance, and it might have been a performance in
  front of… I mean, I think the start of it getting confusing or
  kind of interesting was when Matthew started asking about,
  you know: So who's the audience to be? Do we invite people?
  Is it open to anybody? And then… you know, that, that
  sense of it being a performance in front of a group of people
  became a little bit… began to feel a bit wooden, somehow.
– You sitting and there's like a… an audience
– Yeah, me sitting and there's a group of people there and
  I do the thing
– And you do your thing
– So that's when it seemed to be, it seemed a bit dense and
  a bit dull somehow to do it that way. It seemed a bit…

– It's just quite, It's just quite involving because it occupies
  you. It occupies your mind. I guess it seems as if one's
  you know, good at doing it.
– In what way? Like one hundred per cent occupying of
  the mind?

–   At times yes, almost.
–   Because the Spanish and the English.
–   Yeah, and because it's trying to think about the word and
    trying to think about, you know. I mean, I find I drift in and
    out. You know, sometimes I'm conscious or if I find myself
    performing kind of gestures, sometimes I catch myself being
    aware of that gesture even if it wasn't, you know… So that's
    why in a way for me… the space seems like it should be
    seems like a starting point.

★

–   If you were to do the performance where would it be?
–   What if, well, I don't know, but I mean, I guess…
–   Well if you had to, if there was audience coming.
–   I mean, I guess if you had audience coming you'd have
    to have a consideration about where you sat and what
    they looked at and…
–   You'd have to be sitting down?
–   Yeah, you'd probably be sitting down
–   You would be sitting down?
–   Yeah

–   It would what, again?
–   Well there's more kind of… there's more… of a sort of
    making an effort to perform if he's standing up, isn't there.
–   Yeah, I mean
–   Rather than kind of going through…
–   It depends what the performance is I guess

★

–   There is a box full of bones. From the last artist who
    showed in this gallery!

★

–   There, it's the biggest wall, people think that's the more
    important bit. That's the kind of… but that's okay

– Size is not necessarily related to importance, is it?
– No, but I think that…
– Size doesn't really matter
– I think that's kind of how people think whether or
   not it's true.

★

– Yeah, I think it's over there, No, there, there.
   That's better, no?
– Yeah. From the beginning or from where we stopped?
– Let's try from where we stopped. A bit, like five
   sentences before.
– From where we stopped the first time, maybe.
– Okay, yeah

– So, I don't know… Shall we do it sentence by sentence?
– Slowly
– Slowly
– And quietly
– And quietly
– Because there's an echo. The goat jumped from stone
   to stone like a rubber ball. A rubber ball.

– Sometimes she turned to look back. Tall… Tall and upright.
   With her black hair and the big satanic beard. She hid
   among the bushes and… Somersault? Did somersaults in
   the air and jumped. The dog walked behind her. Achieving
   territory in a way that was difficult for him. The boy chased
   both of them. Out of an understanding that the chase would
   have to end quickly. Because of the… Because the abrupt
   part of the mountain finished shortly.

– The boy tried to catch her by the horn. Hanged desperate
   from the edge of the cave. When he saw how impossible it
   was he came back to the place where the shepherd was and
   told him what happened. Damn beast, murmured the old
   man. We'll go back now boy, we'll go back now boy. First
   we'll out the… the… flock – the flock in the stable. Flock.

Between them both they locked the goats and when they'd done this the shepherd and his grandson descended towards the… deserted land and they approached the edge of the cave. The goat continued on her legs in the bushes. The dog barked at her from outside. Give me, give me your hand grandfather. I'll go down said the boy. Careful boy. I'm very scared you're about to fall. Don't worry grandfather. The boy… em… the boy, no, the boy pushed out the bushes from the mouth of the cave. He sat on the edge and he pushed himself, around until he held himself with his hands really until the edge of the cave. He slid down… he scratched his feet down until the edge of it, until he, landed on one of the… the bits that stick out from the entrance. He grabbed the animal's horns in one hand and pulled them. The animal, seeing that she was being held, kicked so strong backwards that she lost grip on the earth. She fell and with her fall dragged the boy down to the bottom of the… hole. Not a scream was heard, not one complaint, not even a small murmur. The old man looked into the mouth of the cave. Boy, boy, he screamed in a desperate way. Nothing was heard. Boy, boy. It seemed mixed with the murmur of the wind, could be heard a cry of pain that was rising from the bottom of the hole. Standing alongside himself.

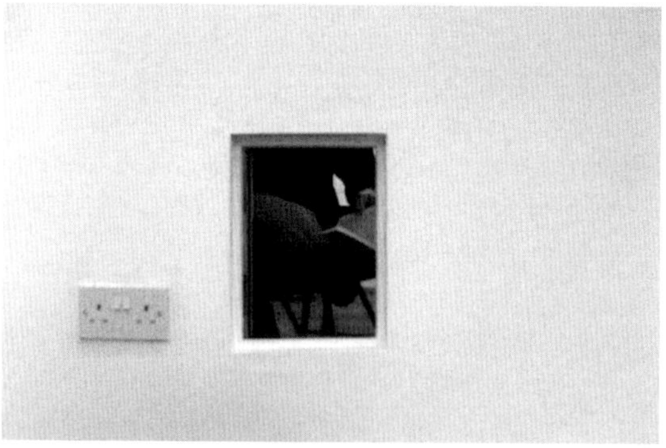

–   Look. What is this?
–   Well it's a hole, there's a little door here.
–   Can you open it?
–   I think you can

–   And where's it leading? No?
–   I just need to bash it, hang on
–   Maybe you can do it from there?
–   From the other side?

★

–   This is, you know, it's a dark place isn't it.
    It's just off the high street but…

★

–   Do you want a drink? I'm getting a pretty dry mouth.
–   Glass of cream

★

–   Okay, let's… Yeah, I think that's quite a nice frame.
    The Chasm
–   I'm not sure why it's funny
–   It's just, it's just so… The landscape was severe.
    Very, very severe

★

–   It's a really authentic question, it's absolutely worth asking
    I think but it… but, I'd never want to answer it myself.

–   People do carry around an idea of this is why something
    can be art and this is why something else can't be. And you
    know, even people with very radical pretensions tend to
    have those sort of definitions lodged in their head because
    they need those definitions to have an everyday life. And
    occasionally they slip out and someone will say, you know,

you're kind of saying this can't be art, or you know, this is
this and it's not that. People are always caught out on that,
they think that there's kind of a...
— It's probably a good sign that this question keeps popping
up, yet to be defined. You know, that it does manage
somehow to escape.

★

— Is that it?
— That's it
— That's the end of the story?
— Yeah
— You translated everything?
— Yeah
— But you don't want to go on a ladder?

★

— That's my phone. Hi Robin. No problem. I was just calling
to say. I left you a note about it. I went out onto the terrace
and... a chair must have been blown over by the wind and it
must have fallen on... on the... on that... fish bowl that we
lumbered you with when we left.
— Okay, see you soon. Speak to you in a bit, bye.
Yeah, the fish bowl smashed
— The fish?
— The fish bowl
— And the fish with it?
— No, the fish were... they were the fish that we had
before we... before we left London and...
— You ate the fish!
— No, no, we didn't eat them. We freed them.
We released the fish, back into the canal.

★

294

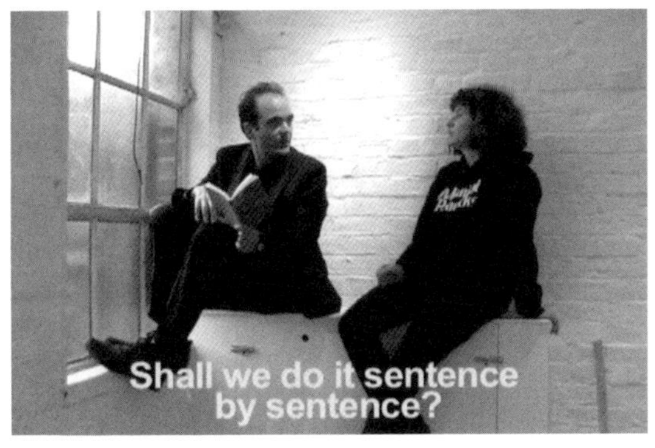
Shall we do it sentence
by sentence?

Perdendosi

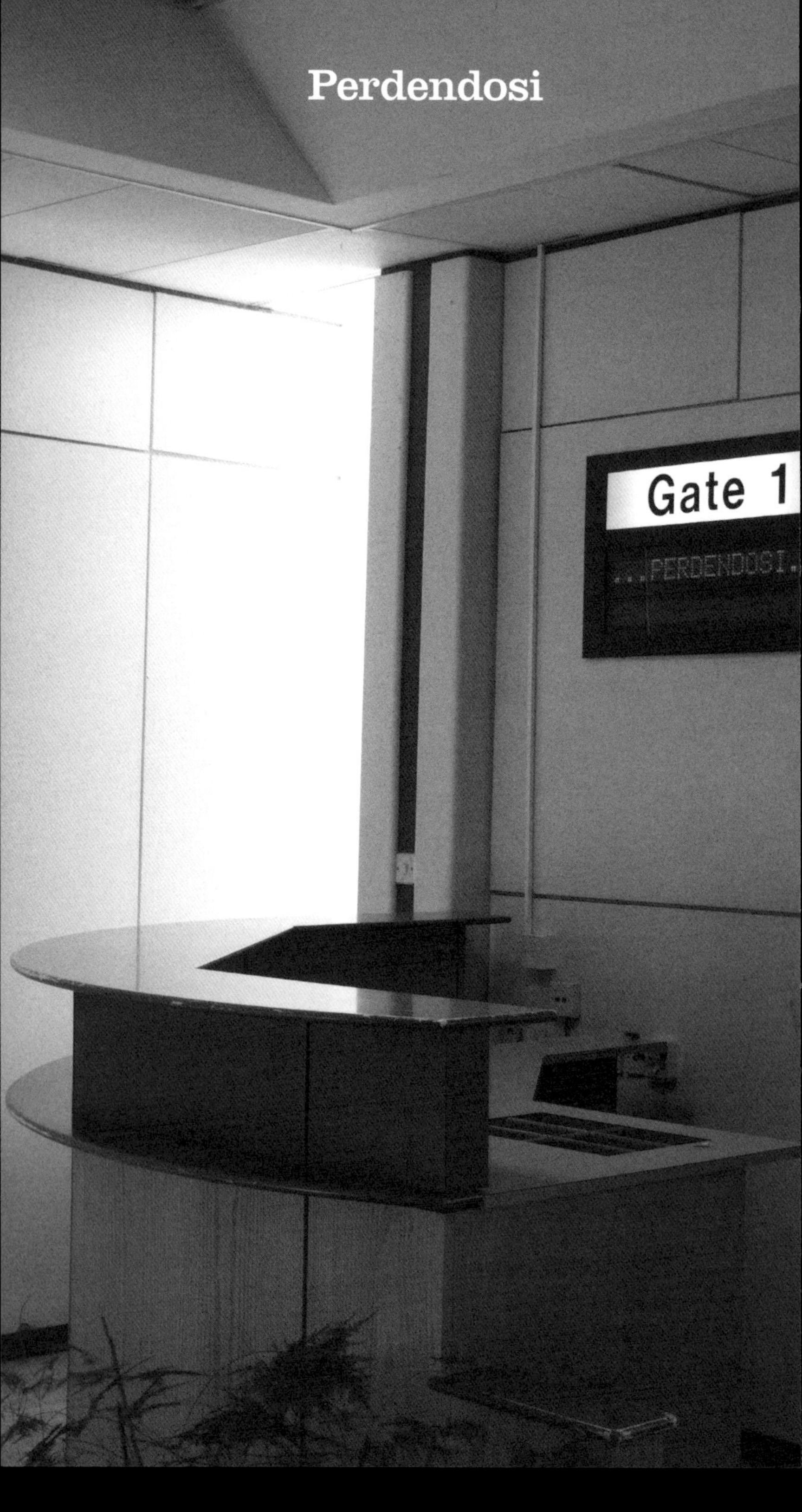

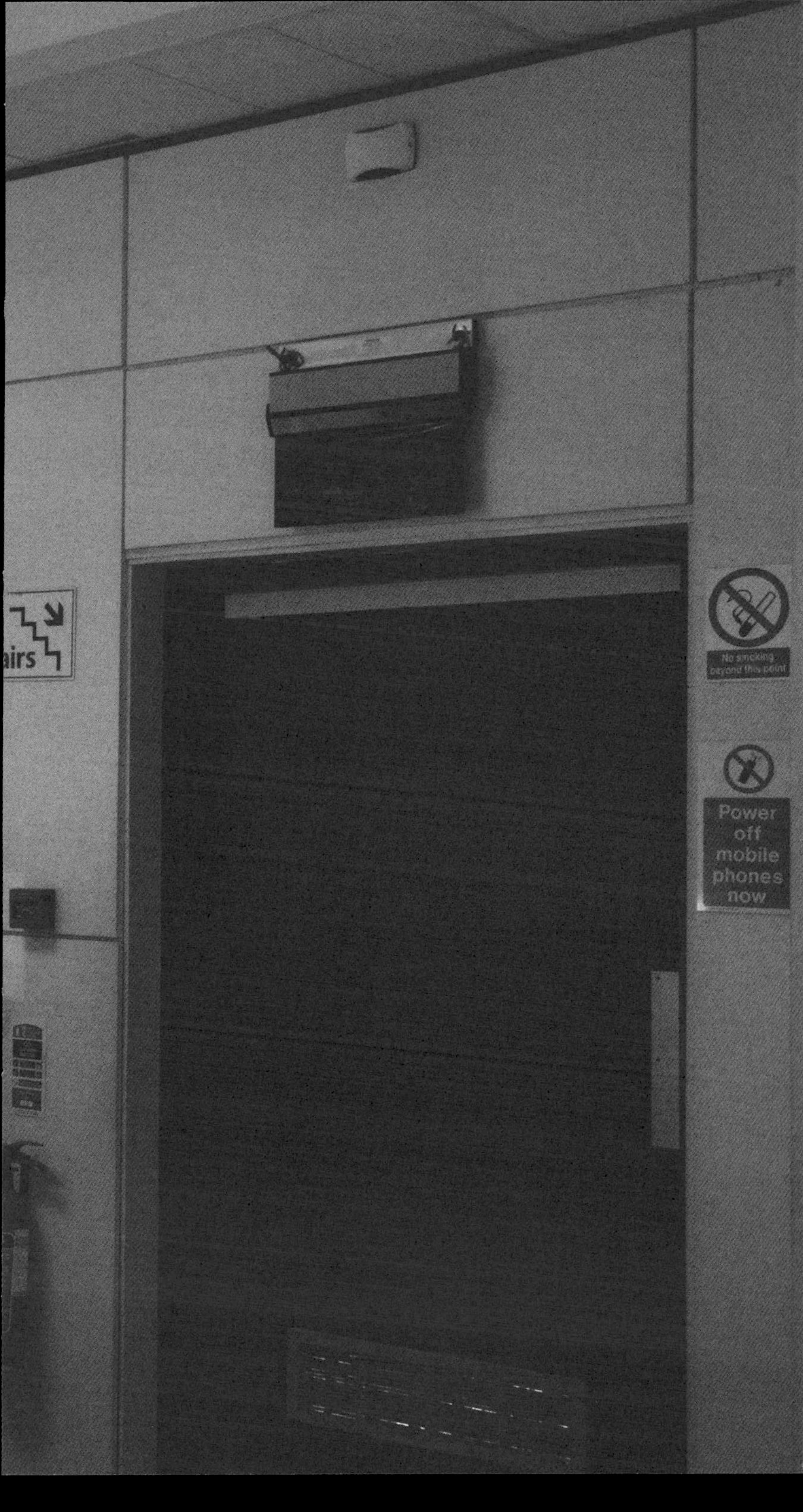
airs
No smoking
beyond this point
Power
off
mobile
phones
now

Carborundum Prints

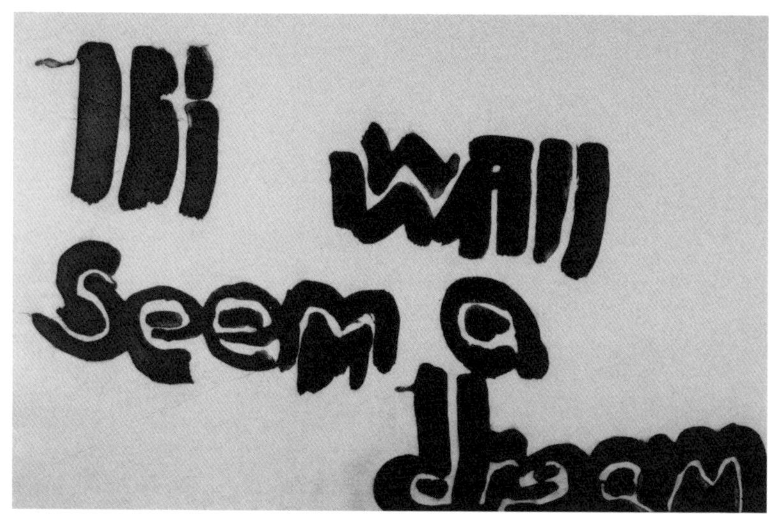

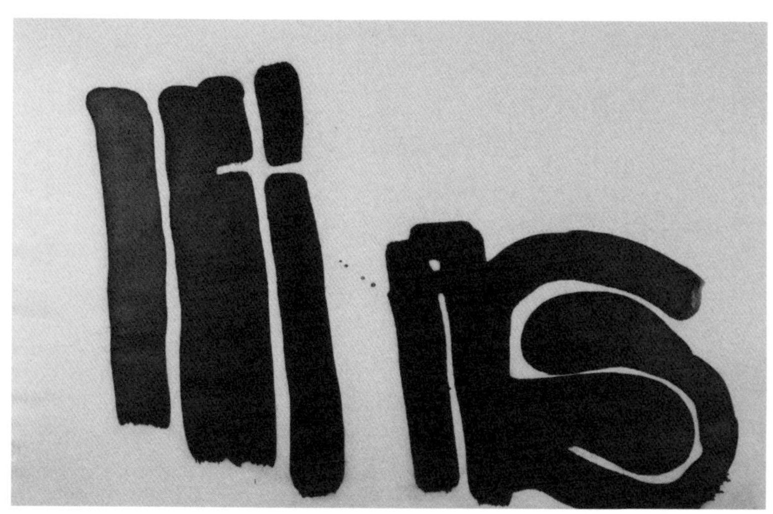

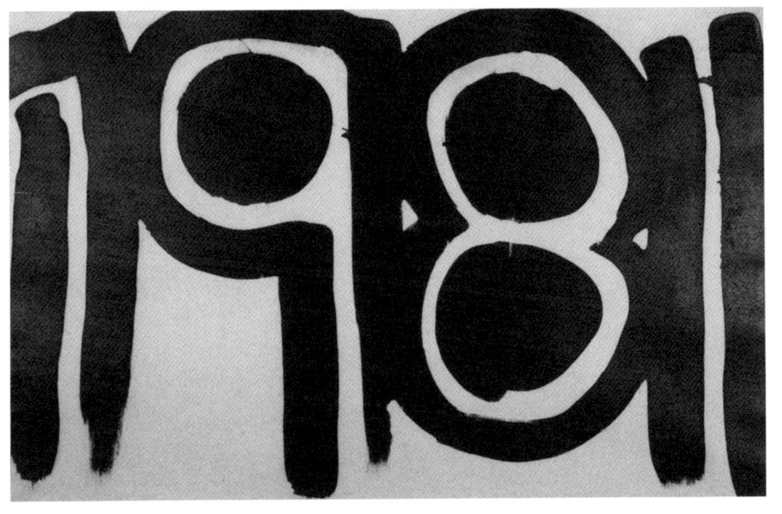
1981
Barnabas

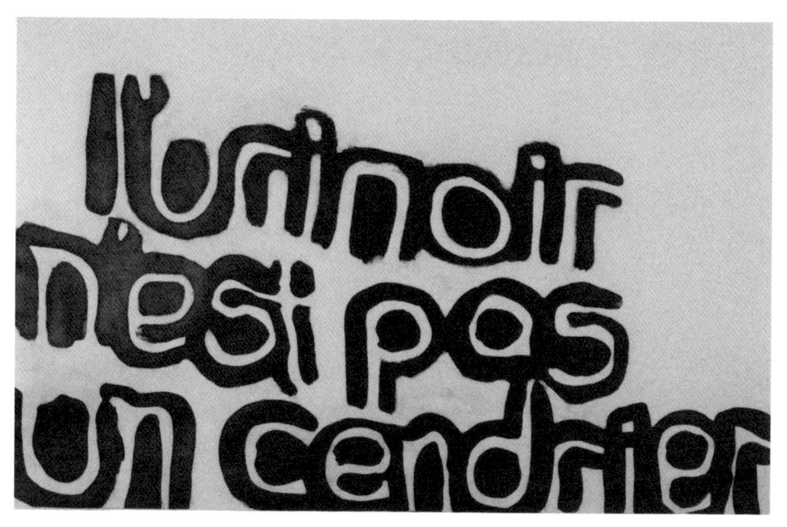

l'urinoir
n'est pas
un cendrier

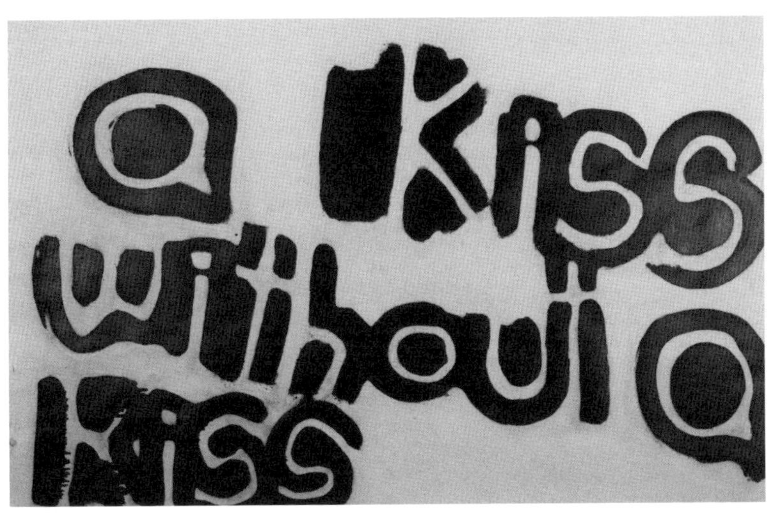

a kiss
without a
kiss

Offset Litho Monoprints

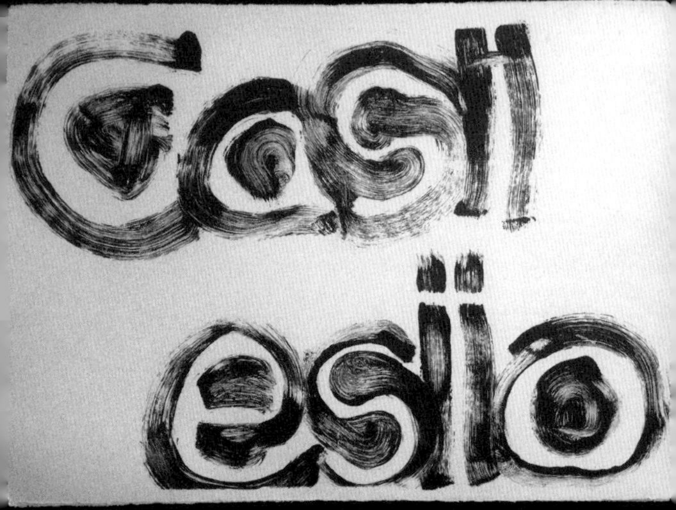

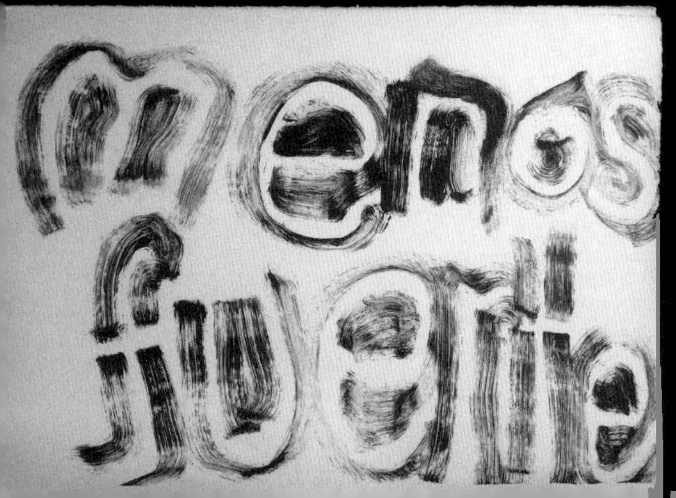

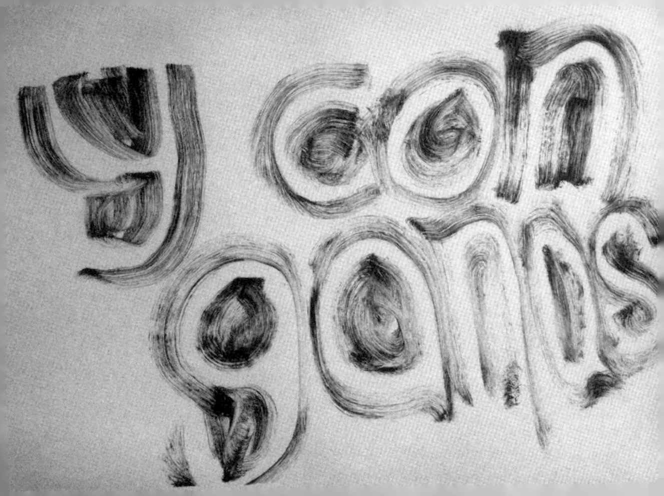

y con
ganas

Index

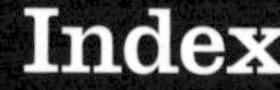

1

When taking photographs
you have to decide whether to
choose a subject and then look
for it or to go out open minded and allow-subjects to make
themselves apparent.

1a

If you choose the subject beforehand you might well end
up trying to find examples of
the subject and then arrive at
a typology that will be hard to
value in anything other than
documentary terms.

1aI

You might well think that by
persisting with the documentary approach you will bypass
it; as if taking it to ludicrous
extremes would turn it into
something else. The risk is
that this won't happen and
that your work will become
increasingly entrenched and
inescapable.

1b

If you don't choose the subject
beforehand and leave it to
reveal itself, you might feel
that you are giving excessive
priority to your taste or vague

things like your 'eye'. You
might also wonder whether
you have any criteria for your
work or whether it's just about
chance.

1bI

So you accept that and let
yourself go with it, thinking
that the problem is really with
you, that you're maybe too up-
tight about things and that it's
a question of the work loosen-
ing your critical parameters.
It might, but if it doesn't you
could look quite foolish.

1a & bII

You might consider captioning
your photographs or showing
them in such a way – through
framing or sequential presentation with a slide projector
– that the value of the work
is not seen to reside in the
quality or the specifics of the
photograph but in its relation
to another whole. But this
opens up the problems of
making objects and staging
installations of things that are
not in themselves the work.

2

When doing a show some-
where you have to decide

whether you're going to engage with the context or use it as a space to house your work.

2a

If you engage with the context you will probably end up with a work that will be meaningless in any other place. You will also run the risk of appearing to be aggrandising what might be quite a shallow and instrumental understanding of any given place.

2aI

Perhaps you think that by dealing with enough contexts you will develop a looseness and fluidity in relation to contexts, a lightness of touch which might lead to the work disappearing and becoming a kind of tuning or focusing of the context. But it might be the case that your work does actually disappear.

2b

If you just use the space to house the work then the installation might feel a bit like window dressing. You might also feel that what you consider to be the particularities of your own work are unable to survive those of the context in which they're placed. It will be hard to deal with the inevitable shifts in meaning and even harder to claim them.

2bII

But you could claim that these inflections of context interest you, at least until your obvious lack of concern leads you to make an enormous blunder. Fine if you can keep faith in your work in isolation and deal with it not appearing in any context.

2a & bII

Go to 6

3

When you start a painting you should know whether you're going to insist on the image you start with or whether you're going to allow the image to change and be transformed into something you hadn't imagined.

3a

Insist on the image and you could find yourself slavishly depicting something even when you have lost confidence

in its meaning. You might
find that you ask yourself
whether other processes
wouldn't be more appropriate.

3aI

Plenty of arguments you
could make as to why it was
appropriate to paint the image
rather than to make it in any
other way. But you might not
want to keep on having to
argue yourself into a tenable
position, you might think
that you want it to seem
less defensive.

3aII

It might be wise to accept
that your work will only be
supported in a limited world
where your concerns will
not be questioned. But it
will be a very conservative
world and it might destroy
your motivation.

3b

If you allow the image to
change you might wonder
whether the effects that
emerge are pure chance. You
might make something fan-
tastic but from which you feel
completely alienated – as if
you had somehow cheated.

3bI

You could perhaps carry it off
though, develop for yourself a
persona full of mystique, as if
your intuitive judgments and
chance discoveries were somehow unique and special. Your
on suspicion that they might
not be is hard to take.

3bII

Wise as it may be to begin
now to engage with the
physicality of the work – depth
of stretcher, type and density
of paint, weave of backing… –
you have to bear the possibility of seeing yourself as
a demonstrator in an art
material shop.

4

You might start with an idea
of what you want your video to
be, and you can establish the
way to shoot it to achieve this
end. You can never though be
certain that you won't engage
with the editing process to a
significant extent.

4a

If you start with a very fixed
idea you will feel stuck if the
piece doesn't work because

your principles will tell you that it must be-good even when you're noticing that it's rubbish.

4aI

You might decide that this might be remedied by securing appropriate viewing conditions – a huge projection in a sound-insulated room perhaps. But this might make you feel that you are straying too far from your idea and engaging in a process almost as arbitrary as editing.

4b

If you understand from the beginning that you will be doing a lot of editing then your filming might seem random and purposeless to you – as if you might as well be using any material and just putting it together nicely.

4bI

So you tell yourself that there's more to it than that. That you are engaging with your own informed and sensitised intuition, that every small decision contains in-depth analysis of film and video history – the critique, you tell yourself, is implicit. You may though find it difficult to discuss your work.

5

You might start a piece of writing imagining it to be a way of avoiding the formal and aesthetic decisions that frustrate you about more material kinds of work. But you will find that at some stage the same problems will surface.

5a

Avoid formalising it and you end up with loads of endless rambling texts, which you will not know what to do with.

5aI

You can convince yourself that you are engaged in a pure form of writing that will one day be discovered and published. More likely though is that you start to see yourself as one of the many who have a novel in them but are incapable of maintaining the discipline to complete it.

5b

Formalise them into novels, short stories or poems and

find yourself without criteria by which to judge them. You might then have to look at them in relation to other formalised examples of writing only to discover that you are beginning with the same problems again.

5bI

So you enter the literary world, thinking that with your fresh perspective you will take it by storm. Your letters go unanswered, you find that you don't have the history or knowledge to engage in meaningful discussion. Then you meet a novelist who thinks that really he might be an artist – he shows you his work.

5a & bII

You turn to the short story as a form that seems less ponderous and weighed down. You wonder whether you should write about art, about the art-world or whether to try to come up with a story about something else that might or might not have some metaphorical link to the worlds of art.

5a & bIIa

Choose art as your subject and you accept a certain ghettoisation of your work. You could also risk making rather glib commentary on a field that will only care for you as long as you entertain it. This could be a very brief moment, and once they abandon you, you will have no-one else.

5a & bIIb

However beautiful your stories and metaphors you might find that your audience will need some catch to tell them why they should be interested in this thing you're telling them about. It might be that in doing something that you may consider to have broad relevance you may be alienating yourself from the only audience to which have any access.

6

You might come to the conclusion that being an artist is not for you, and that you would rather get involved with being a curator or a critic. These activities are likely to leave you feeling equally despondent.

6a

If you try to go to the limits of
the activity you might begin
to wonder why you are not
making the work that you
are enabling or writing about
yourself.

6aI

So you return to being an
artist, but people resent
the influence you may have
garnered as a critic or curator
and imagine that whatever
success you have is tainted.
Other critics and curators will
also be eager to see you fail
and will therefore not help
you with their activities. This
is not to mention all the other
inherent problems of trying to
be an artist.

6b

Adhere to the discipline of the
activity and begin to feel as if
you are becoming something
which you do not recognise or
want to be.

List of Works

Descriptions of Works in the Collection of the South London Gallery 1997
Book/Installation
Commissioned by graduating students of the Goldsmiths MA Curating programme for the exhibition *Summer Collection* at the South London Gallery

Sancti Petri 1998
Tape/Slide Installation
38 mins
Commissioned by Matt's Gallery, London, and now in the Arts Council Collection, Southbank Centre, London

James: Grey Doors 1998
Typescript/Installation
First exhibited in *Artists of the World,* Passage de Retz, Paris

James: Woodyard 1998
Typescript/Installation
First exhibited in *Soon,* curated by Dermot O'Brien, Het Consortium, Amsterdam
James: Grey Doors, Woodyard and The Golden Heart
Typescript/Installation
First exhibited in *Backspace,* Matt's Gallery, London

That That Which 1998
Silkscreen on Poster Paper
648 × 478mm
First exhibited in *A to Z,* Curated by Matthew Higgs for The Approach, London 1998

Lock and Quarry 1999
Typescript/Installation
First exhibited in *Lucy Gunning – Juan Cruz,* curated by Susanne Gaensheimer, Künstlerwerkstatt, Munich

Driving Back 2000
Audio Installation
25 mins
Commissioned by Camden
Arts Centre, London
First published as *Driving
Back* [CD] London:
Camden Arts Centre, 2000
ISBN 1900470144

Meter 2000
Aluminium Multiple
Commissioned by Camden
Arts Centre, London

Santa Maria 5 O'Clock 2000
Video Installation
32 mins
Commissioned by Kettle's
Yard, Cambridge

Portrait of a Sculptor 2001
Installation with Video
Projection, Video on Monitor,
Architectural Interventions
and Pamphlet
62 mins
Commissioned by
Matt's Gallery, London
First published as *Portrait
of a Sculptor*, London:
Matt's Gallery [monograph]
ISBN 0907623387

*Application for Planning Permit:
Proposal to Build a Metaphor*
2001
Planning permit applications
in twelve sites throughout
Melbourne and project lodged
permanently in Melbourne
city archives
Commissioned by
Juliana Engberg for the
Melbourne Festival
First published as *Application
for Planning Permit: Proposal to
Build a Metaphor* Melbourne:
Melbourne Festival 2002
ISBN 0958039208

Two Cameras 2002
Typescript/Installation
First exhibited in *Geometers*,
curated by Simon Morrissey
for Geometers, Nylon,
London

Disappearing Streets 2002
Typescript, Photographs,
Cable Clip Sculptures,
Slide Projections
7 mins
Versions of this work
have been exhibited in
*TECHNIKEN DES
VORUEBERZIEHENS/
techniques of passing-alluding*,
curated by Verena Gfader,
Fotoforum, Innsbruck and at
Galeria Elba Benitez, Madrid

Palms 2003
Slide Projections
15 mins
Not previously exhibited

Index 2003
36 Typed Index Cards ea.
127 × 75mm
Not previously exhibited

Three Shows 2004
Performance/Slide Projections
20 mins
Commissioned by Mark
Wilsher for The Tabernacle
Theatre, London

Two Clamped Books
Photograph 2009
previously reproduced in
NOIT, London:
Camberwell Press; 1st issue
(November 2013)
ISBN 1908971282

In the Shape of what we Know
2007
Video Installation
6 minute loop
Commissioned by Remise
Bludenz, Austria

Un Aire de Actividad
2008
Video Installation
17 minute loop
Commissioned by PAC,
Murcia for Estratos, curated
by Nicolas Bourriaud

Mensch 2009
Bluetooth Transmissions
Commissioned by
Juliana Engberg for
The Enlightenments, Edinburgh
International Festival

Translating: Chapter 2 2009
Video, 19 mins
Commissioned by Matthew
de Pullford for *Bad
Translations*, Crate, Margate
and made in collaboration
with Naama Yuria

Perdendosi 2011
Carborundum Print,
380 × 285mm

Perdendosi 2012
Adapted Airport Signage
Commissioned by Peter
Gorschluter for *Terminal
Convention*, Cork – a Static,
Liverpool, project

It will seem a dream / *1981* /
It is / *A kiss without a kiss*
L'urinoir n'est pas une cendrier
All 2012
Carborundum Prints, ea.
745 × 485mm

Casi esto / *Menos fuerte* /
Y con ganas
All 2014
Offset Litho Monoprints, ea.
765 × 565mm

Juan Cruz

Born in Palencia, Spain (1970) and educated at Chelsea College of Art & Design, Juan Cruz is an artist and writer currently based in London. Exhibitions of his works are, more often than not, responsive to the particularities of the context where they are installed, but the work itself is almost always based on personal content. Cruz writes autobiographical narratives and shorter descriptive texts, which he has deployed through videos, installations, typescripts, prints and performances; he has also worked with translation, performing several oral translations of works from Spanish literature, including Don Quijote, into English and, more recently, of American art magazine *Artforum* into Spanish. In 2006 Juan Cruz *A translation of Niebla (Fog) by Miguel de Unamuno* was published by Forma and in 2007 another translated work, *SEDA, an Interesting Story* was included in *The Alpine Fantasy of Victor B. and Other Stories*, Serpent's Tail, London.

His work has been exhibited at Matt's Gallery, London; Camden Arts Centre, London; Witte de With, Rotterdam; Serralves Foundation, Porto; Galeria Elba Benitez, Madrid; the Edinburgh International Festival and the Melbourne Festival. In 1999 Cruz was awarded a Paul Hamlyn Foundation Award for Artists and in 2000 named Artist Fellow at Kettle's Yard, University of Cambridge. Between 1995 and 1998 Cruz was a regular contributor to the London-based magazine *Art Monthly* and has continued to write on the work of other artists throughout his career. Cruz is represented by Galeria Elba Benitez, Madrid and Matt's Gallery, London.

Since 2014 he has been Professor of Fine Art at the Royal College of Art in London, where he is also Dean of the School of Fine Art. Formerly he was Senior Lecturer in Fine Art at Goldsmiths and Director of Liverpool School of Art and Design at LJMU, where he remains a visiting professor.

Juan Cruz
Catalogue:
It will seem a dream
17.02 – 04.06.2017

MUSAC
Museo de Arte
Contemporáneo
de Castilla y León

DIRECTOR
Manuel Olveira

GENERAL COORDINATOR
Kristine Guzmán

EXHIBITIONS AND
PROJECTS COORDINATION
Eneas Bernal
Helena López Camacho
Carlos Ordás

REGISTRAR
Koré Escobar
And Professional Services
by Dalser S.L.

EDUCATION AND
CULTURAL ACTION
Belén Sola
Julia R. Gallego

LIBRARY-DOCUMENTATION
CENTER
Araceli Corbo
And Professional Services
by Dalser S.L.

COMMUNICATION
AND PRESS
Izaskun Sebastián

RESTORATION
Professional Services
by Albayalde S.L.

ADVISORY COMMITTEE
Neus Miró, Luis Francisco
Pérez, Sergio Rubira, Blanca
de la Torre, Manuel Olveira

www.musac.es

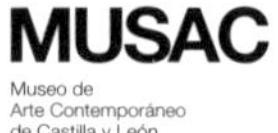

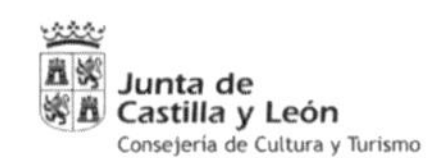

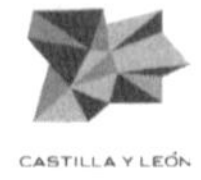